Heredity, Environment, & Personality

Heredity, Environment, & Personality

Heredity, Environment, & Personality

A Study of 850 Sets of Twins

John C. Loehlin & Robert C. Nichols

University of Texas Press, Austin & London

Library of Congress Cataloging in Publication Data

Loehlin, John C
    Heredity, environment, and personality.

    1. Nature and nurture. 2. Personality. 3. Twins—
Psychology. I. Nichols, Robert Cosby, 1927– joint
author. II. Title. [DNLM: 1. Genetics, Human.
2. Environment. 3. Personality. 4. Twins. BR698
L825h]
BF341.L63  155.7   75-33794
ISBN 0-292-73003-9

Second Printing, 1977

Contents

Figures

Tables

Preface

In this brief note we would like to indicate our respective involvements in this book and to acknowledge the help of some of the many others who have contributed in one way or another to it.

The study was originally planned and the data gathered under the supervision of Nichols at the National Merit Scholarship Corporation while he was a member of its research staff. The two authors first met at a conference on Methods and Goals in Human Behavior Genetics held in Louisville, Kentucky, in the spring of 1963, at which time Nichols reported the selection of the twin sample and the plans for the questionnaire study and Loehlin presented some ideas for analyzing twin data. Subsequently, Loehlin was invited to come to the National Merit Scholarship Corporation in Evanston, Illinois, for two months in the summer of 1967 as a consultant. During that period Nichols and Loehlin planned the present book, which was to be jointly written with Nichols as senior author. In addition, Loehlin carried out some of the analyses that are reported in its pages. Several basic analyses of the data had earlier been made by Nichols and have been reported in other publications (Nichols 1965; 1966). A later dissertation by N. S. Breland (1972) has independently analyzed some of these same data.

As it turned out, conflicting obligations arose for Nichols; Loehlin wound up writing the book and shares responsibility with various computers for the particular data analyses reported in it. Nichols read the draft manuscript and contributed a number of suggestions and corrections. "Nichols and Loehlin" turned into "Loehlin and Nichols," but Loehlin reminds the reader that Nichols, not Loehlin, should receive full credit for the design and execution of the research, even though Loehlin must take most of the responsibility for the particular form in which it is reported here.

It is with pleasure that we jointly acknowledge the many contributions that others have made to this enterprise. John M. Stalnaker, as president of the National Merit Scholarship Corporation, was always supportive of the entire research operation, and he encouraged the use of the National Merit data for basic research as well as for studies more relevant to the day-to-day operation of the scholarship program. It was his broad intellectual approach that made possible the collection of twin-study data within the framework of an action program. Alexander W. Astin participated in the early planning of the study and contributed to the questionnaire design. Sally Carson, Virginia Chalmers, Henri Fellner, and Mary Alice Meyer did most of the work involved in mailing, editing, coding, and preparation of nearly error free computer tapes.

The National Merit research program, within which these data were collected, was supported by grants from the National Science Foundation, the Carnegie Corporation of New York, and the Ford Foundation. Support for a number of the data analyses was provided by the Computation Center of the

University of Texas at Austin and by NSF Grant GU-1598. The writing of the initial draft of the book during the summer of 1970 was greatly facilitated by access to Steven G. Vandenberg's extensive personal library on twin research. The final manuscript was capably typed by Marilyn Hatfield.

But, most of all, we are indebted to the twins, who devoted about three hours each (for a total of 5,100 hours) to completing questionnaires. Without them, this research would obviously have been impossible.

Chapter 1

Introduction

Since 1875, when Galton published an article entitled "The History of Twins, as a Criterion of the Relative Powers of Nature and Nurture,"[1] the study of twins has been actively pursued by psychologists and biologists seeking to learn how heredity and environment influence the development of the biological and psychological characteristics of individuals. While there sometimes has been confusion on this point, it is now clear that the conventional comparison of identical and fraternal twins provides information concerning the relative influence of heredity and environment in accounting for the *differences* among the individuals in a population rather than direct information concerning the development of traits as such. The inferences to developmental processes from such studies are necessarily indirect, and genetic (or environmental) factors operating uniformly for all members of the population will not be detected by them. Two-leggedness in humans is highly genetically determined, but differences in leggedness among humans are mostly due to environmental accident. A conventional twin study will detect the latter, not the former, fact.

Individual differences in psychological traits are, however, of great interest to parents, teachers, and society in general, as well as to scientists attempting to understand psychological development. It is a common observation that people differ widely in abilities, personality characteristics, and interests. To some extent, these differences may reflect genetic differences among the individuals concerned. To some extent, they may reflect differences in the environmental influences to which the individuals have been exposed. A sufficiently sensitive analysis of individual differences on any behavioral trait would undoubtedly discover that both kinds of factors are reflected to *some* degree. The obvious next question, and the one the twin study has typically attempted to answer, is, How much of each? Are the differences among individuals on one trait (say, intelligence) more closely associated with genetic differences among the individuals concerned, and less closely associated with environmental differences, than are the differences among individuals on some other trait (say, honesty)? We can always give a simple answer to the question "Are poets (or quarterbacks, or whatever) born or made?" since the answer is clearly "Both." But it is likely to make a considerable practical and theoretical difference whether the influences of heredity and environment on differences in performance in a given population are in the proportions 90%:10% or 10%:90%.

The key to the ability of the twin-study method to tackle this kind of question lies in the existence of two kinds of twins: (1) identical, or monozygotic, twins, who originate from the splitting of a single fertilized ovum and often show striking resemblances in appearance and behavior, and (2) fraternal, or dizygotic, twins, who originate from the separate fertilization of two ova and typically show only the ordinary family resemblances of brothers and sisters.

If we know the average degree of genetic resemblance for the two sorts of

1. References are in a single list at the end of the book, preceding the Index. They will normally be cited in the text by author and year, e.g., "Galton (1875)."

twins (deducible from genetic theory) and know—or guess—the average degree of environmental resemblance (often, but not necessarily, taken to be the same for both), then it is possible to infer from the observed resemblance what the relative contributions of genes and environment are in accounting for differences in the trait. There are some additional complexities in applying this general formulation to the actual estimation of trait heritabilities, but this is the central notion: how does the observed difference in degree of resemblance between the two kinds of twins compare to the differences expected on genetic and environmental hypotheses?

It has not always been fully appreciated in the past that even moderately accurate estimates of this type require quite large samples of twins. To illustrate, if identical twins are correlated .50 on a personality trait, and fraternal twins .30, a rough estimate would be that around 40% of the variation of this trait is genetic. If this estimate were based on, say, 50 pairs of each type, its standard error would be approximately 33%; that is, there would be only about two chances out of three that the true value in the population lay within the range 7% to 73%.[2] With 200 pairs of each kind, the error would be about ±17% for a corresponding range of 23% to 57%. With 400 pairs of each kind of twin, the standard error would be about ±12%, giving two chances out of three of the population figure being located within the limits 28% to 52%. While this is still hardly precise, it is perhaps enough to let one begin to make rough distinctions among the heritabilities of different traits. With this level of accuracy one could, for example, be reasonably confident (i.e., 19 chances out of 20) that a trait with an estimate of 60% genetic variance based on correlations of .60 and .30 was indeed higher in heritability than one with an estimate of 25% genetic variance based on correlations of .40 and .275. If one wished to estimate heritabilities fairly closely (for example, to the nearest 5%), he would need much larger samples than 400 pairs—on the order of tens of thousands of pairs.

Most twin studies of psychological traits have used far fewer than 400 pairs of twins of each kind. Newman, Freeman, and Holzinger's classic 1937 study used 50 pairs of each kind. Gottesman's 1963 Minnesota study of twin per-

2. The figures should not be taken as exact, especially at the high end. They are based on a heritability estimate via $\frac{r_I - r_F}{\rho_I - \rho_F}$ (Jensen 1967) whose standard error may be given as approximately

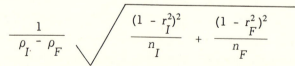

$$\frac{1}{\rho_I - \rho_F} \sqrt{\frac{(1 - r_I^2)^2}{n_I} + \frac{(1 - r_F^2)^2}{n_F}}$$

where r_I and r_F are the observed identical and fraternal correlations .50 and .30, and ρ_I and ρ_F are the theoretical genetic correlations 1.0 and .5 (the latter assumes zero correlation between the spouses for the trait and purely additive genetic variance—or at least assumes that departures from these conditions tend to cancel each other out).

sonality used 34 pairs in each group, and his 1966 Boston study had 79 and 68 pairs. Vandenberg's Louisville studies have typically involved twin groups in the 30 to 110-pair range (Vandenberg, Stafford, and Brown 1968). The reasons for this are not hard to understand: if there are only two or three twin pairs in the desired age range in a given school, the recruiting of even 100 pairs of twins for a study will require substantial effort. Unfortunately, it remains the case that, while studies on this scale are capable of detecting significant departures from 0% or 100% of genetic (or environmental) variation, they cannot make meaningful estimates of genetic and environmental influence in the middle range.

A few studies using psychological measurements have managed to reach considerably larger samples of twins. Most of them have done this by identifying twins in mass testings being carried out for other purposes. Nearly all such studies have involved some form of intelligence testing. An early study of this type was one by Byrns and Healy (1936), which located 412 twin pairs among 119,850 Wisconsin high school seniors who had been given the Henmon-Nelson intelligence test in a state-wide testing program in 1933–1935. Another was the well-known Scottish study. Mehrotra and Maxwell (1949) report data on 525 twin pairs from among the 75,451 children in the 1947 intelligence testing of all 11-year-old schoolchildren in Scotland. In France, Tabah and Sutter (1954) located 375 twin pairs in a representative sample of 95,000 schoolchildren given a nonverbal test of reasoning. And in Sweden, Husén (1959) obtained induction test data on 904 pairs of twins from among youths registering for compulsory national service in 1948–1952, from a total of 196,000 registrants, constituting nearly all the male population of Sweden reaching the age of 19 during that period.

In two more recently completed studies along similar lines, Record, McKeown, and Edwards (1970) reported data on a verbal-reasoning test from the British Eleven-plus examination for 963 twin pairs born between 1950 and 1957 in Birmingham, England, and Schoenfeldt (1968) obtained a sample of 524 twin pairs from among the 400,000 U.S. high school students in the nationwide Project TALENT sample. This last study was unique in having scores on personality and interest measures available in addition to ability measures.

In addition to studies that have taken advantage of mass testing, some Scandinavian investigators have studied large groups of twins traced from birth records and tested via mailed questionnaires. A Swedish study of smoking habits (see Cederlöf et al. 1961) tested about 520 pairs, and a Finnish study of drinking behavior (Partanen, Bruun, and Markkanen 1966) tested 346 pairs. Existing U.S. social records probably would not permit such a study for the whole U.S. population, although it may be feasible to trace twins from special subpopulations, as evidenced by the group of over 15,000 twin pairs identified among U.S. military veterans (Jablon et al. 1967).

The study to be described in the present book began with twins identified in the large group of high school juniors who took the National Merit Scholarship Qualifying Test (NMSQT) in the spring of 1962. This test, administered annually to some 600,000 to 800,000 students in a large proportion of U.S. high schools, was used to identify academically talented students for recognition in the National Merit Scholarship Program and for guidance in the local schools.

For a group of twins identified from among NMSQT participants, scores for the five NMSQT subtests were automatically available. In addition, a battery of personality and interest questionnaires was mailed to the twins; to their parents, a questionnaire inquiring about the twins' early experiences; and to teachers and friends of the twins, brief questionnaires and rating scales. Since most of these questionnaires had previously been sent to a random sample of students taking the NMSQT, a control group of nontwin National Merit participants was available with which to compare the twins. Finally, for the diagnosis of the twins as identical or fraternal, a mail questionnaire was developed along the lines of those used in the Scandinavian studies (Cederlöf et al. 1961; Sammalisto 1961).

The present book reports a number of analyses of the data from the 850 twin pairs, 514 identical and 336 fraternal, who formed the final sample in this study. The plan of the book may be outlined briefly as follows: In the next chapter, we describe in more detail the design and procedures of the study, describe the twin diagnosis, and discuss the sampling and the quality of the data. In chapters 3 to 6 we report various analyses and results. Chapter 3 focuses on the twins as individuals, comparing the two twin types to each other and to the members of the nontwin sample. Chapter 4 considers the twins as pairs and examines the differential resemblance of the two types of twins on measures of personality, abilities, and interests. Chapter 5 reports the data from the parent questionnaire and relates it to the present resemblances between the twins. Chapter 6 contains several special analyses focused on points of theoretical interest: the twinship itself, left- and right-handedness, the covariation of traits within and between pairs, and the form of the distribution of twin differences. Finally, in chapter 7 the main empirical conclusions of the study are discussed in the light of the broad question toward which the study was directed: what are the respective contributions of heredity and environment to individual differences in personality, ability, and interests? We will not attempt here to anticipate our conclusions, except to note that some of our findings provide challenges to conventional views of the influences important in the development of personality.

Chapter 2

**Design of
the Study**

In this chapter we will describe some of the details of how the twin sample was derived, how the questionnaire data were gathered, and how the twins were diagnosed as identical or fraternal. In addition, we will comment on the biases inherent in the method of sampling and present some information concerning the quality of the data.

As the reader will recall from the previous chapter, the study basically involved the gathering of personality and interest data by mail from a large group of twins identified among U.S. high school students taking the nationwide National Merit Scholarship Qualifying Test. Data on ability, in the form of subtest and total scores on the NMSQT, were therefore available for the sampled twins. In addition, the design of the study called for supplementary information from parents, teachers, and friends of the twins, but of these only the parent data are reasonably complete and will be reported here.

PROCEDURE

In 1962, the National Merit Scholarship test was administered to just under 600,000 U.S. high school juniors—596,241 to be precise. On the answer sheet of the questionnaire, among a number of other information items, was a set of three answer spaces labeled "single," "twin," and "triplet." The test administrator, when this part of the face sheet was reached, read the following instruction: "In the final column with the three ovals, you are to indicate whether you are a triplet, a twin, or neither. If you are neither a twin nor a triplet, blacken the oval *above* the word 'single' in the grid. If you are a twin, blacken the oval *above* the word 'twin' in the grid. And if you are a triplet, blacken the oval *above* the word 'triplet' in the grid." (The instructions to the administrator added, "If there are any students who are of a multiple birth greater than triplets taking the test, ask them to mark the oval above the word 'triplet' in the grid.")

When the tests were scored by computer, a card was punched for all students who indicated that they were a twin. These cards were sorted in order by high school and last name, and all sets of two or more individuals in the same school with the same last name were tentatively identified as twin pairs. Since the scope of the present study included only same-sex twins, all opposite-sex pairs were dropped at this point. The test answer sheets containing the students' home addresses were retrieved, and the few pairs with different home addresses were discarded.

The names and addresses of 1,507 prospective same-sex twin pairs were obtained by this procedure. Each of the individual twins was sent a four-page questionnaire (reproduced in Appendix A) designed to yield information permitting the diagnosis of the twin pair as identical (monozygotic) or fraternal (dizygotic) and to solicit further participation of the twins in the study. The last item of this questionnaire read:

16. Your responses to the above questions will be helpful in determining the factors which influence students' scores on the National Merit Examination, and we greatly appreciate your cooperation. We now have another favor to ask you. We are conducting a large study of twins in which we would like for you and your twin to participate. If you agree we will send you a questionnaire which will take from two to three hours to complete. We think you will find this questionnaire interesting and when some results are available we will send you a newsletter describing the findings. Your help in this research will make a valuable contribution to knowledge about the factors which determine human behavior.

Will you participate in the larger study?   (Check one)

———— Yes, Please send the questionnaire.

———— No, I do not want to participate.

This questionnaire was mailed out in May of 1963, slightly more than a year after the twins had taken the NMSQT and toward the end of their senior year in high school. Of the 1,507 presumed twin pairs who were sent questionnaires, both twins returned the questionnaires in 1,188 cases, a response rate of 79%. (In a few additional cases, one twin responded but not both.) This exceptionally high level of response to a mailed questionnaire was in part due to effective follow-up of the original request by postcard and letter, in part to the fact that the population of students that take the NMSQT is above average in ability and academic achievement, and in part, undoubtedly, to the generally good reputation and prestige enjoyed by the National Merit Scholarship program. Virtually all those returning questionnaires agreed to participate further, and to these were mailed a battery of personality and interest tests, including the California Psychological Inventory (CPI), the Holland Vocational Preference Inventory (VPI), an experimental Objective Behavior Inventory (OBI), an Adjective Check List (ACL), and a number of other, briefer self-rating scales, attitude measures, and other items. In addition, a parent was asked to fill out a questionnaire describing the early experiences and home environment of the twins. Other brief questionnaires were sent to teachers and friends, asking them to rate the twins on a number of personality traits; because these ratings were available for only part of our basic sample, they have not been analyzed in detail and will not be discussed further in this book. (The parent and twin questionnaires, except for the CPI, are reproduced in Appendix A.)

The test battery was, with minor exceptions, the same as one that had previously been mailed to a random sample of all the students who had taken the

Table 2-1. Final Twin Sample, by Sex and Zygosity

	Males		Females		Total	
Type of Twin	Pairs	%	Pairs	%	Pairs	%
Identical	217	61.3	297	59.9	514	60.5
Fraternal	137	38.7	199	40.1	336	39.5
Total	354	100.0	496	100.0	850	100.0
% of total		41.6		58.4		100.0

NMSQT the previous year, which will be referred to in this book as the *non-twin sample*. The chief difference between the two batteries was that the questionnaire sent to the twins included some items that referred specifically to the twin relationship itself.

Reasonably complete data from both members of the twin pair plus a filled-out parent questionnaire was in due course received for 850 sets of twins. This represented about 72% of the 1,188 pairs who responded to the first questionnaire, or about 56% of the twin pairs initially matched by the computer. The response rate for the nontwin sample, who received essentially the same follow-up procedures as did the twins, was 64%. The somewhat lower overall response rate for twins than for nontwins is presumably due to losses in the two-stage questionnaire procedure used for twins and to the fact that responses from both twins of a set were required for a twin response to be counted.

The composition of the twin sample in terms of sex and zygosity is shown in table 2-1. As is evident from the table, there were more female than male twin pairs in the final sample and more identical than fraternal pairs—about 60%:40% in each instance. The numbers of pairs in the four major subgroups range from a low of 137 for fraternal-twin males to a high of 297 for identical-twin females. The proportion of identicals and fraternals is about the same for both sexes. Since there are roughly equal numbers of identical- and same-sex fraternal-twin pairs born in the United States in a given year, about half male and half female, this suggests that females and identical-twin pairs are overrepresented in our sample. We will pursue this matter in more detail in the next section.

SAMPLING CONSIDERATIONS

In 1945, the year in which the majority of 1962 high school juniors were born, 2,735,456 live births were registered in the United States. These included 27,393 sets of twins in which both partners were born alive (U.S. Public Health Service 1947). Almost exactly one-third of these, 9,132 sets, were of unlike sex, leaving 9,286 male and 8,975 female pairs, or 36,522 individuals who were members of intact like-sex pairs at birth; this would represent 1.34% of the total newborn population.

But twin mortality rates during the first weeks of life are considerably higher than those of nontwins, due to birth difficulties and the higher prematurity rate of twins, so the proportion of intact pairs to be expected later in life would be less than this. Probably the most satisfactory estimates of early twin mortality for our purposes are those of Barr and Stevenson (1961) based on a study of all live births in England and Wales in 1949–1950. In their data, 84.2% of male twin pairs born alive were intact at the end of the first year of life, and 89.1% of female pairs. Applied to our figures, this would represent about 7,820 male and 8,000 female pairs at age 1. Barr and Stevenson's corresponding survival figure for singleborns at the end of the first year is 96.8%, so members of intact same-sex twin pairs at this age would represent about 1.19% of the population.

After the first year of life, the mortality rate among twins is not thought to differ appreciably from that of nontwins (Allen 1955). Such mortality as does occur between the ages of 1 and 17 would tend to decrease intact pairs at a greater rate than individuals, but, because of the low overall death rate in the United States during this period (about 1.3%), the effect on the proportion of paired same-sex twins in the population would be slight—reducing it to perhaps 1.18%.

If we estimate that there were about 2,600,000 17-year-olds in the United States in 1962, this would mean about 30,800 individuals in intact same-sex pairs, or 15,400 pairs. Our group of 850 pairs thus represents about a 5.5% sample of the U.S. same-sex twins of that age.

It is not, however, an unbiased sample. First, National Merit Scholarship test participants tend to be above average in academic achievement. The average score for NMSQT participants is about one standard deviation above the mean for all eleventh-grade students. In some high schools, the test is administered to all students, but, in most, participation is voluntary, and typically the test is taken by students who are planning to go on to a four-year college. Second, as we have noted, the sample contains an excess of females and of identical twins. The figures cited above would suggest that only slightly over half the surviving same-sex pairs should be female (50.6% at age 1, and not much change from that should occur by age 17). But about 60% of the pairs in our sample are female. In addition, almost exactly one-third of the twins born in the United States in 1945 were unlike-sexed. From this, we can deduce via Weinberg's rule that approximately half of the same-sex pairs at birth should be fraternal, with the other half identical. According to Barr and Stevenson's data, early mortality is higher among identical twins, which would lead us to expect a slight preponderance of fraternal same-sex pairs later on. In our sample, however, about 60% of the pairs were diagnosed as identical.

The 596,241 U.S. high school juniors who participated in the 1962 National Merit Scholarship testing represent about 23% of their age group. Even the 1,507 same-sex pairs initially matched represent only about 10% of U.S. same-sex twin pairs of that age. This deficit could reflect a shortage of twins among National Merit test takers. It could also reflect cases in which twins were in different schools or grades or lived at different addresses or in which one twin took the NMSQT while the other did not. A third possibility would be mechanical errors in the matching processes resulting from misrecorded names or the like.

All three of these alternatives have some plausibility. As will be discussed in more detail in the next chapter, twins as a group tend to average slightly lower than single-born children on tests of intellectual and academic ability, and this might well lead to their underrepresentation in the National Merit test-taking population. Second, the twins of a pair obviously sometimes differ in their life experiences, their educational careers, and their vocational plans in ways that could lead one twin to be included in our sample but not the other. If we assume that such differences are more likely to occur in male pairs than in female pairs and in fraternal pairs than in identical pairs, this could account for the relatively greater underrepresentation of male and fraternal pairs in our sample. And, finally, errors in data transcription and matching do occur in any large-scale information-handling process, although we have reason to believe that ours was fairly efficient. Genuinely random errors would shrink the sample but should not otherwise disturb its representativeness. Errors stemming from some attribute of the test taker (e.g., carelessness) could introduce bias. It seems likely that this would mostly parallel other biases present, which we consider next.

Discussion so far has focused on factors that could lead to fewer matched same-sex twin pairs in the initial sample than we might otherwise expect from a population of this size. But an equally critical selective factor occurs after this stage in the selection process: the willingness to respond to mailed questionnaires. As noted earlier, about 56% of the same-sex twin pairs initially identified wound up in the final sample, after roughly equal attrition at two stages, the short zygosity diagnosis questionnaire and the longer personality battery and parent questionnaire. Attrition at the first stage is compounded of some unknown proportion of failure to receive the questionnaire because of changed address, or the like, after the lapse of a year, and of failure to respond to it. Attrition at the second stage is presumably largely a function of the latter (although now including a parent as well as the twins).

Presumably, many failures to respond to mail questionnaires are due to situational and accidental factors occurring randomly with respect to variables of interest. Such failures, beyond reducing sample size, are of no great scientific concern. But, in other instances, failures to respond to mail questionnaires may be related to personality and ability characteristics of the nonrespon-

Table 2–2. NMSQT Selection Score in Twin and Nontwin Samples

Sample	Males	Females	Total
		Means	
Identicals	104.8	99.6	101.8
Fraternals	107.8	100.0	103.2
Nontwins	106.5	103.5	104.9
		Standard deviations	
Identicals	22.9	21.4	22.2
Fraternals	21.9	21.1	21.8
Nontwins	18.1	18.3	18.2

Note: The NMSQT selection score is the sum of the scaled scores for the five subjects. The mean for all NMSQT participants is 100.

dents and thus do become of concern because they may restrict the range or change the average level of the sample on such measures. Provided that such selection does not restrict the range to zero, this should not preclude finding meaningful relationships within the data, but quantitative estimates and generalizations to other populations may be distorted to some extent in ways related to the selection that has occurred.

One way of evaluating the net effect of the selection that has taken place at various stages of deriving the sample is to compare the final twin sample to normative data on personality and ability for National Merit test takers and for U.S. adolescents in general.

Our twins, like other NMSQT test takers, do well academically. The twins rank on the average at about the seventy-ninth percentile of their high school classes in grades. (This is by self-report, but other National Merit studies have shown such self-reports to be reasonably accurate.) The twins' means and standard deviations for the NMSQT total selection score (the total test score) are shown in table 2–2. They suggest that these twins are generally similar to the NMSQT participants in terms of ability. (The NMSQT mean for participants is approximately 100, and the standard deviation is approximately 20.) There is evidence in the table of higher mean scores for males and for fraternals, which would be consistent with a greater degree of selection in these groups. The standard deviations do not suggest much restriction in range, however. Indeed, those for the twins are somewhat elevated. Chapter 3 of this book contains a more detailed comparison of the twins with the sample of nontwin NMSQT testees, who were presumably subject to similar questionnaire-answering biases.

The twin and nontwin samples can be compared in terms of personality to

Table 2-3. Means on the CPI Scales for Twin and Nontwin Groups and High School and College Standardization Samples

CPI scale	Male					Female				
	HS[a]	IT	FT	NT	Coll.[a]	HS[a]	IT	FT	NT	Coll.[a]
Dominance	23.2	27.9	28.1	27.5	28.3	23.7	26.7	27.1	27.2	28.5
Capacity for Status	15.3	18.2	18.3	18.6	20.9	16.0	18.6	18.7	18.8	22.2
Sociability	21.5	24.9	24.6	24.7	25.4	21.4	24.2	24.1	23.8	26.0
Social Presence	32.7	34.8	34.5	34.7	37.3	31.1	32.9	33.0	32.1	37.0
Self-Acceptance	18.7	21.3	21.3	21.4	22.3	18.9	20.8	21.0	21.2	19.5
Sense of Well-being	33.5	36.2	35.9	35.1	36.6	34.6	35.8	35.3	35.3	37.5
Responsibility	26.7	31.3	31.6	30.6	30.8	30.0	33.2	33.2	33.4	33.3
Socialization	36.3	39.5	38.9	37.9	36.8	39.4	41.3	41.0	40.4	39.5
Self-Control	25.3	28.4	27.7	25.8	27.6	27.6	29.9	28.8	28.3	30.8
Tolerance	17.8	22.2	22.4	21.2	23.3	18.7	22.7	22.7	22.4	25.0
Good Impression	15.1	17.3	16.7	15.8	17.2	15.7	17.1	16.2	16.4	19.1
Communality	25.2	26.0	26.0	25.9	25.5	26.1	26.5	26.5	26.4	25.5
Achievement via Conformance	22.3	27.4	26.9	26.0	27.4	24.1	27.7	27.0	27.1	28.8
Achievement via Independence	14.6	19.3	19.4	18.5	20.9	15.5	19.8	19.6	19.5	21.9
Intellectual Efficiency	33.6	38.6	38.9	38.1	39.8	34.4	38.9	38.6	38.6	41.4
Psychological-Mindedness	9.2	11.2	10.9	10.7	11.4	8.7	10.7	10.6	10.4	11.4
Flexibility	9.1	9.4	9.4	9.4	11.1	8.9	9.4	9.2	9.3	11.6
Femininity	15.4	16.9	16.5	16.9	16.7	24.1	24.1	23.9	24.5	22.8
Number of persons	3,572	414	252	325	1,133	4,056	582	386	385	2,120

[a]From *CPI Manual* (Gough 1957).

HS: High School.
IT: Identical twin.
FT: Fraternal twin.
NT: Nontwin.
Coll.: College.

U.S. normative samples on the California Psychological Inventory. Tables 2-3 and 2-4 show comparisons of means and standard deviations for our sample to the high school and college norms presented in the *CPI Manual* (Gough 1957).

We may briefly characterize these tables as showing that the NMSQT twin sample tends mostly to fall in between high school and college norms on personality variables, is restricted in range on some traits, but not too severely, and closely resembles the nontwin sample. An average position between the

Table 2-4. Standard Deviations on the CPI Scales for Twin and Nontwin Groups and High School and College Standardization Samples

Scale	Male					Female				
	HS[a]	IT	FT	NT	Coll.[a]	HS[a]	IT	FT	NT	Coll.[a]
Dominance	6.0	6.0	5.9	6.6	6.3	6.1	5.8	5.9	6.0	5.9
Capacity for Status	4.4	3.9	4.1	4.1	3.8	4.9	3.9	4.1	4.0	3.6
Sociability	5.4	5.0	5.4	5.2	5.0	5.7	5.0	5.0	5.2	4.8
Social Presence	5.7	5.4	5.9	6.0	5.8	5.8	5.3	5.6	5.8	5.9
Self-Acceptance	4.1	3.6	3.5	4.1	3.8	4.4	3.8	3.9	4.0	8.1
Sense of Well-being	5.6	4.8	4.7	5.4	4.6	5.7	4.4	4.7	5.2	4.4
Responsibility	5.7	4.6	4.4	4.7	4.5	5.2	3.7	3.6	3.7	4.1
Socialization	6.0	5.1	5.2	5.6	5.2	5.6	4.7	4.8	5.2	5.0
Self-Control	8.0	8.0	7.6	8.0	7.5	8.5	7.8	7.2	7.8	7.4
Tolerance	5.3	5.1	5.0	5.2	4.8	5.5	4.5	4.7	4.6	4.2
Good Impression	6.2	6.0	6.3	6.2	6.2	6.2	5.9	5.6	5.9	6.2
Communality	2.8	2.3	1.7	2.0	2.0	1.9	1.6	1.6	1.6	2.0
Achievement via Conformance	5.3	4.6	4.8	4.8	4.5	5.3	4.2	4.3	4.3	4.4
Achievement via Independence	4.1	4.7	4.3	4.3	4.2	4.2	4.0	3.9	3.9	3.9
Intellectual Efficiency	6.3	5.4	4.7	5.5	5.0	6.5	4.9	4.9	5.1	4.8
Psychological-Mindedness	2.6	2.6	2.8	2.6	3.0	2.6	2.7	2.6	2.5	2.9
Flexibility	3.4	3.8	3.8	3.8	3.8	3.2	3.7	3.4	3.4	3.7
Femininity	3.6	3.8	3.7	4.1	3.7	3.5	3.1	3.3	3.5	3.3

[a]From *CPI Manual* (Gough 1957).

HS: High School.
IT: Identical twin.
FT: Fraternal twin.
NT: Nontwin.
Coll.: College.

high school and college populations seems quite reasonable for high school juniors who plan to attend college. For most of the CPI scales, then, our samples appear to be reasonably representative of the portion of the population from which they come. The strongest selection, as evidenced by elevated means (and, to some extent, reduced standard deviations), appears to have occurred for the scales Self-Acceptance (especially for girls), Responsibility, Socialization, Communality, and Femininity. A relationship of these traits to the tendency to return mail questionnaires is quite plausible. There is, however, ample variation left on these scales to permit us to detect any strong relationships of these traits to others within the data.

In evaluating any questionnaire data, a social scientist is immediately concerned with the possibility that subjects may have filled out the questionnaire casually or carelessly—in the extreme case, merely marking the answers randomly—or may have biased their responses in an effort to make a good impression, to please the experimenter, or the like. He is apt to be especially concerned about the possibilities in the case of a questionnaire administered by mail, although it is perhaps debatable whether his extra concern is appropriate, since many persons who in a captive population might be careless or biased responders in a mail survey simply become nonresponders.

Nevertheless, the skeptic is always a bit doubtful about what he cannot see; so certain checks were built into the present questionnaires. On the sixth page of the 324-item Objective Behavior Inventory, which consists of a long list of descriptions of activities that the student is to mark as having done frequently, occasionally, or not at all during the past year, is inserted the following item: "As a check on accuracy of recording make no response at all to this item." A few respondents did mark it—33 males and 39 females, or about 4.3% of the total sample. In other words, somewhat over 95% of the twins correctly followed the instruction to omit. The majority of those that failed to follow the instruction marked the third alternative, "not at all," and, since the phrasing of the item is not wholly unambiguous, probably some fraction of these should be counted as legitimate responders. The 13 males and 6 females (1.1% of the total) who marked "occasionally" are clearly in error, however, so we can assess the correctness of response to this item as lying somewhere between 95% and 99%. Clearly, most of the respondents were, in fact, reading and responding to the items of the questionnaire.

Another evidence of the presence of content sensitivity is virtually unanimous response to a given alternative on certain items. An item farther along in the inventory was "Jumped in a parachute." Only 6 out of the 1,673 respondents indicated that they had done this during the past year—and quite possibly some of them had. Clearly, sheer random responding on the part of very many respondents (or a very high level of random error in the data transcription process) can be fairly well excluded on the basis of data like these. Similar evidence may be drawn from the health items later in the questionnaire (p. 19)—for example, less than 1% of any group marked "Epilepsy" and less than 1% of males marked "Menstrual dysfunction."

Another check is afforded by the 12 repeated items within the 480-item California Psychological Inventory. One measure of the care with which the subjects filled out this inventory may be obtained by examining the amount of agreement between the first and second encounters with the same items (in general, widely separated within the questionnaire). We obtained these figures for the present sample. The percentages of agreement, omitting those few individuals who on one or both occasions failed to respond to the item, ranged from 85% to 96% for the different items, with a median of 89%. These levels of agreement may be compared with those obtained in three college-student samples by Goldberg and Rorer (1964), in which agreement on the 12 repeated CPI items ranged from 83% to 98%, with a median value of 91% (our calculations from their data, treating omissions as above). Two of their samples were tested under classroom conditions; the third consisted of paid volunteers. Thus, the consistency of the twins' responses, at the end of a long mail-questionnaire battery, is clearly of the same general order as that of Goldberg and Rorer's college students.

So far, we have concerned ourselves with the questionnaires filled out by the twins. We also need to evaluate the quality of the data obtained from the parent of the twins on the parent questionnaire. One might anticipate a slightly lower level of conscientiousness among the parents, who, after all, did not volunteer their services for this study quite as explicitly as did the twins. On the other hand, their task was easier, since their questionnaire was considerably shorter. On the whole, their level of performance seems to have been comparable to that of the twins. On page 11 of the parent questionnaire, among a set of items comparing the twins, were the following pair of items: "Started menstruation first (for boys leave blank)" and "Voice changed first (for girls leave blank)." Eight mothers of boys marked the first, and sixteen mothers of girls marked the second, or about 2.9% altogether. In each instance, the majority of these marked either the alternative "Neither twin" or "Don't know"; in only nine instances (about 1.1%) was there actually a positive response to the item.

The evidences we have cited of consistency and accuracy of response can simultaneously serve as testimony to the quality of the basic data-processing steps involved, in the editing of the returned questionnaires, the punching of the data on cards, and the transcription to magnetic tape. For it could, of course, be a careless keypuncher and not a careless mother who introduces a menstruating son into the data. One of us (JCL) checked a sample of the parent-questionnaire data recorded on tape back against the original questionnaires and found gratifyingly few instances of apparent editing or keypunching errors. We were extremely fortunate in having the experienced research staff and facilities at National Merit, well equipped for investigations involving large-scale data processing, to handle this critical phase of the study.

ZYGOSITY DIAGNOSIS

An important step in a genetic study involving twins is the classification of pairs as identical (monozygous, or MZ) or fraternal (dizygous, or DZ). Where fraternal twins are of opposite sexes, their identification is automatic. (It is *possible*, through chromosomal accident, to have monozygous twins who are phenotypically of opposite sexes, but such cases are so rare as to be negligible for practical purposes—see Turpin and Lejeune 1969.) The differentiation between monozygotes and dizygotes among same-sex pairs is not quite so easy. The most accurate methods that are practicable for general use are based on extensive blood typing of the pair members. Any discordance in blood groups between the pair members classifies the pair as fraternal. The failure to find such a difference leaves the pair classified as presumptively identical. This procedure will result in the misclassification of occasional dizygous pairs who happen to be alike on all the blood groups tested. With current procedures, this may be expected in 2% or 3% of cases. The opposite error, classifying identicals as fraternals, is more likely to result if there are errors in the blood-typing procedure itself, since a single mistyping will classify an MZ pair as DZ, but seldom the other way around. However, with proper procedures and appropriate double-checking, such errors should be infrequent.

The nature of the present sample of twins scattered across the United States made blood typing of the whole sample clearly impracticable, so a questionnaire procedure was used for zygosity diagnosis. Such a questionnaire, asking only two questions about similarity in childhood and frequent confusion by others, had given better than 90% agreement with a blood-grouping criterion in a Swedish study (Cederlöf et al. 1961); similar good results with a mail questionnaire have subsequently been reported for a sample of twins from among U.S. military veterans (Jablon et al. 1967). The latter study yielded approximately 93% agreement with a combined blood-group-anthropometric criterion of zygosity.

The development of the zygosity questionnaire used in the present study has been reported in detail elsewhere (Nichols and Bilbro 1966) and hence will only be summarized briefly here. The questionnaire itself is given in Appendix A. It asks for information about the physical similarity of the twins (eye and hair color, height, etc.) and for confusions of identity by parents, teachers, and peers.

Scoring rules for the questionnaire were developed and cross-validated on part of the present twin sample. Blood-group zygosity diagnoses were obtained for 124 sets of twins—82 monozygotic and 42 dizygotic. An additional 81 sets of twins diagnosed as dizygotic on the basis of distinct differences in eye color were used with 40 of the blood-diagnosed monozygotic pairs in the development of the scoring rules for zygosity. The remaining 42 monozygotic pairs and the 42 blood-diagnosed dizygotic pairs were kept for cross-validation purposes.

The rules developed called for a three-stage process. At the first stage, twins were diagnosed as fraternal if they showed decided differences in height or in hair or eye color or reported that they were never mistaken by teachers; they were diagnosed as identical if they reported being frequently mistaken for one another by parents or close friends. About half the pairs in the cross-validation sample (38% of the identicals and 55% of the fraternals) were diagnosable at this level, 92% of them (36 of 39) in agreement with the blood diagnosis. At the second level, a point system was applied to less clear-cut items of evidence, and the remaining pairs were classified in this way, with the exception of 6 pairs (7%) who wound up with tied scores and were diagnosed at the third level, on the basis of general impression from reading their questionnaires. The second-level diagnoses proved to be no less accurate than the first level: 37 of 39, or 95%, were in agreement with the blood-type diagnosis. And, even at the third level, 5 out of 6, or 84%, were correct.

Of the six disagreements, four were in the direction of classifying blood-grouped fraternals as identicals, and two were in the opposite direction. These numbers are too small to make much of, but they suggest a slight tendency for the rules to overclassify as monozygotic—the more so if one or both of the opposite "errors" were in fact true dizygotics missed by the blood typing.

The entire twin sample was then diagnosed using the rules as developed above, with a few minor revisions based on the cross-validation experience. A total of 1,239 twin pairs were diagnosed (1,188, plus 51 more who were diagnosed on the basis of a questionnaire returned by only one twin); 737 of the 1,239, or 59.5%, were classified as identical and the remaining 40.5% as fraternal. The subgroup of 850 pairs that in due course remained as the final sample showed very nearly these same proportions of the two twin types—60.5% and 39.5%, respectively.

THE 1965 SAMPLE

While most of the analyses described in the present book are based on the sample of 850 twins from the 1962 testing, in a few instances we report data from a larger group of twins identified in the 1965 National Merit testing. These twins did not receive the personality questionnaire battery, but NMSQT scores are available for them. They have taken part in a separate study using the Strong Vocational Interest Blank, which is reported elsewhere (Roberts and Johansson 1974). In 1965, the NMSQT was given to nearly 800,000 students, and slightly over 2,900 same-sex pairs were tentatively matched on the basis of the same criteria of school, surname, and address used in 1962. The larger proportion of pairs located in 1965 is presumed mainly to reflect fewer pairs missed due to misspelling of names and the like—more extensive hand checking of such matters was employed in the 1965 study.

The return on the zygosity questionnaire was 78%, virtually the same as the 79% achieved in the 1962 study. This yielded a total of 1,300 identical- and 864 same-sex fraternal-twin pairs for whom NMSQT scores were available, which is the relevant sample size for the analyses reported here. The proportions of female and identical pairs were 60.1% and 60.9%, respectively, quite close to the 58.4% and 60.5% of the final sample in the 1962 study.

Chapter 3

Twins and Nontwins

In this chapter we will consider our sample of twins primarily as individuals, rather than as pairs, with a view to discovering the personality, interest, and ability differences, if any, between the two types of twins in the sample and between the twins and nontwins. These matters are important for any consideration of heredity and environment; for example, most methods of estimating the heritability of traits from twin data assume the comparability of identical and fraternal twins as individuals. Furthermore, if the heritability values so obtained are to be generalized meaningfully to nontwin populations, the question of the comparability of twins and nontwins becomes important. If twins are a very special breed in their psychological development, then one may raise real doubts as to how safely conclusions derived solely from twin data may be applied to nontwins.

But, in addition to serving as groundwork for later considerations of genetic and environmental influences, the comparison of twins and nontwins is of interest in its own right. For instance, the extensive investigation by Helen Koch (1966) of 5- and 6-year-old twin and nontwin groups was almost solely concerned with the characteristics of various subgroups of twins as such and only minimally with heredity-environment comparisons. Being a twin has often been supposed to lead to special difficulties in development of a separate sense of identity, to deficiencies in interpersonal relationships outside the twinship, and to acute rivalries and jealousies within it. On the other hand, twins may perhaps escape some of the stresses of loneliness and inferiority feelings that can be the lot of the single child alone in a world of adults or siblings of different ages, interests, and competence than his.

In the intellectual realm, there is a well-documented tendency toward slightly lower average intelligence-test scores of twins (references given later in the chapter). This is sometimes attributed to minor brain damage resulting from the low birth weights common in twins and sometimes to a slower socialization of language due to less individual attention from adults or to private forms of communication within the twinship. The latter interpretations gain support from one study in which twins whose partners were stillborn or died in infancy tended not to show the typical twin retardation (Record, McKeown, and Edwards 1970). But, in another study, singly reared twins did show retardation (Myrianthopoulos et al. 1972), so the question remains open.

Since Koch's investigation (1966) is relevant to ours in a number of ways, we will summarize its design and findings briefly. Koch's subjects were 5- and 6-year-old twins from the Chicago area; they were the only children in their families and were matched with control children from 2-child nontwin families from an earlier study. All children were white, native-born, and in regular classes in the public schools. There were 34–36 children in each of the following four twin groups: identical-twin males, identical-twin females, fraternal-twin males, and fraternal-twin females (i.e., 17 or 18 pairs in each category). Koch also studied a group of unlike-sex fraternal twins, but we will not dis-

Table 3–1. Comparisons between Identical- and Fraternal-Twin Individuals in Koch's Study (Data from Table 72 in Koch 1966)

Fraternals higher

Number of female playmates
Mother's age at birth
Ratings of:
   Speech form
   Gregariousness
   Leadership
   Indirectness

Identicals higher

Number of male playmates
Male preference
Closeness composite

Sex × zygosity interaction

Health (DZm poor)
CAT speech (DZf good)
CAT syntax (DZf good)
Ratings of:
   Criticalness (MZf high)
   Moodiness (MZf low)
   Finality (DZf high)

Social class × zygosity interaction

CAT mother mentions
Rating of selfishness

No significant difference

Birth weight
Weight at time of study
Height at time of study
Mother's age at marriage
PMA—total
PMA—5 subscales
CAT—12 scores
Involvement with children
Number of playmates
Number of same-age playmates
Involvement with adults
Emotion-tension complex
Masculinity complex
Femininity complex
Female preference
Nervous habits
Sissyness
Tomboyishness
Hostility complex
Quarrelsomeness
Ratings—32 traits

cuss these here, since there is no comparable group in our study. Each twin pair was matched with from 1 to 4 control children; the control children were matched to the twins on sex, age, sex of sibling, and social class.

The children in all groups were studied by means of interviews with them, their mothers, and their teachers. The teachers also filled out a trait-rating scale describing the children. In addition, two tests were used, the Thurstone Primary Mental Abilities test (PMA) and a storytelling projective instrument, the Children's Apperception Test (CAT).

From these tests, ratings, and interviews, some 84 measures were scored (66 for the twin-nontwin comparisons). Table 3–1 summarizes the results for the comparison of the identical- and fraternal-twin groups. The nominal level

Table 3-2. Comparisons between Twin and Nontwin Individuals in Koch's Study (Data from Table 73 in Koch 1966)

Variables on which at least two of the four twin groups differed significantly from their matched nontwin controls:

> PMA Verbal (lower, all 4 groups)
> PMA Perceptual (higher, 2 female groups)
> Number of same-age playmates (higher, all 4 groups)
> Weight at time of study (lower, 3 of 4 groups)
> Height at time of study (lower, 2 male groups)
> Number of younger playmates (lower, 2 female groups)
> Ratings of:
> > Friendliness to adults (higher, 2 female groups)
> > Involvement with other children (higher, 2 female groups)
> > Leadership (higher, 2 female groups)
> > Popularity (higher, 2 female groups)
> > Social apprehensiveness (lower, 2 female groups)
> > Tendency to project blame (lower, 2 male groups)[a]

[a]After correcting an apparent typographical error—cf. Koch's table 42.

of significance for the measures that differ is .05, but where results are selected, as here, from a large number of comparisons between two groups, such a probability cannot be taken seriously for individual measures. Assignment of scores by means of a random number table would be expected to yield some differences of this magnitude.

For two of the observed differences—the greater psychological closeness of identical twins and the greater age of mothers at the birth of fraternal twins—there is independent support from other studies in the literature. The other differences may perhaps best be taken as hypotheses to be tested in subsequent investigations. The principal trend seems to be toward slightly better social and speech skills in the fraternal twins, especially the females, although there are more measures of social and speech skill that do not distinguish between the groups than there are that do. Indeed, the major conclusion to be drawn from table 3-1 is that identical- and fraternal-twin individuals are very much alike in most respects at age 5. The greater closeness, say, of the identical twins does not appear to have had such broadly ramifying implications for their personality development as to make them very different individuals from the same-sex fraternal twins.

How about the effects of being a twin, compared to membership in a nontwin same-sex sibling pair? The relevant comparisons are summarized in table 3-2. Shown are the 12 of the 66 variables for which there was a significant difference between twins and nontwins that occurs for more than one sub-sample.

The lower PMA Verbal score is in agreement with a rather consistent finding in the literature that twins tend to show a disadvantage in intellectual performance compared to nontwins. For example, Byrns and Healy (1936) located 412 twin pairs in a population of 119,850 Wisconsin high school students given IQ tests in 1933–1935 and found the twins averaged at about the fortieth percentile of the entire group. In the 1947 Scottish Survey (Mehrotra and Maxwell 1949; Scottish Council for Research in Education 1953), which tested a nearly complete population of Scottish 11-year-old schoolchildren, the 974 twins obtained lower scores, on the average, than the 69,831 nontwins. This difference held for both sexes and in five maternal age and nine occupational categories. Tabah and Sutter (1954), in a study of 6- to 12-year-old French schoolchildren, found 750 twin individuals to score lower on the average than some 95,000 nontwins. The difference held across ages and within four occupational levels. Husén (1959), with a virtually complete population of Swedish males 19–21 years of age over a 4-year period (2,339 twins and 155,244 nontwins), again found the twins consistently lower scorers on an intelligence test by about one-fourth of a standard deviation. Husén also obtained similar results using standardized achievement tests sampling essentially complete populations of fourth- and sixth-grade Swedish schoolchildren (Husén 1960 and 1963). An English study of 2,164 twins born in Birmingham between 1950 and 1957 found a below-average performance of twins on the Eleven-plus examination (Record, McKeown, and Edwards 1970). And, finally, in a U.S. collaborative study coordinated by the National Institutes of Health, 164 white and 232 black 7-year-old twins averaged 5 and 7 IQ points below large groups of single-born white and black children on the Wechsler Intelligence Scale for Children (Myrianthopoulos et al. 1972).

Another difference shown in table 3–2 is a tendency for the twins to be smaller than matched nontwins. Twins are often born at low birthweights, and this may persist. Husén (1959) found his twins as young adults still averaging slightly shorter and lighter than nontwins. Other differences in table 3–2 involve playmates. The greater frequency of same-age playmates (and the lower number of younger playmates) no doubt stems from the presence of twin children of one age in the family, as against two children of different ages in the nontwin sample. Most of the remaining differences in table 3–2 suggest that the girl twins tended to be seen by their teachers as something of social stars. On the whole, however, perhaps the most important data are the 54 variables *not* listed in table 3–2, which failed to show significant differences between twins and nontwins across any two of the four subgroups studied.

To summarize Koch's findings: by and large, the two types of twins were very much alike as individuals and much like nontwins from comparable family backgrounds. Among the observed differentiating variables were certain biological factors connected with twinning (such as the maternal age difference between fraternals and identicals and the tendency toward light weight and small stature of the twins), as well as certain social factors connected with the twin situation (such as the closeness of the identical twins and the tendency toward more same-age playmates among the twins). There was no strong evidence of social disadvantage for twins; indeed, the girls, at least, gave some indication of an average social advantage over the corresponding nontwin groups.

How do our own results compare with these?

In chapter 2 we described the overall design of the present study. It will be recalled that questionnaires were obtained from 850 sets of twins: 217 pairs of male identical twins, 297 pairs of female identical twins, 137 pairs of male fraternal twins, and 199 pairs of female fraternal twins. In addition, we have, for comparison purposes from an earlier study, a similar questionnaire filled out by 334 nontwin males and 394 nontwin females. We can thus carry out an analysis of differences between identical and fraternal twins, and between twins and nontwins, that is roughly parallel to Koch's, keeping in mind that (a) our twins are some ten years older, (b) our data are derived mainly from questionnaires, rather than ratings, (c) our twins and nontwins come from families of various sizes, not just two-child families, (d) our nontwins are not individually matched to our twins, and (e) our samples are larger by a factor of about 10.

Some basic data relevant to this analysis are presented in Appendix B. The major findings will be summarized in the present chapter. But first, a statistical matter or two. We have chosen to express all differences in terms of the point-biserial correlation between the variable in question and the identical-fraternal or twin-nontwin dichotomy. (For two-choice items, this becomes the fourfold point correlation, or phi coefficient.) A test of the significance of such a correlation is equivalent to a corresponding t test or chi-square test on means or frequencies, and the use of the correlation coefficient permits an easier comparison of the relative strengths of associations involving differently scaled variables. In addition, expressing a relationship by a correlation coefficient of .15 is apt to induce a more sensible spirit of proportion all around than stating that the relationship could have arisen by chance only once in some astronomically large number of times.

We have included in our tables in this chapter only variables showing a correlation of at least .130 with the relevant dichotomy. We arrived at this cutting point from the following considerations. Take the smallest group, the 714 individuals involved in the male identical-fraternal-twin comparisons. The standard error of a zero correlation based on 714 cases is approximately $1/\sqrt{714}$, or .037. If we are dealing with a single variable, we could accept a difference as significant at the .05 level if it gave rise to a correlation 1.96 times its standard error, in this case a correlation of .073. However, we are *not* dealing with a single variable; we are looking through some 1,600 variables in search of high

Table 3–3. Variables on Which Identical- and Fraternal-Twin Means Differ[a]

Variable	Males			Females		
	r	M_I	M_F	r	M_I	M_F
365. OBI: pretended to be twin	.54	71	15	.50	73	21
41. Religion of rearing	.15	1.70	1.44	(.05	1.64	1.54)
290. OBI: told female dirty joke	(.02	35	36)	.14	52	66
675. ACL: high-strung	.14	6	15	(.00	16	16)
1033. Regional music contest	.13	8	16	(.05	9	12)

[a]Based on all 1,610 variables. See text for description of entries and criteria for inclusion, and Appendix A for full specification of variables. Variable numbers in this and later tables refer to numbering in appendixes.

r: Point-biserial or phi coefficient.
M_I: Identical-twin mean.
M_F: Fraternal-twin mean.

1. A level of .00044, because $.99956^{1600} \approx .5$. For a two-tailed test based on the normal curve, this represents a cutoff at approximately 3.5σ—and $3.5 \times .037$ is .130. We can put the argument this way: if all our scores had been assigned from a table of random numbers, we would have a 50:50 chance of obtaining some correlations as high as ±.13 in our male identical-fraternal comparisons. This does not, of course, guarantee that all observed correlations higher than .13 are meaningful, but at least they are more likely to be than not.

2. We took one other precaution to avoid finding spurious relationships. Some of our dichotomous variables, such as questionnaire items requiring yes-no responses, yielded extremely disproportionate divisions of response, close to 0% or 100%. Such extreme splits produce notoriously undependable correlations. Therefore, we excluded from this analysis any correlation based on a fourfold table in which the smallest cell frequency was less than five cases.

correlations. How high should a correlation be in a search of this magnitude to yield an acceptably small risk of it having resulted simply from chance in drawing our sample? The present writers do not know of a completely unobjectionable way of answering this question (for discussions of related issues the reader is referred to Ryan 1959 and 1962, and Petrinovich and Hardyck 1969), but on a simple probability basis, to have an even chance of escaping any false claims in 1,600 independent comparisons, one should use a probability level of .00044 for each comparison. This implies a minimum correlation of .130 for a sample of this size.[1]

The other comparisons all involve larger numbers of individuals, and in addition, the twin-nontwin comparisons are based on a much smaller set of variables. Thus, the correlation required for a comparable degree of confidence would be lower in these cases. However, since we are less concerned with statistical significance than with degree of relationship, we will use a uniform cutoff of ±.13 for all tables. We can simply have added confidence in the case of the other comparisons that the relationships we are reporting are nonchance ones.[2]

Table 3–3 shows those variables having a mean difference between identical and fraternal twins that, expressed as a correlation, exceeds .13 for at least one sex (the values for the other sex are shown in parentheses). The identical and fraternal means are given in the columns headed M_I and M_F; for dichotomous items, percentage of "yes" responses is given. The means are expressed as decimal numbers in the units of the original questionnaire scale (see Appendix A); the percentages are given as integers. The values in the columns headed r represent point-biserial or phi coefficients. The variables are listed in the table in descending order of correlation.

Table 3–4. Variables on Which Twin and Nontwin Means Differ[a]

Variable	Males			Females		
	r	M_T	M_N	r	M_T	M_N
495. SR: take it easy	.18	1.90	2.31	(.04	2.03	2.11)
1591. CPI: factor I	.16	71.7	66.8	(.04	73.7	72.5)
1581. CPI: Self-Control	.15	28.2	25.8	(.07	29.5	28.3)
1585. CPI: Achievement via Conformance	.13	27.2	26.0	(.04	27.4	27.1)

[a]Based on 131 selected variables (NMSQT scores, religion, life goals, attitudes, dating, self-ratings, and CPI and VPI scales). Otherwise, same as table 3–3.

r: Point-biserial or phi coefficient.
M_T: Twin mean.
M_N: Nontwin mean.

The conclusions to be drawn from table 3–3 seem fairly clear. It is evident that on very few of the comparisons are the two kinds of twins, as individuals, appreciably different. There are exactly 5 variables among the 1,610 that show a correlation with zygosity exceeding the .13 criterion, and in only one case does this difference hold up across the two sexes. This is the Objective Behavior Inventory (OBI) item, "Confused people by pretending to be your twin," a behavior engaged in during the past year by nearly three-quarters of identical twins and only about one-fifth of like-sex fraternals. Indeed, this item might be a reasonable candidate for use in a questionnaire diagnosing zygosity. Since the other four items form no clear pattern, are not replicated across sexes, and show differences that are not large in absolute size, we forbear to interpret them further.

The twin-nontwin comparisons are shown in table 3–4. The general arrangement of the table is the same as for the identical-fraternal comparisons in table 3–3. The comparison in this case is based on 131 representative variables for which data were available in convenient and comparable form for the two samples; these included NMSQT scores, rated importance of different life goals, self-ratings on 57 traits, California Psychological Inventory and Holland Vocational Preference Inventory scales, and a few miscellaneous variables related to background, attitudes, and interpersonal behavior.

Again, there were only a few variables showing differences between the groups equivalent to a correlation coefficient of .13 or better. All of these discriminated only for males. This time there appeared to be some degree of consistency among the variables: the twin boys rated themselves as harder working than did the nontwin boys and scored higher on three CPI scales—Self-Control, Achievement via Conformance, and the first factor scale of Nichols and Schnell (1963), interpreted as representing value orientation or emotional maturity.

Since the selective factors in the twin and nontwin samples, while similar, were not exactly the same (the twins, it will be recalled, had to pass the extra hurdle of filling out a zygosity questionnaire), we are not prepared to assert with any confidence that twin males are on the average better socialized than nontwin males, although that is the suggestion in our data. The difference is, in any case, not large in absolute terms. By far the most impressive fact emerging from the analysis is that, on nearly all the variables surveyed, average differences between twins and nontwins, like the differences between identical and fraternal twins, were small or nonexistent. This does not imply that it never makes a difference to one's personality to be a twin (or, if a twin, to be a member of an identical pair); it merely suggests that whatever effect this may have is not in any consistent direction from pair to pair.

How do our results fit with the observations of Koch on her much-smaller but better-controlled samples of 5- and 6-year-old twins and nontwins discussed earlier (tables 3–1 and 3–2)?

★ Our data agree with Koch's in finding a great many more similarities than differences between identical and fraternal twins and between twins and nontwins. With respect to the differences between the two kinds of twins, the data we report in this chapter do not bear on the better established differences (greater closeness of identicals, older fraternal mothers), although we will offer some positive evidence later on these points. The present data offer no great support for the other differences tentatively reported by Koch: more gregariousness, leadership, indirectness, and better speech in the fraternals and a relatively greater preference for males in the identicals (table 3–1). We cannot, of course, say whether Koch's findings represent true but transient differences in the 5-year-olds or whether they are simply chance differences resulting from comparing a small number of subjects on a large number of variables.

For the twin versus nontwin comparisons, we do not have comparable evidence on height, weight or on age of playmates. As far as personality variables go, there does not appear to be in the present data the extra social involvement, popularity, and leadership among the female twins that Koch reports. This difference, if not due to chance sampling, could plausibly be a function of age level: the novelty of twins is likely to be greater in kindergarten than in high school and could well provide a transient social advantage for 5-year-olds.

There is only weak evidence in the present data of the well-established average ability difference between twins and nontwins. The differences do lie in this direction, but the correlations with the NMSQT total score are only $-.01$ for the boys and $-.09$ for the girls—the latter is significantly different from zero but is only on the order of two-tenths of a standard deviation $(.2\sigma)$ in magnitude. Previous large-scale studies (Byrns and Healy 1936; Husén1959; Mehrotra and Maxwell 1949; Record, McKeown, and Edwards 1970; Tabah and Sutter 1954; Myrianthopoulos et al. 1972) have tended to find average twin-nontwin differences in the $.25\sigma$ to $.50\sigma$ range.

There are several reasons why one might expect to find smaller twin-nontwin ability differences in the present study. First, in the previous studies there is some tendency for older samples to yield smaller differences than those observed among preadolescents. Second, Husén found in his study that the differences were larger at the lower end of the intellectual scale (where any effects of brain damage due to the twins' unfavorable prenatal circumstances would be most likely to show up). Our sample is, of course, drawn mostly from the higher end. And, finally, with a sample like the present one, which is selected for above-average ability, one might anticipate that at least part of any existing discrepancy in the population at large would be reflected, not in lower averages for the twins, but in a smaller proportion of twins than nontwins taking the NMSQT.

Thus, on the whole, the twins of the present sample appear to be generally comparable to similarly selected nontwins on personality, ability, and interest measures, and, within the twin group, those who are members of identical-twin pairs show few if any consistent differences from those who are members of fraternal pairs. This means that there will be less difficulty in making comparisons between the two twin types and in generalizing the results to non-twins than there would have been if the differences among the groups had been large. It does not, of course, imply that the hazards in such generalizations vanish altogether.

Chapter 4

Twin Resemblance

In the previous chapter we considered the average scores of identical- and fraternal-twin individuals on the measures of our study and compared these to the average scores obtained by nontwin individuals. We concluded that the two twin groups were very much alike, as well as being generally similar to the nontwins.

In the present chapter we will be looking at the twins as members of pairs. We will be concerned chiefly with the degree of resemblance between members of twin pairs, both identical and fraternal. As discussed in chapter 1, the greater resemblance of identical twins on a behavioral or physical trait has often been interpreted as evidence that the trait is to some degree under genetic control. Identical twins are genetically identical; fraternal twins share on the average only about one-half their genes. Thus, if the environments of the two kinds of twins are equally similar, a greater resemblance among identical pairs than among fraternal pairs can be taken as reflecting genetic influence on the trait in question and, indeed, can be used to estimate what proportion of the trait variance is genetic, that is, the heritability of the trait.[1]

Environmental resemblance may not, of course, be the same for identical and fraternal twins. In this case, the greater resemblance of identicals might partly or wholly reflect a greater similarity in their environments.

To put it differently: if heritability is uniformly low, differences in the observed degree of resemblance between identical and fraternal pairs on different traits should mainly reflect differences in the similarity of their environments with respect to those traits. If heritability is high, the observed differences should mainly reflect differences in the heritability of the traits. In either case, we will be interested in the patterns of identical-fraternal resemblance in our data; we will now examine these, deferring for the present their possible interpretation in terms of heredity and environment.

The basic data on twin resemblance are presented in Appendix B, which gives for each of the 1,600-odd variables the intraclass correlation for identical and fraternal twins, separately for male and female pairs.

Even a casual glance through these correlations should convince the reader (a) that the correlations for both identical and fraternal twins are preponderantly positive; (b) that the identical-twin correlations tend generally to be higher than the fraternal-twin correlations; and (c) that appreciable inconsistencies often exist between the two sexes in the magnitude of a particular identical- or fraternal-twin correlation, which might represent either a true difference or a sampling fluctuation. The effective sample sizes are considerably smaller now that the pair, rather than the individual, is the unit.

We may explore these matters more fully in a small portion of the data. Table 4–1 gives the relevant intraclass correlations for the 18 standard personality scales of the CPI in two random halves of the total sample. Note that virtually all the correlations are positive, with two minor exceptions in one male fraternal subgroup. Also note that, on the whole, the identical-twin cor-

1. Terminology varies. Some authors prefer to call this the "degree of genetic determination"; others refer to it as heritability "in the broad sense."

Table 4–1. Intraclass Correlations on 18 Standard CPI Scales for Identical and Fraternal Male and Female Pairs in Random Subsamples I and II

| CPI scale | Identical | | | | Fraternal | | | |
| | Male | | Female | | Male | | Female | |
	I	II	I	II	I	II	I	II
1573. Dominance	.58	.56	.48	.50	.14	.11	.36	.35
1574. Capacity for Status	.56	.52	.52	.66	.33	.36	.52	.56
1575. Sociability	.60	.41	.56	.53	.40	.09	.36	.29
1576. Social Presence	.62	.39	.48	.60	.21	.08	.20	.42
1577. Self-Acceptance	.43	.40	.50	.58	.23	.04	.36	.37
1578. Sense of Well-being	.54	.54	.54	.35	.33	.32	.38	.14
1579. Responsibility	.65	.49	.39	.47	.18	.39	.46	.32
1580. Socialization	.46	.60	.61	.49	.17	.15	.51	.45
1581. Self-Control	.55	.56	.52	.61	.16	.35	.33	.39
1582. Tolerance	.63	.55	.44	.50	.17	.39	.41	.35
1583. Good Impression	.40	.57	.45	.47	.15	.41	.39	.16
1584. Communality	.34	.28	.49	.37	-.01	.47	.16	.05
1585. Achievement via Conformance	.45	.50	.43	.45	-.10	.19	.18	.34
1586. Achievement via Independence	.61	.53	.57	.48	.33	.44	.41	.42
1587. Intellectual Efficiency	.59	.55	.42	.52	.24	.33	.36	.40
1588. Psychological-Mindedness	.52	.42	.36	.37	.29	.27	.29	.05
1589. Flexibility	.47	.35	.52	.49	.12	.34	.06	.29
1590. Femininity	.37	.45	.23	.36	.30	.23	.12	.17
Pairs	113	89	135	153	54	70	98	95

relations exceed the fraternal-twin correlations: the median for identical-twin correlations over all scales and subgroups is .50; the corresponding fraternal twin median is .32. The identical-twin correlation is higher than the corresponding fraternal correlation in 69 of the 72 possible comparisons in the table (the three discrepant instances fall on different scales and are divided between sexes and subsamples). Finally, absolute agreement ranges from reasonably good for the female identical twins, where the samples are largest (135 and 153 pairs), to considerably poorer for the male fraternals, where the samples are smallest (54 and 70 pairs).

Now, the question of most immediate interest is whether there is a dependable pattern of identical-fraternal difference among these scales. That is, are there some scales on which identical pairs are much more alike than fraternal pairs and other scales on which there is relatively little difference in resemblance between the two groups? In short, are the *differences* between identical- and fraternal-twin correlations consistent over the various subgroups?

The relevant evidence is presented in table 4–2, which shows the differences in correlation between identicals and fraternals; in the right-hand portion of the table, these differences are ranked in order of magnitude. Inspection of

Table 4–2. Differences between Identical- and Fraternal-Twin Correlations and Their Ranks for 18 CPI Scales (Based on Data of Table 4–1)

CPI scale	Differences				Ranks			
	Male		Female		Male		Female	
	I	II	I	II	I	II	I	II
1573. Dominance	.44	.45	.12	.15	4	1½	10	12
1574. Capacity for Status	.23	.16	.00	.10	13½	12	17	16
1575. Sociability	.20	.32	.20	.24	16½	4	5	4
1576. Social Presence	.41	.31	.28	.18	5	5½	3	10
1577. Self-Acceptance	.20	.36	.14	.21	16½	3	9	6½
1578. Sense of Well-being	.21	.22	.16	.21	15	8	7½	6½
1579. Responsibility	.47	.10	-.07	.15	2	15	18	12
1580. Socialization	.29	.45	.10	.04	10	1½	12	18
1581. Self-Control	.39	.21	.19	.22	6	10	6	5
1582. Tolerance	.46	.16	.03	.15	3	12	16	12
1583. Good Impression	.25	.16	.06	.31	12	12	14½	3
1584. Communality	.35	-.19	.33	.32	8	18	2	1½
1585. Achievement via Conformance	.55	.31	.25	.11	1	5½	4	15
1586. Achievement via Independence	.28	.09	.16	.06	11	16	7½	17
1587. Intellectual Efficiency	.35	.22	.06	.12	8	8	14½	14
1588. Psychological-Mindedness	.23	.15	.07	.32	13½	14	13	1½
1589. Flexibility	.35	.01	.46	.20	8	17	1	8
1590. Femininity	.07	.22	.11	.19	18	8	11	9

$W = .209$ $\bar{\rho} = -.054$

these rankings suggests little tendency for certain scales to show consistently greater identical-fraternal differences than others, an impression that is borne out by calculating a coefficient of concordance over the four sets of ranks: $W = .209$, which is equivalent to an average Spearman rank correlation of -.054 between pairs of rankings (Siegel 1956).[2] In short, there is no consistency. Some individual correlations are males, samples I and II, $\rho = -.09$; females, samples I and II, $\rho = .30$; sample I, males and females, $\rho = .04$; sample II, males and females, $\rho = -.22$. None of these correlations differs significantly from zero.

Thus, in the CPI data, we fail to find evidence of any consistent tendency for some scales to show greater differences in identical-fraternal resemblance than other scales do; the identicals are consistently more alike than the fraternals but about equally so on the various scales. There is some indication in table 4–2 that the males show a larger average difference between identicals and fraternals than do the females (the male difference is larger on 15 of the 18 scales in sample I and on 12 of the 18 in sample II); however, this does not lead to any greater consistency for the males—if anything, the difference is in the other direction ($\rho = .30$ for females, -.09 for males, as noted above).

2. Here and elsewhere, W is uncorrected for ties. This correction has only a slight effect on W unless ties are quite numerous.

Is this some peculiarity of the CPI scales, or does the same phenomenon hold more broadly in the data? Before describing an analysis designed to answer this question, a minor point should be made about reliability of measurement. It is quite conceivable that, in an analysis of this sort, one could achieve a degree of quite spurious consistency simply by including some scales of sufficiently low reliability. For, if a scale has zero reliability, one should, with a large enough sample, obtain zero correlations in both identical and fraternal groups and, hence, "consistently" smaller identical-fraternal differences than on, say, one of our CPI scales, which have reliabilities around .80. In fact, one reason for using the CPI in the analysis above was that the CPI scales do not differ too greatly in reliability. A few of the shorter scales—for example, Communality, Psychological-Mindedness, and Flexibility—tend to have reliabilities lower than the others, but the differences are not too drastic, and allowing for them does not greatly change the figures reported above (i.e., the correlation of the males becomes –.13 and that for the females .28, instead of –.09 and .30, if one adjusts the correlations for differences in reliability before ranking them).

Were it not for the reliability considerations mentioned, a plausible approach to examining the generality of our CPI findings across our data would be to draw one or more random samples of our variables and repeat with them the analysis carried out with the CPI scales. But, since many of the variables are single items, some almost certainly of very low reliability, this would run into the difficulty mentioned above. (The problem would not, of course, be alleviated by using *all* the variables rather than just a sample.) Consequently, a series of cluster analyses was carried out on subsets of the data to yield a number of composite variables. The criterion for inclusion in a cluster was a correlation of at least .30 with every other variable in the cluster, and a minimum of three variables was required to define a cluster. Thus, every composite variable is guaranteed a moderate degree of internal-consistency reliability at least.

The cluster-analysis program used begins a cluster with the highest correlation between any two variables in the correlation matrix and each time adds to the cluster that variable whose lowest correlation with the existing members of the cluster is highest. When that correlation is less than .30, the program deletes the variables in the cluster from the correlation matrix and repeats the process, stopping when no correlation as high as .30 is left in the matrix. Only those clusters with at least three members are retained. Thus, no variable enters into more than one cluster, and every variable in a cluster correlates at least .30 with every other.

Computational practicability dictated limiting the variables in a single analysis to a maximum of 160; the desirability of restricting each analysis to variables of roughly similar scale properties led to an analysis of the variables in 13 groups: 3 of CPI items; 2 of OBI items; 1 each of VPI, ACL, and honors items; and then separate groupings for 2-alternative, 3-alternative, 4- to 6-alternative, 7-alternative; and quantitative items from the remainder of the questionnaire. Certain variables were excluded from the cluster analysis in the interests of avoiding statistical artifacts—in particular, the CPI and VPI scales were excluded, as was the NMSQT total score; also, the second occurrences of the 12 repeated items from the CPI were omitted.

The analyses were carried out separately for each of the two half-samples; identical and fraternal and male and female data were combined in each subsample so that the correlations were based on 800 or so cases. With the first half-sample, 73 clusters were obtained, and with the second, 77. Agreement between the samples appeared to be reasonably good: 47 of the clusters were identifiable in both (criterion: at least half their variables shared), and most of the others were minimal clusters emerging in one but not both of the two analyses. Drastically different clustering of the same variables was gratifyingly rare.

For the purpose of examining the consistency of identical-fraternal twin differences, 70 clusters based on the first half-sample were used (the last 3 clusters derived from the CPI items were omitted—for no more profound reason than an error in setting up the computer run). Scores were obtained for each individual on each of the composite cluster variables by summing his scores on the items comprising the cluster. Intraclass correlations were obtained, separately for identical and fraternal males and females in each of the two subsamples. (Note that the correlations in both half-samples are based on the same variables—namely, the clusters as defined in sample I.)

The correlations for the composite variables are presented in table 4–3. In that table, each composite is given a brief label, followed by a list of the variables comprising it.[3] These are given in the order of extraction; that is, the correlation between the first two variables is the highest, and the minimum correlation of each with the preceding ones drops off from left to right. In most cases, interpretation of the clusters was reasonably straightforward; a few rather heterogeneous collections of variables have a question mark after the label (often these represented the last cluster extracted from a particular matrix). It is worth noting that, in general, the intraclass correlations drop off very little from sample I, in which the clusters were derived, to sample II, which speaks well for the coherence of our composites.

The general features of the correlations in table 4–3 resemble those we have noted earlier. Again, the correlations are generally positive (although there are occasional small negative correlations in the fraternal group). Again, the identical-twin correlations tend to run higher than the fraternal correlations. And, again, there is often appreciable group-to-group fluctuation.

In addition, we may note some differences in the levels of twin correlation in different groups of clusters. For example, those clusters based on specific activities (clusters 53–67, derived from the OBI) tend to show generally higher correlations than those based on self-concepts (3–13 and 22–30), occupa-

3. The variable numbers refer to the lists in the appendixes.

Table 4–3. *Intraclass Correlations of 70 Cluster Scores for Identical and Fraternal Male and Female Pairs in Random Subsamples I and II*

| | Identical | | | | Fraternal | | | |
| | Male | | Female | | Male | | Female | |
Cluster	I	II	I	II	I	II	I	II
1. Ability (9, 7, 8, 5, 6, 14)	.73	.80	.86	.89	.48	.52	.59	.66
2. Social aspiration (?) (34, 33, 32)	.01	.01	.24	.26	.06	.10	.56	.26
3. Masculine (549, 502, 543, 496)	.41	.17	.43	.57	.09	.14	.39	.11
4. Confident (503, 486, 464, 488)	.41	.40	.28	.48	.06	-.09	.24	.32
5. Shy (505, 483, -498, -474)	.43	.36	.49	.54	.01	-.04	-.01	.06
6. Popular (493, 481, 490, 463)	.62	.44	.50	.62	.47	.04	.41	.17
7. Responsible (471, 467, 477, 495, 468)	.58	.40	.36	.47	.17	.29	.20	.16
8. Careless: ideal (532, 525, 526)	.08	.22	.37	.41	.21	.06	.14	.18
9. Well-adjusted: ideal (514, 513, 511)	.46	.10	.44	.45	.17	.11	.12	.15
10. Kind (494, 465, 487)	.35	.32	.13	.29	.14	.03	.04	.01
11. Popular: ideal (540, 528, 537)	.39	.20	.42	.50	.15	.25	.36	.10
12. Kind: ideal (541, 512, 546)	.27	.23	.07	.49	.12	.20	.36	.12
13. High-strung (479, 470, 480)	.27	.05	.31	.41	-.18	.10	-.07	-.08
14. Science goals (383, 382, 369)	.44	.28	.31	.32	.16	.25	.02	.14
15. Religious (42, 41, 402, 397)	.81	.76	.83	.83	.75	.47	.85	.77
16. Leader goals (378, 377, 398, 386)	.45	.42	.50	.40	.38	-.02	.39	.25
17. Artistic goals (390, 371, 384, 389)	.33	.42	.53	.56	.34	.00	.23	.10
18. Enjoy life (?) (388, 381, 393)	.28	.24	.33	.29	.09	.05	.22	.05
19. Symptoms (800, 791, 790)	.27	.15	.35	.36	.14	.21	.35	.18
20. Music honors (1029, 1028, 1033, 1034)	.74	.79	.77	.69	.57	.53	.68	.61
21. Professsional music (1032, 1027, 1026, 1030)	.42	.45	.54	.20	.66	-.01	-.03	-.02
22. Tense (756, 710, 774, 675)	.06	.20	.51	.37	-.19	.08	-.03	.15
23. Messy (703, 653, 633)	.09	.24	.23	.06	.21	-.09	.17	-.07
24. Timid (759, 742, 723)	.25	.27	.37	.38	.19	-.14	-.06	.03
25. Reliable (729, 650, 733)	.29	.28	.22	.34	.26	.26	.06	.24
26. Warm (767, 718, 674, 693, 670, 743)	.28	.47	.36	.31	.27	.06	.09	.35
27. Original (713, 680, 625)	.38	.38	.34	.55	.14	.14	.02	.14
28. Cheerful (673, 635, 692)	.25	.09	.32	.35	.27	.01	.22	.05
29. Argumentative (722, 624, 755)	.21	.07	.31	.33	.21	.14	.07	.11
30. Practical (720, 696, 724)	.24	.34	.37	.37	.15	-.06	.14	.29
31. Literary career (888, 884, 904, 974, 854, 954, 897, 864, 874)	.46	.44	.38	.59	.23	.22	.42	.28
32. Military career (917, 886, 975, 990, 839, 880)	.43	.41	.36	.32	.12	.14	.25	.28
33. Crime fighter (842, 840, 945, 976, 906, 946, 966, 993, 968, 956, 926)	.46	.48	.46	.44	.10	.19	.47	.29
34. Science career (970, 920, 910, 877, 980, 848, 930, 940, 870, 950, 960, 850, 900)	.57	.34	.37	.49	-.07	.50	.32	.32
35. Construction (889, 878, 865, 935)	.29	.35	.23	-.05	-.13	.15	-.09	.03
36. Stage director (964, 934, 933)	.36	.43	.30	.34	.05	.02	.22	.27
37. Mechanical (898, 849, 958, 979, 949, 908, 899)	.36	.48	.20	.20	.18	.10	.25	.27

Cluster	Identical				Fraternal			
	Male		Female		Male		Female	
	I	II	I	II	I	II	I	II
38. Diplomatic (896, 876, 856, 858)	.34	.31	.32	.50	.18	.08	.41	.24
39. Adventure (965, 955, 855, 905)	.48	.36	.47	.53	.08	.30	.18	.25
40. Social service (961, 891, 981, 987, 871, 971, 881, 941)	.31	.28	.39	.48	.17	.08	.28	.02
41. Child education (867, 857, 911)	.12	.23	.38	.45	.05	.16	.31	.30
42. Sports (973, 927, 907)	.44	.49	.37	.39	.16	.28	.25	.23
43. Artistic (944, 914, 957)	.41	.38	.30	.43	.03	.28	.31	.34
44. Banking (918, 912, 982, 994)	.27	.36	.30	.26	.34	.27	.20	.08
45. Dangerous (985, 925, 885)	.24	.46	.44	.35	.05	.02	.06	.26
46. Teaching (951, 868, 931, 861, 948)	.39	.30	.39	.37	.05	.15	.37	.26
47. Financial (952, 872, 922, 962, 932)	.30	.11	.10	.27	.03	.12	-.04	-.12
48. Biological science (890, 860, 859)	.47	.38	.40	.35	.17	.30	.24	.32
49. Sales (953, 938, 873)	.42	.27	.18	.29	.16	.08	.20	.02
50. Drawing (984, 894, 991)	.23	.34	.17	.47	.06	-.09	.26	.09
51. Business (913, 883, 963)	.32	.18	.33	.34	.28	.18	.34	.07
52. Bluecollar boss (?) (959, 909, 947)	.24	.43	.34	.09	.08	.26	.10	.47
53. Participation in sports (159, 72, 152)	.71	.54	.71	.52	.48	.42	.62	.41
54. Masculine activities (188, 67, 100, 64)	.77	.73	.50	.53	.51	.56	.54	.35
55. Water sports (167, 73, 158)	.68	.69	.73	.74	.65	.45	.65	.73
56. Party (122, 60, 149, 172)	.71	.58	.70	.79	.55	.38	.59	.58
57. Domestic activities (168, 112, 111, 92, 102, 198)	.55	.58	.63	.57	.53	.37	.31	.38
58. Religious activities (54, 53, 177)	.68	.78	.72	.84	.66	.45	.77	.66
59. Speech activities (305, 249, 275)	.43	.50	.67	.64	.29	.13	.55	.66
60. Tough male (289, 209, 301, 266, 274, 269)	.65	.52	.60	.58	.49	.48	.58	.48
61. Alcohol (312, 228, 316, 268)	.69	.62	.71	.74	.55	.70	.72	.47
62. Personal exchange (?) (295, 237, 260, 250)	.53	.61	.69	.57	.39	.58	.54	.47
63. Family quarrel (340, 257, 255)	.52	.64	.63	.40	.27	.36	.42	.33
64. Tough female (290, 208, 236)	.47	.45	.66	.64	.45	.34	.49	.52
65. Band/orchestra (307, 300, 205)	.75	.79	.85	.67	.52	.53	.71	.58
66. Feminine activities (282, 280, 347, 351)	.47	.43	.53	.39	.14	.35	.32	.29
67. Dating (357, 224, 288)	.72	.67	.71	.74	.59	.42	.60	.34
68. Like parties (1310, 1255, 1334)	.67	.31	.60	.48	.57	.39	.31	.27
69. Shy with strangers (1319, 1278, 1376)	.22	.40	.36	.43	.17	-.02	.09	.13
70. Feel no good (1371, 1344, 1335, 1349)	.35	.37	.33	.27	.06	.21	.19	.25

tional interests (31–52), or life goals (14–18)—except for religion (cluster 15). It is, of course, not altogether surprising that twins should often share activities or that family membership should be more important than individual inclination in determining religious attitudes and practices. However, we will be returning to discussion of some of these matters later.

We now wish to address ourselves to the issue that prompted this general analysis: are identical twins consistently more similar than fraternal twins on some variables than on others?

Table 4–4. Intraclass Correlations of 5 NMSQT Subtests for Identical and Fraternal Male and Female Pairs in the 1962 and 1965 Twin Samples

| NMSQT subtest | Reliability[a] | Identical | | | | Fraternal | | | |
| | | Male | | Female | | Male | | Female | |
		'62	'65	'62	'65	'62	'65	'62	'65
5. English Usage	.91	.72	.73	.78	.71	.65	.50	.50	.53
6. Mathematics	.88	.74	.70	.71	.71	.41	.52	.46	.49
7. Social Studies	.84	.75	.69	.79	.68	.44	.47	.57	.57
8. Natural Science	.83	.71	.63	.65	.65	.52	.45	.53	.44
9. Vocabulary	.96	.85	.87	.87	.88	.61	.63	.66	.60
Pairs		216	575	293	725	135	371	195	493

[a]Split-half, based on 1962 NMSQT.

To answer this question, we may rank order the identical-fraternal differences in each of the four subsamples (male and female pairs in the two half-samples) and compute a coefficient of concordance and Spearman rank correlations as before. We did this. The coefficient of concordance turned out to be .263, which is equivalent to an average correlation of .02 among the rankings. The male-female correlations are .01 in sample I and −.05 in sample II. The correlations between random subsamples are −.12 and .12 for males and females, respectively. None of these differs significantly from a correlation of zero. In short, this broader survey of our data fully agrees with the results of the analysis of the CPI scales: no consistent tendency is found for certain variables to show larger differences in correlation between identical and fraternal twins than others. And this is true for comparisons both within and across the sexes.

It is of interest to make the same kind of analysis for the ability measures, the NMSQT subtests. Here, we can base conclusions on considerably larger samples, since these scores were also available for the twins of the 1965 sample. Table 4–4 shows the intraclass correlations for the 1962 and 1965 samples. Note that with these larger numbers of cases and with fairly reliable measures (the split-half reliabilities of the subtests range from .83 for Natural Science to .96 for Vocabulary) the correlations are reasonably stable. The resemblances are higher in the identical-twin group, as usual, and there do not appear to be striking sex differences. The Vocabulary subtest appears to show somewhat higher correlations than the others. (This is probably attributable in part to its higher reliability, but adjusting for reliability would not wipe out the difference altogether.)

The differences between identical- and fraternal-twin correlations are shown in the left-hand portion of table 4–5, and their rank ordering on the right.

Table 4–5. Differences between Identical- and Fraternal-Twin Correlations and Their Ranks for the 5 NMSQT Subtests (Based on Data of Table 4-4)

| NMSQT subtest | Differences | | | | Ranks | | | |
| | Male | | Female | | Male | | Female | |
	'62	'65	'62	'65	'62	'65	'62	'65
5. English Usage	.07	.23	.28	.18	5	2	1	4
6. Mathematics	.33	.18	.25	.22	1	4½	2	2
7. Social Studies	.31	.22	.22	.11	2	3	3	5
8. Natural Science	.19	.18	.12	.21	4	4½	5	3
9. Vocabulary	.24	.24	.21	.28	3	1	4	1

$W = .228$ $\bar{\rho} = -.029$

There appear to be no consistent tendencies for identical-fraternal differences in resemblance to be greater for some subtests than for others. This is borne out by a coefficient of concordance of .228, corresponding to an average correlation of -.03 among the rankings. (With the correlations adjusted for differences in reliability, these become .075 and -.23, respectively.) Thus, the ability measures show us the same picture as the personality measures: identical twins are more alike than fraternals, but not consistently more so on some variables than on others.

Table 4–6 may serve as a kind of summary of our data on twin resemblance. Here we present the median intraclass correlations for groups of measures representing different areas of personality. These include four groupings of composite variables from the cluster analysis—representing self-concepts, ideals and goals, vocational interests, and activities—plus the NMSQT subtests and the CPI scales (9 special scales as well as the 18 standard scales are included). Median correlations are given for each of our basic subgroups; thus, the .74 under Identical Male I represents the median of the five NMSQT subtest intraclass correlations for male identical-twin pairs in the first half-sample.

Various general trends may be noted in table 4–6, including the obviously higher correlations among the identicals; the greater twin resemblance for both groups on the abilities and activities measures, the intermediate resemblance on the CPI scales, and the lower resemblance on self-concepts, ideals, and vocational interests; and the generally similar patterns of resemblance for males and females, with perhaps the female pairs showing slightly greater resemblance (in 18 of the 21 comparisons where there is a difference, the females are higher).

The differences between the typical correlations for the identical twins and the fraternal twins are given in table 4–7, which shows much the same picture

Table 4–6. *Typical Twin Resemblances in Different Areas of Personality*

	Median correlation							
	Identical				Fraternal			
	Male		Female		Male		Female	
Variables	I	II	I	II	I	II	I	II
5 NMSQT subtests	.74	.71	.79	.74	.47	.55	.47	.60
15 self-concept clusters[a]	.28	.32	.34	.37	.17	.04	.07	.14
9 ideals and goals clusters[a]	.39	.24	.42	.45	.17	.06	.23	.14
22 vocational interest clusters[a]	.36	.36	.35	.36	.09	.16	.25	.26
17 activities clusters[a]	.68	.61	.69	.64	.52	.42	.58	.47
27 CPI scales	.56	.50	.49	.50	.22	.23	.36	.30

[a]The clusters are self-concept, 4–7, 10, 13, 22–30; ideals and goals, 8, 9, 11, 12, 14–18; vocational, 31–52; and activities, 20, 21, 53–67.

Table 4–7. *Differences between Typical Identical- and Fraternal-Twin Correlations in Different Areas of Personality (Based on the Data of Table 4–6)*

| | Differences | | | | Ranks | | | |
| | Males | | Females | | Males | | Females | |
Variables	I	II	I	II	I	II	I	II
NMSQT subtests	.27	.16	.32	.14	2½	6	1	5
Self-concept clusters	.11	.28	.27	.23	6	1	2	2
Ideals and goals clusters	.22	.18	.19	.31	4	5	3	1
Vocational interest clusters	.27	.20	.10	.10	2½	3	6	6
Activities clusters	.16	.19	.11	.17	5	4	5	4
CPI scales	.34	.27	.13	.20	1	2	4	3

$$W = .195 \qquad \bar{\rho} = .074$$

as previous similar tables in this chapter. Its message might roughly be translated: "Identical twins correlate about .20 higher than fraternal twins, give or take some sampling fluctuation, and it doesn't much matter what you measure—whether the difference is between .75 and .55 on an ability measure, between .50 and .30 on a personality scale, or between .35 and .15 on a self-concept composite."

This is not *literally* true, of course; we have measures in our study, such as self-report of race (40),[4] for which both groups correlate in the .90's, and others, such as handedness (13), for which the intraclass correlations in both

4. Variable numbers are shown in parentheses (see Appendix A).

groups are essentially zero. It is, indeed, with some feeling of relief that we are able to report that the identical-twin pairs are *not* noticeably more alike than the fraternals in the size of their high school classes (15), the size and urbanization of their hometowns (18 and 19), and the presence of various items in their homes (575–615). Otherwise, we might have to start worrying about some pervasive response artifact, such as collaboration of the identicals in filling out the questionnaire.

The findings reported so far in this chapter were hardly of a sort to make us optimistic, but it seemed possible that, if a fairly large number of rather specific variables were screened, one might still locate a few that showed a consistent tendency to be high or low in difference between identical and fraternal resemblance. We decided to attempt such an analysis with the CPI item pool.

First, in order to avoid the difficulties presented by low item reliability, we selected only those CPI items that could stand alone psychometrically. Goldberg and Rorer (1964) obtained 3- to 4-week test-retest data for the CPI item pool for three samples of college students, ranging in size from 95 to 179. We retained only those items that had test-retest reliability coefficients (phi coefficients) of at least .50 in *each* of the three samples. There were 179 such highly dependable items out of the 468 nonduplicated items on the CPI.

Next, we sorted out from among these reliable items those in which the intraclass correlation between identical twins was at least .20 higher than that between fraternal twins ("high-difference" items) and those in which either the correlation between identicals was no more than .02 above that between fraternals or the fraternal correlation was higher ("low-difference" items). This procedure was carried out separately in the two random halves of our total sample. The question was simply, Are high and low identical-fraternal differences consistent properties of particular items, or are we screening chance sampling fluctuation? And, if consistent, what sorts of items fall into the two categories?

There were 55 and 54 items meeting our criterion of high difference in the two half-samples and 38 and 31 items meeting our criterion of low difference. Table 4–8 shows the answer to our critical question: Is there cross-sample consistency on such items? The answer is yes, a very little. There are a few more high-high and low-low cases (27) than high-low and low-high (18). A closer examination of table 4–8 suggests that this modest amount of consistency derives mostly from the low-difference items. Given the marginal totals, one would predict 16.6 chance matches of high-difference items—and 16 occurred. However, only 6.6 chance matches of low-difference items would be predicted, and 11 were observed. In slightly different terms, if one collapses table 4–8 into a 2 × 2 table of "high" versus "other," one finds no relationship ($\chi^2 = .04$), whereas if one collapses it into a 2 × 2 table of "low" versus "other," a significant association appears ($\chi^2 = 4.57$, 1 *df*, $p < .05$).

Table 4–8. The Consistency of High- and Low-Difference CPI Items across Random Half-Samples (See Text for Explanation)

| | | Second half-sample | | | |
		High	Neither	Low	Total
First half-sample	High	16	32	6	54
	Neither	27	46	14	87
	Low	12	15	11	38
	Total	55	93	31	179

In short, it appears that one can dependably select items from the CPI on which identical-twin pairs are not noticeably more similar than fraternal-twin pairs but not items on which the identical-fraternal difference in resemblance is exceptionally large.

The 16 items from the high-high cell of table 4–8 and the 11 items from the low-low cell are listed in table 4–9. The high items appear to constitute a varied group describing various aspects of personality, abilities, and interests. All are clearly self-descriptive in character. Several items like these also appear in the group of low items, but the distinctive feature here is a number of items expressing social attitudes: "A person who doesn't vote is not a good citizen," "I do not like to see people carelessly dressed," "I believe women should have as much sexual freedom as men," "People have a real duty to take care of their aged parents, even if it means making some pretty big sacrifices."

The proposition that items expressing political and social attitudes tend to show little difference in identical- and fraternal-twin resemblance receives some support elsewhere in our data. For example, the three opinion items (402–404) on attitudes toward God, racial integration, and federal welfare programs show intraclass correlations of .57 and .67, .37 and .40, and .27 and .14, for identical and fraternal pairs, respectively. It is perhaps plausible that twin resemblance on political and social attitudes is primarily a function of family membership and, thus, is essentially similar for both groups. And, again, it is reassuring, in terms of possible response artifacts, that identical twins are not more similar than fraternal twins on *everything*.

Thus, this analysis, like the preceding ones in this chapter, fails to find consistent tendencies for some CPI items descriptive of personality, abilities, and interests to show larger identical-fraternal differences than others do, although we do find a suggestion that differences on items expressing political and social attitudes may show relatively little association with zygosity.

We began this chapter with a discussion of how differences in identical-fraternal resemblance on various traits might be used to estimate the differen-

Table 4-9. CPI Items Classified as High and Low in Differentiation in Both Half-Samples in Table 4-8

Variable
no.

High in both
1096. A person needs to "show off" a little now and then.
1100. I liked "Alice in Wonderland" by Lewis Carroll.
1130. It is hard for me to start a conversation with strangers.
1138. I think I would like the work of a school teacher.
1187. The idea of doing research appeals to me.
1216. I am likely not to speak to people until they speak to me.
1273. I have always tried to make the best school grades that I could.
1297. I enjoy a race or game better when I bet on it.
1331. I like to talk before groups of people.
1388. I would like to be an actor on the stage or in the movies.
1415. I have never done any heavy drinking.
1451. I think I am usually a leader in my group.
1483. I am quite a fast reader.
1535. I'm not the type to be a political leader.
1557. I must admit that I am a high-strung person.
1571. I sweat very easily even on cool days.

Low in both
1105. I am very slow in making up my mind.
1110. A person who doesn't vote is not a good citizen.
1180. I do not like to see people carelessly dressed.
1215. I think I am stricter about right and wrong than most people.
1224. I fall in and out of love rather easily.
1240. I believe women should have as much sexual freedom as men.
1313. People have a real duty to take care of their aged parents, even if it means making some pretty big sacrifices.
1350. In school I found it very hard to talk before the class.
1420. I find that a well-ordered mode of life with regular hours is congenial to my temperament.
1477. It is pretty easy for people to win arguments with me.
1568. I had my own way as a child.

tial heritability of these traits (or the differential pressures of the environment upon them). We emerge with no such differences to interpret! We defer a consideration of the implications of this finding until our final chapter; we have other relevant data and analyses to report first. It is appropriate, however, to

Table 4–10. Identical- and Fraternal-Twin Correlations on Measures of General Ability in Various Twin Studies

Test	Correlations		Pairs		Source
	I	F	I	F	
National & Multi-Mental	.85	.26	45	57	Wingfield & Sandiford (1928)[a]
Otis	.84	.47	65	96	Herrman & Hogben (1933)
Binet	.88	.90	34	28	Stocks (1933)
Binet & Otis	.92	.63	50	50	Newman, Freeman, & Holzinger (1937)
I-Test	.87	.55	36	71	Husén (1947)[b]
Simplex & C-Test	.88	.72	128	141	Wictorin (1952)
Intelligence factor	.76	.44	26	26	Blewett (1954)
JPQ-12	.62	.28	52	32	Cattell, Blewett, & Beloff (1955)[c]
I-Test	.90	.70	215	416	Husén (1959)
Otis	.83	.59	34	34	Gottesman (1963)
Various group tests	.94	.55	95	127	Burt (1966)
PMA IQ	.79	.45	33	30	Koch (1966)
Vocabulary composite	.83	.66	85	135	Huntley (1966)
PMA total score	.88	.67	123	75	Loehlin & Vandenberg (1968)[c]
General-ability factor	.80	.48	337	156	Schoenfeldt (1968)
ITPA total	.90	.62	28	33	Mittler (1969)
Tanaka B	.81	.66	81	32	Kamitake (1971)
Median of above	.85	.59			
NMSQT 1962	.87	.63	687	482	Nichols (1965)
1965	.86	.62	1,300	864	

Note: Where more than one test used, averaged r's are given; studies with less than 25 pairs in each group not included.

[a] As recalculated by Stocks (1933).
[b] Cited in Husén (1959, p. 46).
[c] Correlations derived from data presented in another form.

inquire at this point whether there is precedent for findings such as ours in previous twin studies in the literature.

It will be convenient to discuss the evidence on abilities first and then to proceed to the data on personality.

First—to document the obvious—previous studies have generally reported a greater resemblance of identical than of fraternal twins on measures of ability. Table 4-10 presents correlations from a number of studies in the literature involving IQ's or other fairly general measures of intellectual ability. In only one instance do the identicals fail to be more similar than the fraternals.

Similar results have been reported for special abilities. Vandenberg (1968) summarizes the results of 10 twin studies, most of them fairly recent, in which tests measuring a number of mental abilities were administered to identical- and fraternal-twin groups. The tests included the Thurstone Primary Mental Abilities test, the Differential Aptitude Tests (DAT), the Wechsler Adult Intelligence Scale (WAIS), and others. On a total of 76 different subscale measurements reported in these studies, the identicals failed to be more similar than the fraternals only once (on a test of paired-associate memory in a Swedish study). Not all the differences were large or statistically significant, but the consistency is impressive. Schoenfeldt (1968) also found, for both sexes, identicals to be more similar than fraternals on three differential aptitude factors extracted from the Project TALENT test battery.

How much more similar are identicals than fraternals on ability measures? In table 4–10 the median correlations of identical and same-sex fraternal twins on general-ability measures are .85 and .59, respectively—a difference of .26. The nearest thing we have to a general-ability measure in the present study is the NMSQT total score, which presumably contains appreciable academic achievement variance as well. The correlations among identical twins on this measure are .87 and .86 in the 1962 and 1965 samples and, among fraternals, .63 and .62—a difference of .24 in each case. Our figures are thus not very different from typical values reported in other twin studies in the literature. We should, however, note that the compilations made by Erlenmeyer-Kimling and Jarvik (1963; Jarvik and Erlenmeyer-Kimling 1967) and Burt (1966) yielded slightly higher median correlations for identical twins reared together (.87 to .88) and slightly lower median correlations for same-sex fraternal twins (.53 to .56) than we found in our survey of the literature—thus, slightly larger identical-fraternal twin differences (.31 to .35). These authors have apparently included some studies involving only one kind of twin or having very small samples in one or both groups—conditions that make comparability of sampling difficult to assess. But they also may have located some studies that we have missed.

Our results for measures of different abilities (the NMSQT subtests) are compared with results from several studies in the literature in table 4–11. This table contains for each study the median identical- and fraternal-twin correlations reported for the various measures of specialized intellectual abilities used in the study. It will be noted that the medians of the NMSQT subtests in our study lie slightly above the average of previous studies. This could be due either to higher reliability or to the presence of academic achievement variance. The difference between identical- and fraternal-twin correlations is .23 in the other studies cited and .22 in ours.

Have other studies, like ours, failed to show consistent differences in twin

Table 4-11. Median Correlations on Measures of Special Abilities in Various Twin Studies

No. of scales	Population	Median correlation		Pairs		Source
		I	F	I	F	
12	Schoolchildren (Sweden)	.67	.58	128	141	Wictorin (1952)
4	Military recruits (Sweden)	.78	.60	215	415	Husén (1959)
7	Aged (New York)	.68	.44	75	45	Jarvik et al. (1962)
8	Adult males (Finland)	.70	.42	157	189	Partanen, Bruun, & Markkanen (1966)
15	High school (Michigan & Kentucky)	.66	.50	123	75	Loehlin & Vandenberg (1968)[a]
3	High school (United States)	.65	.40	337	156	Schoenfeldt (1968)
21	High school (Kentucky)	.64	.43	137	99	Vandenberg (1969)
	Median of above	.67	.44			
5	Present study	.74	.52	509	330	

[a]Derived from data presented in another form.

resemblance on measures of different abilities? Despite the existence of some assertions to the contrary, this appears to be the case.

For example, the Thurstone Primary Mental Abilities test has been given to at least four different twin samples; the results have been tabulated by Vandenberg (1968). Table 4-12 shows the rank orders of a measure of differential twin resemblance for the five scales used in all four studies. The agreement can hardly be described as striking. The coefficient of concordance of .322 is not statistically significant; it corresponds to an average correlation of .10 between the rankings. Most of whatever correlation there is derives from the relatively low status of the Reasoning scale—which has reliability problems.

The first three of Thurstone's primary abilities—verbal comprehension, spatial ability, and numerical ability—are fairly widely represented in cognitive test batteries. Measures of these three abilities are available in 10 studies included in Vandenberg's review. Table 4-13 shows the rank ordering of differential twins resemblance on these measures. There is obviously no very strong tendency for the identicals to show a consistently greater difference than fra-

Table 4–12. Rank Ordering of F-Ratios of Identical- and Fraternal-Twin Within-Pair Variance on PMA Scales in Four Twin Studies (Based on Data from Vandenberg 1968)

	Study			
	Blewett	Thurstone	Vandenberg (Michigan)	Vandenberg (Kentucky)
Verbal	1	2	1	4
Space	4	1	4	1
Number	5	4	2	2
Reasoning	2½	5	5	5
Word Fluency	2½	3	3	3
	$W = .322$	$\bar{\rho} = .096$		

ternals on one of these dimensions than another. Typically, the identical-twin pairs are more similar than the fraternals in cognitive abilities—but to roughly the same degree, it would appear, in different ones.

One possible exception to this generalization should be mentioned. One or more tests of rote memory were included in four of the studies cited in Vandenberg's review, and in only one of the four studies were identical twins significantly more alike than fraternal twins on any rote memory measure. Thus, rote memory *may* differ in this respect from other cognitive abilities. However, it should be noted that (1) rote memory tests often have reliability difficulties, which could lead to spuriously low identical-fraternal differences; (2) in the one study in which identicals *did* show up as significantly more similar in rote memory, the two memory measures used were quite comparable to measures of other abilities in the magnitude of this difference; and (3) Schoenfeldt (1968) reports identicals to be more similar than fraternals on a memory factor in the Project TALENT study—the difference is statistically significant for both sexes and fairly large for the males. Thus, the picture regarding memory abilities is not altogether clear.

The Project TALENT data, by the way, show the same lack of consistency that we have observed elsewhere: the three special-ability factors rank in the order memory, spatial visualization, and perceptual speed, for the males, and in the order spatial visualization, perceptual speed, and memory, for the females.

A recent study by Vandenberg (1969) reports identical- and fraternal-twin correlations for a large battery of spatial perception and other cognitive tests. It is difficult for us to share Vandenberg's view that "the results of this study add further evidence for the fact that different mental abilities are determined,

Table 4–13. *Rank Ordering of F-Ratios of Identical- and Fraternal-Twin Within-Pair Variance on Verbal, Spatial, and Numerical Abilities in Various Twin Studies (Based on Data from Vandenberg 1968)*

Test and scales		Rankings		
		V	S	N
PMA (Verbal, Space, Number): Blewett		1	2	3
Thurstone		2	1	3
Michigan		1	3	2
Louisville		3	1	2
DAT (Verbal Reasoning, Space Relations, Numerical Ability):	1961	1	2	3
	1965	1	2	3
WAIS (Vocabulary, Block Design, Arithmetic)		1	3	2
Wictorin (Verbal Analysis, Form Perception, Arithmetic)		3	2	1
Husén (Synonyms, Matrices, Number Series)		1	3	2
Bruun (Verbal Opposites, Paper Formboard, Addition and Subtraction)		2	3	1

$$W = .120 \qquad \bar{\rho} = .022$$

V: Verbal.
S: Spatial.
N: Numerical.

to different degrees, by hereditary components." While identical twins do indeed show higher correlations than fraternal twins on most of the tests given and while the correlations do indeed vary, the differences among measures of the same type (sometimes between parts of a given test) appear to be fully as large as the differences between types of measures on which this conclusion is presumably based. Among the tests showing relatively large identical-fraternal differences are a couple of spatial tests (Surface Development and Newcastle), a vocabulary test (Heim), and a reasoning test (Ship Destination). And among the tests showing relatively small identical-fraternal differences are a couple of spatial tests (Form Board and Paper Folding), a vocabulary test (Wide Range), and a reasoning test (Logical Inference). While we can think of a number of excellent reasons why different mental abilities *might* be influenced to different degrees by heredity and environment, we can find little consistent evidence, in our own data or in the literature, that they *are*.

What about personality?

Again, it is not difficult to find evidence from other studies that identical twins are generally more similar on personality measures than are fraternal twins, although the data are less unanimous on this point than in the case of abilities. Another Vandenberg review (1967) provides a convenient summary. This covers 14 studies using 10 different multiple-scale personality inventories.

Table 4–14. Median Correlations on Personality and Interest Scales in Various Twin Studies

No. of scales	Population	Median correlation		No. of pairs		Source
		I	F	I	F	
4	High school (California)	.60	.33	40	43	Carter (1933)
7	High school (Michigan)	.55	.00	45	35	Vandenberg (1967)
31	High school (Minnesota)	.45	.21	34	34	Gottesman (1963)
4	Adult (Netherlands)	.50	.34	88	42	Wilde (1964)
18	High school (Massachusetts)	.48	.31	79	68	Gottesman (1966)[a]
4	Adult (Finland)	.26	.18	157	189	Partanen, Bruun, & Markkanen (1966)
12	High school (Kentucky)	.47	.24	111	92	Vandenberg, Comrey, & Stafford (1967)
11	High school (United States)	.44	.33	337	156	Schoenfeldt (1968)
	Median of above	.48	.28			
27	Present study	.50	.28	490	317	(CPI scales)

[a]Data presented in another form; intraclass correlations courtesy of the author.

There are altogether 150 single-scale comparisons possible; the identical twins are more alike than the fraternals on 129 of them. In addition, Schoenfeldt (1968) presents data on 11 noncognitive factors from the Project TALENT data, which include a variety of personality and interest measures derived from questionnaires filled out by his 337 identical and 156 fraternal pairs at the time of the original Project TALENT testing. The male identical twins have higher intraclass correlations than the fraternals on 10 of the 11 measures, the females on all 11.

The magnitude of the typical differences found in a number of studies can be judged from table 4-14. As is evident from the table, our results from the CPI are reasonably comparable to those obtained in other studies with personality inventories. It will be recalled, however, that some of the personality and interest measures in the present study yielded correlations somewhat lower than this (self-concept, ideals and goals, and vocational interests), and some yielded correlations somewhat higher (activities).

Table 4–15. Rank Ordering of F-Ratios of Identical- and Fraternal-Twin Within-Pair Variance on Scales of Two Personality Inventories in Different Twin Studies (Based on Data from Vandenberg 1967)

Scale	MMPI Rankings			Scale	JPQ–HSPQ Rankings		
Hs	7	10	3	I	4½	7½	7
D	3	1	7	Q_4	3	2	10
Hy	10	7	1	C	1	1	8
Pd	2	2	8	Q_3	8½	3	3
Mf	8	8	2	D	6	9½	9
Pa	9	3	5	A	8½	6	6
Pt	5	6	10	H	7	9½	2
Sc	4	4½	9	E	10	7½	4
Ma	6	9	6	J	2	4	5
Si	1	4½	4	F	4½	5	1

$W = .213 \qquad \bar{\rho} = -.180 \qquad\qquad W = .310 \qquad \bar{\rho} = -.035$

Finally, what evidence does the literature present concerning the relative stability of differences in identical-fraternal twin resemblance for different personality traits?

In Vandenberg's review (1967), two inventories are cited that have each been used with three twin samples: the Minnesota Multiphasic Personality Inventory (MMPI) and R. B. Cattell's Junior Personality Quiz (JPQ) and its revised form, the High School Personality Questionnaire (HSPQ). We have rank ordered Vandenberg's measure of twin resemblance for the scales of each of these inventories in table 4–15 and computed coefficients of concordance. They are .213 and .310, neither one significantly different from zero, and they correspond to average correlations of −.18 and −.04 between rankings, respectively.

Table 4–16 shows similar comparisons made for three personality dimensions for which some sort of equivalent could be found in each of eight studies. These dimensions are neuroticism, extraversion-introversion, and dominance. The coefficient of concordance across the eight sets of rankings is .109, again not significant, and it is equivalent to an average correlation of −.02 among the rank orders.

Thompson and Wilde (1973), who have independently made a similar review of the twin literature and arrived at rather similar conclusions, report the rank-order agreement across the two sexes for heritability estimates from a number of twin studies. They found a median correlation of .12. In the Project

Table 4-16. Rank Ordering of F-Ratios of Identical- and Fraternal-Twin Within-Pair Variance for Measures of Neuroticism, Extraversion-Introversion, and Dominance in Various Twin Studies (Based on Data from Vandenberg 1967)

Test and scales	Rankings		
	N	E-I	D
Bernreuter (Neuroticism, Sociability, Dominance)	2	3	1
JPQ–HSPQ (Factors C, A, E): Cattell	1	2	3
Vandenberg	1	2	3
Gottesman	3	2	1
Thurstone (Stable, Sociable, Dominant)	2	1	3
CPI (Psychoneurotic, Sociability, Dominance)	3	1	2
Bruun (Neuroticism, Shyness, Ascendance)	2	1	3

$$W = .109 \qquad \bar{\rho} = -.018$$

N: Neuroticism.
E-I: Extraversion-Introversion.
D: Dominance.

TALENT data (Schoenfeldt 1968), not included in Thompson and Wilde's survey, the rank-order correlation between identical-fraternal differences for male and for female twins over 11 personality and interest factors is -.11. Finally, the correlation between heritability estimates derived from twin differences on the CPI scales in the present data and data from a twin study by Gottesman is -.22 for males and -.24 for females—neither significantly different from zero (Nichols 1966).

In short, for personality and interests, as for abilities, the existing twin literature appears to agree with our own finding that, while identical-twin pairs tend to be more similar than fraternal-twin pairs, it is difficult to demonstrate that they are consistently more similar on some traits than on others.

One implication of this is that, if one sets out to review the literature for evidence of the heritability of a particular personality dimension (as Scarr 1969*b* has done for extraversion-introversion), one should be successful—that is, one should be able to show that identical twins are more similar than fraternal twins on the trait in question. The difficulty is in showing that trait X is more heritable than trait Y. If our average rank correlations were predominantly positive, but merely low, one could argue that what is needed are larger samples or more reliable tests. Correlations fluctuating around zero cannot be dealt with so simply. However, further discussion of this matter, as we have already indicated, must be deferred to a later chapter. We have other evidence to look at first.

Chapter 5

Early Environment

In the two preceding chapters we have considered the current characteristics of the twins: first, as compared to nontwins and, second, in terms of the resemblances between members of twin pairs. Our data were mostly the reports of the twins themselves about their current and recent behaviors and attitudes. And, insofar as our measures sampled actual performances, they, too, were contemporary.

In the present chapter we turn to another source of data—parental report—and a wider time span—events and behaviors from birth onward.

It will be recalled that a parent of the twins (usually the mother) filled out an 11-page questionnaire describing the twins' homes, the parents' child-rearing philosophies and practices, the twins' behavior at different ages, and various incidents of their early lives. We are well aware of the fallibility of parents' retrospective accounts of the early history of their children (e.g., Caldwell 1964, pp. 16–17; Robbins 1963). However, fallible data interpreted with some caution are clearly better than no data at all, and we even have some grounds for supposing that, of their kind, our data are reasonably good. Our mothers were of above-average education—approximately 80% were high school graduates—and the questionnaire shows internal evidence of being filled out with some care (as discussed in chapter 2). Also, a number of our items were phrased in terms of a comparison between the twins, and relative judgments of this kind are probably easier to make than absolute ones. Consider the ordinary mother asked about the age at which Johnny started walking. Unless she happens to have this particular fact stored as such in her memory, she is likely to arrive at an answer only by means of a chain of inference that begins something like "Well, he was walking pretty well at the time we were at Grandma's at Christmas, so that means he must have started about. . ." Such a chain of inference is obviously fraught with opportunities for error: it may have been Thanksgiving or Christmas of some other year and brother Jimmy who was doing the walking; and, even if her facts are correct, her mental arithmetic may not lead to an accurate answer. The mother of twins who is asked whether Jimmy or Johnny walked first is in a much better position to retrieve that fact directly. Similarly, while it may be difficult for a mother to decide whether, in an absolute sense, Johnny should be described as having had a bad temper as a child, it may be considerably easier for her to conclude that, at any rate, Johnny's temper was worse than Jimmy's.

The questionnaire filled out by the parent of the twins consists of six major sections: a page of face-sheet items (4–11); a series of items in which the parent is asked to indicate whether a number of specific things were true of one twin, the other twin, both, or neither at various ages from infancy to adolescence (12–160); several items characterizing the home environment of the twins—child-rearing attitudes and practices, methods of discipline, and specific disruptive events, such as parental illness or absence (161–233); a series of items in which the parent is asked to contrast the twins—to say which twin weighed more at birth, learned to ride a bicycle first, or is more inter-

Table 5-1. Mean Parental Age and Education and Family Income, for Male and Female Identical- and Fraternal-Twin Groups

Variable	Identicals		Fraternals	
	M	F	M	F
7. Mother's age	46.01	46.19	47.34	47.25
8. Father's age	48.92	49.53	50.15	50.34
9. Mother's education[a]	3.34	3.36	3.59	3.48
10. Father's education[a]	3.53	3.57	3.68	3.66
11. Family income[b]	3.00	3.29	3.38	3.31

[a]Scale value 3 is high school graduate; scale value 4 is part college or junior college.
[b]Scale value 3 is $7,500 to $9,999; scale value 4 is $10,000 to $14,999.

ested in science (234-282); and, finally, some items about twin treatment as such—whether the twins were dressed alike, separated in school, and so on, and whether the parent believes the twins to be identical or fraternal (283-289). (The questionnaire is reproduced in Appendix A.)

Let us begin with the information on age, education, and so forth provided by the initial items on the questionnaire. Table 5-1 presents the means for these variables. The well-known tendency for fraternal twins to be born of older mothers is evident in this sample—the fraternal twins' mothers average about a year older than the identical twins' mothers. The fathers do, too, but since paternal age is not thought to affect fraternal twinning (Yerushalmy and Sheerar 1940), this probably is just a secondary consequence of the maternal age difference. (One would, in this case, expect the paternal difference to be smaller, by virtue of statistical regression, and it is, slightly.) The fraternal twins' parents also on the average have a little more education and (possibly) higher income. It seems plausible that both of these variables would sometimes be associated with delay in starting a family and, thus, with a greater probability of fraternal twinning.

The parent questionnaire also contains an item (37) on premature birth. The percentages of premature twin births in our sample were 48% and 41% for identical males and females and 41% and 36% for fraternal males and females. The higher proportion of prematurity in males than in females and in identicals than in fraternals is consistent with the higher proportion of stillbirths and infant mortality in these groups reported by Barr and Stevenson (1961) in their large-scale study of twin births in England. The overall proportion of premature births is within the range of those obtained in other studies of twins, although somewhat lower than the 50%-60% prematurity most often reported (see Koch 1966, p. 28). Since the definition of prematurity differs in different studies (our parents were allowed to provide their own), probably

Table 5-2. Percentage of Parental Judgments of Zygosity Agreeing with Questionnaire Diagnosis

Parental judgment	Questionnaire diagnosis	
	Identical (%)	Fraternal (%)
Certain they are identical twins	70.0	11.0
Think they are identical twins	10.9	4.8
Don't know, or omitted item	1.4	4.8
Think they are fraternal twins	3.7	11.3
Certain they are fraternal twins	14.0	68.1
Total	100.0	100.0

not too much should be made of this difference. However, it does seem plausible that in this group of fairly successful twins, twin pairs handicapped by extreme prematurity might be underrepresented. We find, in any case, no evidence that the premature twins in our sample were disadvantaged in intellectual performance. In fact, the NMSQT total scores for the twin individuals designated as premature averaged slightly higher than for the nonprematures in both half-samples of the data: 105.98 versus 100.63 in the first, and 104.2 versus 101.01 in the second. The difference held for both sexes and for all five NMSQT subtests. This may tend to support Koch's speculation that mild prematurity may be beneficial for twins (1966, p. 39), but we cannot exclude the possibility that differential reporting might also be a factor in our data, since reported prematurity is positively associated with mother's education in both subsamples. (The association is weak, however.)

Next, let us turn to the final questionnaire item, which concerns the parents' belief about the twins' zygosity. Table 5-2 summarizes the relevant information about parental judgments of zygosity and their correspondence to our questionnaire diagnosis. The parents were typically confident that they knew whether their twins were identical or fraternal—their judgments fell in the "certain" category over 80% of the time, and there were less than 3% "don't knows" or omissions. The parent's classification disagreed with ours in about 17% of the cases (20% if "don't knows" are counted as disagreements), with the disagreements being roughly symmetrical: 17.7% of the pairs we diagnosed as identical were judged by the parents to be fraternal, and 15.8% of those we diagnosed as fraternal were believed by their parents to be identical As these figures imply, the overall proportion of pairs classified as identical and fraternal was not greatly different for us and the parents: approximately 60% of the pairs were identicals in our diagnosis and 57% in the parental judgments.

Table 5-3. Mean Scores for Identical and Fraternal Pairs on Six Items Concerning Differential Experience of Twins

Item	Score range	Identical		Fraternal	
		M	F	M	F
283. Dressed alike	1-3	1.66[a]	1.54	2.01	1.82
284. Played together 6-12	1-4	1.28	1.33	1.60	1.55
285. Spent time together 12-18	1-4	1.81	1.68	2.23	1.95
286. Same teachers in school	1-3	1.70	1.65	1.80	1.83
287. Slept in same room	1-4	1.36	1.44	1.66	1.45
288. Parents tried to treat alike	1-5	1.94	1.95	2.31	2.24
312. Composite of above	6-23	9.73	9.56	11.60	10.84

[a]A score of 1.00 indicates maximum similarity. The standard errors of the item means are in the range .03 to .08. The point-biserial correlations of the differential experience composite with zygosity are .33 and .23 for males and females, respectively.

If we were sure that when we and the parents disagreed on the zygosity of a pair we were right and they were wrong, it might be instructive to carry out a special analysis of the misclassified pairs, in the manner of Scarr (1968). However, since our diagnosis is probably in error some 5%–10% of the time (see chapter 2), a fair proportion of the 17% disagreements presumably represents cases in which it is the parents who are accurate and we who have misclassified the pair. We *can*, however, report that parental opinion about zygosity, when actual zygosity is largely controlled, is not highly predictive of differential treatment; we have computed correlations *within* our diagnosed identical and fraternal groups between parental diagnosis and the six differential twin-treatment items that precede it in the questionnaire. These correlations are essentially zero within the group classified by us as identical (they range from –.04 to +.04), and, though positive, they are quite small (+.02 to +.14) in the group classified by us as fraternal. These data tend to support Scarr's conclusion that parental opinion about zygosity is not per se a critical variable (1968, p. 40).

Let us turn next to the six differential twin-treatment items (283–288). Here the parent was asked to indicate to what extent the twins were dressed alike, played together as children, spent time together as adolescents, had the same teachers in school, and slept in the same room The parent was also asked explicitly about twin-rearing philosophy: "Many parents of twins try to treat both children exactly alike. Others make an effort to treat them differently. In raising the twins which of these methods have you followed?" The alternatives offered ranged from "We have tried to treat them exactly the same" to "We have tried to treat them differently."

The mean scores for these six items are presented in table 5-3. It is evident from the table that, according to their parents, the identical-twin pairs have had more similar experience than the fraternals in each of these respects (which is not, of course, to say that the twins' own behavior had nothing to do with this). Quantitatively, the degree of association between zygosity and differential treatment may be judged by expressing it as a point-biserial correlation. If we do so, we obtain correlations of .33 and .23 on the composite scale for males and females, respectively. On the whole, the differences between the sexes are not great, although there is a suggestion that the girl twins were more often dressed alike and spent more time together as adolescents.

Our results on separation in school do not agree very well with Koch's (1966): she failed to find an overall zygosity difference and did find a sex difference—her male twins were more likely to be separated than her females. It is, of course, possible that school policies on the handling of twins tend to vary for different ages or at different times and places. In other respects, our results agree with Koch's in finding that identical twins play together more and are more often dressed alike. Smith (1965), working with adolescent twins, also reports that identical twins dress alike more often, study together more, and share more close friends than do same-sex fraternal pairs. These studies are consistent on these points with earlier investigations from both the United States (Wilson 1934) and Europe (Lehtovaara 1938; Zazzo 1960).

Thus, our data agree with those of others in finding that, in a number of respects, identical pairs are exposed to more similar environments than are fraternal pairs. How much difference does this make in their later personalities? One way of assessing this is to see whether *within* zygosity groups differences in these experiences are associated with personality differences. For example, do identical twins who are dressed alike turn out to be more similar in personality than identical twins who are not? If they do not, then it is perhaps a bit gratuitous to invoke dressing alike as a reason why identical twins are more alike than fraternal twins.

The answer to this question for abilities (NMSQT subtests) is given in table 5-4; for personality traits (CPI scales), in table 5-5; for vocational interests (VPI scales), in table 5-6; and for interpersonal relationships (self-ratings), in table 5-7. In these tables are shown correlations between the differences in scores of the pair members on various personality, interest, and ability measures and the differential experience of the pair, measured by the six parent-questionnaire variables and the composite score derived from them. We will probably not be accused of extravagance if we say that these correlations are not very large. More of them *are* positive than negative (393 to 181, as a matter of fact), but the typical r is not greater than +.05 or +.06 (the median correlation of the composite score over all variables is the latter). The range of correlations in the tables is -.15 to +.22, which is about what one would expect on the basis of chance fluctuation around the average value (the standard

Table 5-4. *Correlations between Absolute Differences on NMSQT Subtests and Differential Experience Measures*

NMSQT subtest	283 Dress		284 Child		285 Adolescent		286 Teacher		287 Room		288 Treatment		312 Composite	
	I	F	I	F	I	F	I	F	I	F	I	F	I	F
5. English	-12	-05	-06	-06	-02	00	07	02	12	-05	-01	-10	00	-08
6. Mathematics	-01	-02	01	-01	-06	-03	-04	20	02	02	06	05	00	07
7. Social Studies	-02	01	-10	03	11	00	05	12	-01	-07	-08	-09	-02	-02
8. Natural Science	-02	06	-09	04	-08	-03	-09	07	-04	10	-06	01	-10	07
9. Vocabulary	-12	05	-10	-04	-09	00	-07	19	-05	-04	-03	02	-11	05

Note: Correlations based on 276 identical and 193 fraternal pairs who had no missing scores on any of the 119 variables (not all shown) that were analyzed. A positive correlation means that twins who were more different in experience obtained more different NMSQT scores. Decimal points are omitted throughout.

error of a low correlation is in the neighborhood of .06 or .07 for these sample sizes). Thus, it is probably inappropriate to attempt further interpretation within these tables.

In any case, it is clear that the greater similarity of our identical twins' experience in terms of dress, playing together, and so forth cannot plausibly account for more than a very small fraction of their greater observed similarity on the personality and ability variables of our study.

There are two obvious doubts that cross one's mind concerning essentially negative results such as these: Could they simply be due to unreliability of measurement? Could there possibly be some sort of error in the computer program that calculated the correlations? Checks on both of these possibilities were carried out. As for reliability, we have some cross-checks on the parent ratings from the twins themselves. There is an item on the twin questionnaire, "How often are you and your twin together?" and another item, "Do you and your twin dress alike?" (with options "always" to "rarely"). The average of the two twins' response to these items was correlated with the corresponding parental judgments .56 and .52 in the identical-twin group ($N = 433$) and .57 and .57 in the fraternal-twin group ($N = 288$). Since the items on the two questionnaires are only similar, not identical, these correlations may under-represent their reliability (a parent could correctly say that twins, who as high school students had recently given up this practice, had usually dressed alike). Thus, it is clear that low reliability cannot be solely responsible for the obtained low correlations. As to the possibility of computer error, in addition to normal checks via the consistency of means and standard deviations with independently obtained values, we reran the correlations for the CPI scales using a different program and a larger subset of the data. We obtained results fully

Table 5-5. Correlations between Absolute Differences on CPI Scales and Differential Experience Measures

CPI scale	283 Dress		284 Child		285 Adolescent		286 Teacher		287 Room		288 Treatment		312 Composite	
	I	F	I	F	I	F	I	F	I	F	I	F	I	F
1573. Do	05	11	10	05	11	08	02	01	02	16	02	05	07	10
1574. Cs	-01	-01	09	18	10	10	06	01	07	-00	06	03	14	06
1575. Sy	04	03	09	13	07	13	09	03	01	14	02	02	06	11
1576. Sp	11	08	02	11	03	16	03	-04	-01	10	10	01	07	12
1577. Sa	08	13	04	09	10	10	03	06	01	07	04	-00	06	06
1578. Wb	-02	07	05	02	04	10	06	09	02	12	06	05	10	10
1579. Re	-03	06	-00	09	-01	13	-00	03	05	13	-00	05	03	15
1580. So	01	05	08	-05	09	04	-00	-01	-01	05	01	04	09	12
1581. Sc	-04	20	03	15	-00	16	01	11	01	09	-03	10	05	22
1582. To	-06	09	04	18	00	08	00	-01	12	11	-02	10	08	17
1583. Gi	-01	19	13	11	08	17	05	10	07	03	-03	08	07	17
1584. Cm	08	04	01	-03	07	04	-01	-01	02	06	-02	-00	04	05
1585. Ac	02	11	07	10	-01	18	04	02	-03	22	01	04	04	20
1586. Ai	-05	-01	-05	03	01	05	00	11	03	06	00	-02	03	07
1587. Ie	-07	-06	-02	11	-08	02	-06	08	00	08	-05	-02	-04	06
1588. Py	06	-00	06	04	06	06	05	-01	02	16	06	-02	11	04
1589. Fx	-04	09	-02	04	03	06	08	06	-02	-03	-08	09	-02	11
1590. Fe	-04	06	06	01	13	04	02	14	-06	-01	05	01	03	09

Note: Full titles of scales given in Appendix A. Correlations based on 451 identical and 301 fraternal pairs with no missing scores on these variables. Decimal points omitted.

Table 5-6. Correlations between Absolute Differences on VPI Scales and Differential Experience Measures

VPI scale	283 Dress		284 Child		285 Adolescent		286 Teacher		287 Room		288 Treatment		312 Composite	
	I	F	I	F	I	F	I	F	I	F	I	F	I	F
1597. Realistic	04	08	-09	01	-02	08	-04	-01	-03	-01	-11	-05	-08	01
1598. Intellectual	15	04	12	10	14	-05	11	-01	17	-03	13	-09	22	-04
1599. Social	-01	04	-06	01	01	09	06	08	04	-11	-04	02	00	03
1600. Conventional	-01	01	-07	-02	-02	04	-09	01	-08	-00	-09	01	-11	01
1601. Enterprising	10	06	03	01	04	09	02	-03	-05	02	00	-13	03	-02
1602. Artistic	02	12	03	16	14	17	09	22	-01	-09	-07	07	04	17
1603. Masculinity	-11	02	-08	00	-01	05	05	06	-01	-15	03	03	-02	-00
1604. Status	-01	-11	-03	-03	-05	-05	00	-04	-00	12	-10	-10	-06	-07
1605. Control	09	13	02	07	10	08	13	01	-00	02	-01	-06	08	05
1606. Aggression	08	09	09	03	10	04	10	-01	01	08	-01	-06	09	04
1607. Infrequency	04	07	-05	-04	03	-01	02	-06	06	-03	-04	-00	02	-02
1608. Acquiescence	11	07	04	-00	10	01	10	00	-02	-05	-04	-14	06	-06

Note: Same sample as for table 5-4.

Table 5-7. Correlations between Absolute Differences on Interpersonal Relationships Ratings and Differential Experience Measures

Rating	283 Dress		284 Child		285 Adolescent		286 Teacher		287 Room		288 Treatment		312 Composite	
	I	F	I	F	I	F	I	F	I	F	I	F	I	F
833. Boys	04	06	−07	08	−04	13	−10	07	02	−06	01	−02	−03	06
834. Girls	03	13	03	03	07	13	05	05	04	12	−05	10	03	17
835. Mother	06	17	08	02	11	10	03	−01	05	10	06	04	10	12
836. Father	06	19	−01	04	09	12	05	02	−00	11	−05	−03	03	12
837. Teachers	06	10	02	07	19	15	17	05	−05	18	−01	07	09	18
838. Adults	02	07	04	04	01	21	05	03	08	−05	06	−02	08	07

Note: Same sample as for table 5-4.

consistent with our initial ones (the values given in table 5-5 are actually from this rerun). Thus, we are reasonably sure that the smallness of the correlations is no accident but represents the true state of affairs in the data.

Let us move on to look at other kinds of information from the parent questionnaire. A major portion of the questionnaire is devoted to a series of fairly specific items about the behavior and treatment of the twins during various periods of their early lives: infancy (up to 2 years), 28 items; preschool (2–6 years), 41 items; childhood (6–12 years), 36 items; and adolescence (12–18 years), 44 items. For each of these items the parent was asked to indicate whether the specified state of affairs had characterized twin 1 only, twin 2 only, both twins, or neither twin during the period in question. Typical items were "Had colic frequently," "Attended nursery school," "Bit his fingernails," "Made his own bed."

On an a priori basis, one of us (JCL) went through the questionnaire and sorted out 56 items that seemed mainly to reflect environmental inputs to the child (examples: "Was usually rocked and held when he cried," "Was breast-fed for two months or longer") and 52 items that seemed mainly to reflect behaviors emitted by the child (examples: "Cried a lot," "Could amuse himself for several hours playing alone"). These were scored as 7- to 18-item subscales in the various age periods (290–298), as well as combined into total scales (299, 300). For the period of infancy, a third group of items having to do with bodily problems was also sorted out (7 items, examples: "Had colic frequently," "Wore corrective shoes or leg braces for one month or longer"); items of these kinds were too infrequent at later ages to justify extending this scale (292) past infancy. The remaining 34 items (examples: was toilet trained before 18 months of age," "Was often picked-on or teased by other children") were judged to be so interactive in character as not to be readily

Table 5–8. *Means for Male and Female Identical- and Fraternal-Twin Pairs on Scales Measuring Differences in Treatment and Behavior at Various Age Periods*

Parent questionnaire scale	No. of items	Identical		Fraternal	
		M	F	M	F
Treatment					
290. Infancy (0–2)	10	.08	.08	.34	.31
293. Preschool (2–6)	16	.05	.08	.19	.29
295. Childhood (6–12)	12	.07	.07	.14	.09
297. Adolescence (12–18)	18	.27	.34	.75	.58
299. Total treatment[a]	56	.48	.57	1.43	1.28
Behavior					
291. Infancy (0–2)	7	.17	.13	.69	.70
294. Preschool (2–6)	17	.75	.92	2.47	2.10
296. Childhood (6–12)	14	.86	.81	2.15	1.91
298. Adolescence (12–18)	14	1.85	2.02	4.07	4.03
300. Total behavior[a]	52	3.63	3.88	9.39	8.71

[a]The point-biserial correlations between total treatment and zygosity are .40 and .31 for males and females, respectively; for total behavior and zygosity they are .54 and .50. Means for total scales may differ slightly from sum of subscale means because of differing numbers of missing cases.

assignable to either category. (The assignment of items to scales, as well as mean scores for items and scales, may be found in Appendixes A and B.) The claim is not made, of course, that the items in the two main scales represent in any sense *pure* input and output: a child who never cries will not "usually be rocked and held when he cries." Nevertheless, there appeared to be a worthwhile discrimination to be made between items that seem mainly to describe what a child does and items that seem mainly to describe what is done to him.

The scales were scored by the number of items on which the twins of a pair were discordant—that is, where the parent marked "Twin 1 only" or "Twin 2 only" rather than "Both twins" or "Neither twin." The mean scores on the scales are shown in table 5–8.

Several facts stand out sharply in this table. First, the means are low; that is, most twins were concordant on most items. Considering just the rows for the total scales, the highest mean (for differences in behavior between fraternal males) was less than 10.0 on a 52-item scale, while the lowest mean (for differences in treatment between identical males) was less than 1.0 on a 56-item scale! Second, the differences on the treatment subscales are consistently less than the differences on the corresponding behavior subscales. Third, the differences for the identical pairs are consistently less than the differences for the fraternal pairs, in both treatment and behavior. Fourth, there appear to be no striking sex differences. And, finally, both treatment and behavior differences appear to be greater at adolescence than at earlier ages. For behavior, there appears also to be an increase in differences for both identicals and fraternals following infancy, but this is not the case for treatment differences. This change is partly confounded with an increase in scale length, but this will not account for the size of the change in behavior or for the absence of change in treatment.

Thus, as far as explicit environmental influences are concerned, the pairs of twins of both kinds appear to have received very similar treatment. In each of the first three age periods, at least, it was exceptional for a parent to mark any treatment item as different for the twins; for the identicals it was, in fact, positively rare. Behavior differences were relatively moderate for both kinds of twins in infancy but became more marked at later ages. Both treatment and behavior were more different for fraternals than for identicals; however, it would be difficult in the whole pattern of data to hold the treatment differences causally responsible for the behavioral differences, because the treatment differences are smaller, both absolutely and relatively (point-biserial r's), and increase at a later age.

It may help give some substance to these trends to look at some of the individual items on which fraternal pairs were more different than identicals, as well as some items on which they were not. Table 5-9 presents this information. The items with the largest identical-fraternal differences are shown along with a selection of items with no difference. Aside from the relatively low concordances on the first two items listed, for which the form of the item is presumably responsible, the concordances are generally high. It is obvious that the items that show no difference between identicals and fraternals are items with virtually complete concordance in both groups. It is perhaps of interest that all eleven items with relatively large differences were scored on the a priori behavior scales, whereas nine of the twelve items with no difference were scored on the a priori treatment scales.

Are there any items with small identical-fraternal differences other than those that are that way because of essentially complete concordance in both groups? Not very many. The four that come the closest to meeting this specification are shown in table 5-10. With the exception of left-handedness (to be discussed in more detail in the next chapter), the items seem to feature adversities in which chance presumably plays a substantial role.

Another of the major groups of items on the parent questionnaire was aimed at obtaining a picture of the twins' homes. Several a priori scales were also de-

Table 5-9. *Items with Large and Small Differences in Concordance between Identical and Fraternal Twins*

Age and item	% Concordance		
	I	F	Diff.
Large difference			
140. Ad.—more like mother than father in personality	64	30	34
141. Ad.—more like father than mother in personality	62	34	28
137. Ad.—liked sweets a great deal	92	69	23
139. Ad.—sensitive feelings, easily hurt	82	60	22
105. Ch.—bit his fingernails	82	62	20
117. Ad.—spent much time at home reading	92	73	19
136. Ad.—liked to spend time alone	89	70	19
24. Inf.—calm, peaceful child, easy to care for	95	77	18
97. Ch.—spent much time at home reading	96	79	17
101. Ch.—had a quick temper	79	62	17
48. Pre.—sometimes wet bed after age three	93	77	16
No difference[a]			
22. Inf.—often allowed to run around house without clothes	100	100	0
25. Inf.—breast fed 2 months or longer	98	98	0
33. Inf.—played around house (not in playpen)	100	100	0
41. Pre.—bedtime story almost every night	100	100	0
42. Pre.—regular Sunday school or church	100	100	0
43. Pre.—would recite for family or friends	99	99	0
83. Ch.—taken on trip to zoo by parents	100	100	0
92. Ch.—a definite bedtime enforced	100	100	0
95. Ch.—wanted to quit school one or more times	98	98	0
119. Ad.—serious discussions with parents about sex	99	99	0
128. Ad.—parents tried to influence occupational choice	98	98	0
130. Ad.—a definite curfew on weekend nights	100	100	0

Note: Inf. = Infancy; Pre. = Preschool; Ch. = Childhood; and Ad. = Adolescence.

[a]Only the first three such items at each age level are shown.

rived from these items. One such scale (311) involved eight items indicating the presence of disruption in home life (e.g., extended parental absence or illness, moving from one city or neighborhood to another, death of a parent or a close relative). While there was considerable variation in the frequency of such events in different families, the identical and fraternal pairs did not appear to be differentially affected—the mean scores were 2.24 and 2.26, respectively, for the two groups.

Table 5-10. Items Averaging Less than 90% Concordance for Which the Identical-Fraternal Difference Was 5% or Less

Age and item	% Concordance		
	I	F	Diff.
142. Ad.—was left-handed	76	79	−3
126. Ad.—auto accident with more than $50 damage	89	85	4
15. Inf.—one or more serious illnesses	89	84	5
60. Pre.—no serious illnesses	92	87	5

Note: Inf. = Infancy; Pre. = Preschool; and Ad. = Adolescence.

In an effort to discriminate homes in which relatively greater and relatively less environmental pressures might be brought to bear on the twins, three a priori scales (307–309) were derived, two based on disciplinary practices (before and after age 6) and one based on childrearing patterns. The discipline scales scored both the frequency and the variety of forms of discipline applied in the home, and the home-impact scale scored items having to do with high parent-child interaction, parental demandingness and control, and the like. A fourth scale (310) was a composite of the preceding three. The assignment of items to scales may again be found in Appendix A. The two discipline scales were intercorrelated .71 and .72 in the identical- and fraternal-twin groups and showed modest positive correlations with the home-impact scale—.23 and .24 in the identical group and .14 and .20 in the fraternal group.

The difference between the means of identical- and fraternal-twin homes on these scales is not large, but it is consistently in the direction of higher mean scores for fraternals; the difference on the composite scale is statistically significant ($p < .05$). One interpretation of this could be that having a pair of fraternal twins in the home generates a bit more action than having an identical pair. It is perhaps relevant that the difference is larger for the male than for the female pairs.

Now, if home influences play a major direct role in shaping personality, the straightforward prediction is that, in homes where such influences are more actively brought to bear, the children in the home should turn out to be more like one another than in homes where such influences are relatively weak. Consequently, we ran correlations between the disciplinary and home-impact scales and the same set of personality variables that we used for the differential treatment items. We obtained, as before, a lot of small correlations (even smaller, this time), which we forbear to present in detail. Table 5-11 shows the median correlations for the various groups of scales. We need merely comment that the trend (such as it is) is in the opposite direction from the predic-

Table 5–11. Median Correlations between Differences on Various Personality and Ability Measures and Three Home Impact Scales[a]

Scales	307 Early discipline		308 Later discipline		309 Impact	
	I	F	I	F	I	F
5 NMSQT subtests	.02	.02	.04	-.00	.01	-.02
6 Interpersonal relations	.02	.04	.03	.02	.04	-.00
18 CPI scales	.01	.02	.04	.04	-.02	.02
12 VPI scales	.08	.02	.11	.00	.00	.03

[a]Same sample as for table 5-3.

tion: the twins from homes that attempt to exert large amounts of control turned out on the average to be just a shade *less* alike than twins from relatively permissive homes.

A last section of the parent questionnaire contains a number of items on which the parents were asked specifically to contrast the twins. Five a priori scales were derived from these items: three of these (301-303) have to do with differences in current traits ("Is more dependable"); current interests ("Is more interested in art"); and current behaviors ("Watches TV more"). One scale (304) has to do with differential previous treatment ("Received more attention from the mother," "Was spanked more often as a child"). The fifth scale (305) has to do with differential physical and social development ("Learned to walk first," "Had a date first"). A composite scale (306) combines the first three scales on current differences. The means for these scales, given in table 5-12, show a pattern much like that for the differential treatment and behavior scales previously discussed (see table 5-8): the treatment scale yields considerably lower means (smaller differences) than do the behavior scales, and for both kinds of scale the fraternals show larger differences than do the identicals.

The scale measuring differences in previous treatment was correlated against differences on selected personality measures, with the same kind of results as those reported earlier, but rather than present these results in detail, let us summarize a similar analysis undertaken with a composite of *all* our measures of differential treatment (313)—which combined this scale, the total of the twin experience items (312), and the total of the treatment items for the four different age periods (299). This composite was correlated with differences on the 41 selected personality measures (5 NMSQT subtests, 6 interpersonal-relations ratings, 18 CPI scales, and 12 VPI scales). The identical-twin correlations ranged from -.09 to +.22 with a median of +.06, and the fraternal-twin

Table 5–12. Means for Male and Female Identical- and Fraternal-Twin Pairs on "Which Twin" Scales

Scale	No. of items	Identicals		Fraternals	
		M	F	M	F
304. Previous treatment[a]	6	.44	.56	1.15	1.13
301. Current traits	11	5.76	6.18	7.97	7.89
302. Current interests	9	3.22	2.82	5.14	4.27
303. Current behaviors[a]	6	2.95	2.81	4.30	4.07
306. Composite, 301–303[a]	26	11.87	11.83	17.48	16.23
305. Differential development	9	4.10	5.11	5.76	6.41

[a]The point-biserial correlations between previous treatment and zygosity are .29 and .22 for males and females, respectively; for current behaviors they are .37 and .36; and for the composite of traits, interests, and behaviors they are .42 and .37.

correlations from −.08 to +.17 with a median of +.07. The correlation of differential treatment with personality differences appears indeed to be positive, but differential treatment (as we have measured it) clearly can account at best for only a tiny fraction of the variance in personality. Note that the correlation, such as it is, is about the same for identical and fraternal twins—a point of some theoretical interest to which we will return in our final chapter.

A weak overall relationship between differences in childhood treatment and differences in personality does not exclude the possibility that considerably stronger relationships might exist between some particular kinds of difference in early experience and some particular aspects of personality. One way of exploring such relationships is to sort out pairs of identical twins who differ in some aspect of early experience and then to look for personality and ability differences between them. Since the number of twins differing on a particular variable of interest may be rather small and since we are examining a number of dependent variables in each case, the risk of "discovering" chance relationships is appreciable. Consequently, we have carried out our analyses separately in the two random halves of our total sample in order to provide some information about internal consistency.

Tables 5–13 to 5–15 show the results of an analysis carried out for 15 parent-questionnaire items against 23 representative personality and ability variables. The 15 parent items were chosen to meet the two criteria of being of theoretical interest and of having an appreciable number of identical-twin pairs scored differently on them—the latter requirement excluded many variables that would have satisfied the former. In particular, on very few items in the first section of the parent questionnaire were there many discordant identical pairs: only 2 items, illness in infancy and handedness, are included in the present analysis. The latter group of items ("Which twin is more . . .") tended to produce more parental discriminations, and the remaining 13 items were selected from among these.

The 23 dependent variables include the five NMSQT subtests, the six ratings of interpersonal relationships, and selected CPI scales and trait self-ratings (six each). Selection of scales in the latter cases was on the basis of a reasonable diversity of content and good psychometric qualities—for the ratings, means near the middle of the scale and few omissions, and, for the CPI scales, high reliability. (The VPI scales were excluded from this analysis, since they tend to suffer excessively from missing scores.)

We are examining a total of 345 (15 × 23) relationships, in search of "significant" ones, and we can ask, as in chapter 3, what probability of making a false claim in each individual comparison in a random experiment of these dimensions would give us at least an even chance of avoiding any such claims in the analysis as a whole. In this case, it is .002.[1] Since we are looking at two independent subsamples, we can achieve this level of security by using a .0634 probability level in each sample.[2]

For ease of comparison, we have expressed all relationships in tables 5–13 to 5–15 as point-biserial correlations between the discordance in early history and the dependent variable. Some of the variables are basically dichotomous in nature (e.g., left- vs. right-handedness), but others might reasonably have called for the ordinary biserial coefficient (e.g., heavier at birth). However, since in most cases we have eliminated a large intermediate group of twins showing no difference, the assumption of an underlying continuous variable could be rather misleading; therefore, we have elected to use the point-biserial throughout. In the tables, those correlations reflecting relationships nominally significant at the .0634 level (see rationale above) are marked with asterisks. These significance levels are based on t-tests of the difference between correlated means; hence, they are not affected by the choice of coefficient. Since the correlations between identical twins tend to be substantial, fairly modest differences in means (and, hence, low point-biserial coefficients) may achieve respectable levels of significance even when the number of pairs on which they are based is not large.

Table 5–13 presents ability and personality differences for the members of identical-twin pairs differing in several specific aspects of early experience. For example, the first two columns of the table reflect the differences in the two half-samples between the twin who, according to his parent, suffered a serious illness in infancy and the twin who did not. A positive correlation means that the twin who was ill tended to score higher than the healthy twin. Thus, in the first half-sample, there appears to be a tendency for the twin who had had the illness to rate himself as less energetic than the other twin did, although it will be noted that this tendency fails to hold up in the second half-sample. (A relationship asterisked in both subsamples will be taken as probably a dependable one, in line with our earlier discussion; we will also sometimes comment

1. $.998^{345} \approx .5$.

2. $.0634^2/2 = .002$.

Table 5–13. *Ability and Personality Differences in Identical-Twin Pairs with Differing Early History: 5 Experience Variables, Subsamples I and II*

Scale	15 Illness in infancy I	II	245 Illness in childhood I	II	238 Mother's attention I	II	264 Spanked more I	II	265 Held more I	II
NMSQT										
5. English Usage	-05[a]	06	-02	02	-02	-03	-02	-12	-04	-02
6. Mathematics	00	09	-01	-07	-15*	-05	02	04	-01	01
7. Social Studies	03	-09	06	-02	-01	-08	03	-12	-06	-02
8. Natural Science	-05	13*	00	-00	-07	-01	02	10	07	-03
9. Vocabulary	02	04	04	02	-05	-09	-04	-12*	-02	-02
Self-ratings										
470. Calm	-16	-05	10	01	00	-10	-02	-05	-03	-35*
472. Energetic	-24*	01	05	08	00	-12	-12	13	03	-17
473. Give in easily	-02	-24*	11	-04	-08	12	-17	-05	05	04
480. Carefree	-04	-01	-01	-07	-13	-17	30*	-18	00	-17
484. Politically conservative	-06	-06	-04	05	06	-20	09	-08	01	-04
505. Outgoing	03	-04	11	-01	03	-13	-10	10	00	-24
Interpersonal problems										
833. Boys own age	-14	-13	-02	-02	-11	08	07	11	-05	17
834. Girls own age	-14	18*	-06	04	-03	04	07	21	-05	04
835. Mother	-10	12	-03	10	-12	-03	11	-13	04	00
836. Father	-10	-06	-10	-03	-18	-24	02	-15	00	-07
837. Teachers	08	-17	-11	04	-03	-04	15	-20	-03	18
838. Other adults	00	-15	03	02	-09	-05	19*	-05	-05	10
CPI										
1573. Dominance	10	-07	12*	-04	-06	-12	02	-05	-04	-09
1575. Sociability	01	09	10*	-05	03	-13	-05	13	03	-25
1577. Self-Acceptance	08	-06	09*	-17*	-10	05	-05	05	-03	-24*
1579. Responsibility	-14	00	05	07	03	-13	-06	-02	02	-13
1580. Socialization	-02	01	-00	-00	00	04	-11	19	-02	-33*
1586. Achievement via Independence	-01	09	04	03	-00	-16	-10	-05	05	-16
No. of pairs: min.	19	28	71	62	28	19	31	20	27	18
max.	22	31	80	66	31	21	35	22	31	19

[a] A positive correlation means that the twin who had the illness tends to score higher on the variable in question. Differences with $p < .0634$ are marked with an asterisk (see text). Decimal points omitted throughout.

briefly on relationships that are starred in one sample and that show a non-significant correlation of the same sign in the other—while we do not consider them as established by our data, such relationships may be worthy of attention in future research or in connection with the findings of other investigators.)

Having had a serious illness in infancy has apparently no consistent effects on adolescent personality, at least as it is sampled by our present set of variables. This is not, of course, to say that such an illness cannot have effects in individual cases but just that it does not appear in our data that being seriously ill in infancy has a general tendency to lead to (say) poor interpersonal relations, worsened academic performance, or a more submissive personality. Essentially the same conclusion can be drawn about having had a greater number of minor illnesses in childhood, as shown in the next pair of columns in table 5-13. We may note that Shields (1962, p. 114) also failed to find substantial associations between differences in childhood health and later personality and ability differences (in a sample of 54 English identical-twin pairs, about half of them reared apart during all or part of childhood).

The third variable shown in table 5-13 is "Received more attention from the mother." The one asterisked relationship of this variable is with poorer scores on the NMSQT Mathematics subtest, occurring in one subsample—the correlation in the other subsample, though small, is in the same direction; we may take this as suggestive of a relationship worth examining in future research. Since mathematics is traditionally sex typed as a masculine activity in our society, a closer association with the mother might plausibly be inversely related to achievement in this area. A further breakdown (not shown) indicates that the relationship in our data is in the same direction and of approximately the same magnitude for both males and females.

In the 57 pairs of identical twins in which one was reported as having been spanked more often as a child than the other, there does not seem to be any very impressive effect on their adolescent personalities—with the possible exception of a marginal negative association with the Vocabulary subtest of the NMSQT. This test is probably the best index of general intellectual ability among the measures in this analysis—maybe the smarter twin just got caught less often.

The remaining variable in table 5-13—"Was rocked and held more often as a child"—shows appreciable negative relationships in one subsample with three adjustment measures: self-acceptance and socialization as measured by the CPI, and self-rating of calm versus highstrung. However, these correlations occur in the smaller subsample of only 19 pairs, and they drop almost to zero (although still negative) in the larger subsample of 31 pairs. Thus, one hesitates to place much faith in them. If they do mean anything, it seems at least as likely that the rocking and holding might be consequences of early manifestation of emotional maladjustment as that they are causally responsible for the poor adjustment as measured in adolescence.

In sum, then, in table 5-13 there are no relationships between specific differential childhood experiences in identical-twin pairs and differences in adolescent personality that are clearly cross-replicated, although there are hints of associations involving several of the variables.

In the next table, 5-14, are shown relationships between five variables re-

Table 5–14. Ability and Personality Differences in Identical-Twin Pairs with Differing Early History: 5 Behavior Variables, Subsamples I and II

Scale	142 Left-handed		240 Better in grade school		241 More friendly		243 Closer to mother		266 Cried more	
	I	II	I	II	I	II	I	II	I	II
NMSQT										
5. English Usage	02[a]	-03	18*	06	-04	-01	05	00	-03	-05
6. Mathematics	04	-01	08*	14*	06	-01	-06	-08	01	01
7. Social Studies	08	-00	13*	09*	-00	00	-01	-04	-06	-13*
8. Natural Science	02	10	13*	08	-03	-04	-00	01	01	-06
9. Vocabulary	06	01	08*	13*	-03	-02	01	01	-02	-04
Self-ratings										
470. Calm	06	11	08	06	-06	13*	-03	01	-05	-24*
472. Energetic	-06	-12	07	00	01	08	12	-14	01	-19
473. Give in easily	-18*	-04	04	-04	01	19*	11	07	21*	07
480. Carefree	-12	-08	05	09	10	05	00	-03	04	-17
484. Politically conservative	-02	-05	-03	-01	-02	-08	-01	01	10	-05
505. Outgoing	-06	-09	05	03	11*	09	-03	08	00	-06
Interpersonal problems										
833. Boys own age	-11	-10	02	11	-01	01	-13*	02	04	05
834. Girls own age	-05	-04	-08	-02	-02	05	-03	-07	05	07
835. Mother	-06	-07	-04	05	08	-08	-15	-18*	-14	00
836. Father	-04	02	04	-04	12*	-08	-06	-15*	-08	00
837. Teachers	02	-03	-01	02	-01	-12	-09	-04	-04	16
838. Other adults	00	02	06	03	-07	07	-18*	-06	-06	21*
CPI										
1573. Dominance	02	03	12*	07	07	12*	-17*	00	-06	-18*
1575. Sociability	04	-05	05	02	07	10	-08	03	-01	-23*
1577. Self-Acceptance	08	01	01	10	04	00	-13*	08	-12	-20*
1579. Responsibility	07	-01	03	10	-03	04	05	21*	08	-17*
1580. Socialization	04	-09	06	05	-02	04	13	07	-05	-17*
1586. Achievement via Independence	-02	-02	07	09	00	-01	-07	00	-08	-16
No. of pairs: min.	52	60	66	57	80	76	40	39	38	30
max.	57	65	72	64	91	82	49	44	45	34

[a]See footnote, table 5-13.

flecting behavioral traits manifested in early childhood and personality differences as measured in adolescence. (One item, handedness, was reported for adolescence, but presumably most of the pairs discordant for handedness at that age had also been so earlier.)

The left-hander of a pair of identical twins showed, on the average, no very substantial difference in personality or ability from his right-handed twin. There is a marginal relationship with a self-rating of stubbornness (vs. give in easily) in one subsample, but it drops off considerably in the second.

We come across our first cross-validated relationships with the variable "Did better work in grade school." The twin who was reported as having performed better academically in his early years of school got better scores on the Mathematics, Social Studies, and Vocabulary subscales of the NMSQT in both samples and on the remaining two scales in one. The correlations are by no means high, but they are of interest in demonstrating a lasting effect of purely environmental influences in producing differences in intellectual performance among members of a given family. Aside from the NMSQT variables, there is a marginal relationship with the CPI Dominance scale (and, in fact, mostly positive—though small— correlations with the CPI scales in general). The CPI scale Achievement via Independence, which might plausibly be correlated with such a measure, fails to achieve asterisk status in either subsample, although it does show positive correlations in both. Shields (1962, p. 114) reported a tendency toward a positive association between earlier school achievement and current intelligence test score within his twin pairs, but most of the relationship occurred in the group of separated pairs, where between-family environmental factors would also enter in. Shields also noted a slight tendency for the twin with poorer school achievement to have generally poorer personality adjustment.

The variable "Was more friendly as a young child" fails to show strong associations with adolescent personality; the borderline relations with CPI Dominance and the self-ratings of "outgoing" and "give in easily" suggest, however, that the hypothesis of some environmentally induced stability in the extraversion area should not be rejected out of hand. The variable "Was closer to the mother" again shows no cross-validated relationships, although one, a self-rating of current good relationships with mother, comes close. The other marginal associations of closeness to mother tend to link it with good interpersonal relations with other adults and with CPI Responsibility. It will be recalled that we earlier noted a tendency toward a negative association between "More attention from mother" and the Mathematics subtest of the NMSQT. This tendency is supported by the direction of correlation in the present case, though the correlations are certainly not large. Also, since a number of the same twin pairs could be involved in both instances, this cannot be taken as altogether independent support.

The final variable in this set, "Cried more as a child," again shows only weak associations with current personality and ability variables. The possible negative associations with a number of CPI and self-concept scales are plausible enough, if real; the negative association with the Social Studies subtest, if not an accident of sampling, is nonobvious in its significance.

The third table, 5–15, gives the relationships of five developmental variables to adolescent personality and abilities. The first two, birth order and birth

Table 5-15. *Ability and Personality Differences in Identical-Twin Pairs with Differing Early History: 5 Developmental Variables, Subsamples I and II*

Scale	234 Born first		235 Heavier at birth		236 Walked first		237 Toilet trained first		267 Swam first	
	I	II	I	II	I	II	I	II	I	II
NMSQT										
5. English Usage	02[a]	03	03	02	-02	-02	-01	-03	01	-08
6. Mathematics	03	02	05*	04	03	-06	-02	05	03	10*
7. Social Studies	-00	04	02	02	04	-07*	04	-05	-05	-07
8. Natural Science	02	-00	02	02	02	02	01	-01	-02	10
9. Vocabulary	02	-01	-00	02	02	01	-02	-01	00	-01
Self-ratings										
470. Calm	05	-02	08*	02	03	01	-03	12	-10	03
472. Energetic	06	-05	08*	-01	02	-02	-01	25*	13*	03
473. Give in easily	-01	-03	-08*	-08	02	-07	07	08	-07	-08
480. Carefree	00	-04	00	09*	07	05	-08	00	17*	13
484. Politically conservative	00	-00	-00	-04	-05	02	-06	12	-10	13
505. Outgoing	02	-06	01	01	00	05	04	15*	-08	09
Interpersonal problems										
833. Boys own age	-07*	05	-04	02	-02	07	02	13	13	11
834. Girls own age	-01	03	00	04	-02	04	-15*	00	-04	-01
835. Mother	01	04	03	01	-01	-05	-06	-17*	08	05
836. Father	04	05	04	06*	-01	-03	-04	-05	08	08
837. Teachers	-07*	04	-03	03	02	-01	-15*	10	08	-05
838. Other adults	-05	00	-06	01	02	06	-14	-07	03	00
CPI										
1573. Dominance	-01	02	07*	11*	03	09*	05	05	-04	03
1575. Sociability	-00	-05	03	03	-00	08	-03	06	-01	05
1577. Self-Acceptance	-01	01	02	08*	-02	05	05	07	-07	05
1579. Responsibility	-02	03	01	-01	02	04	-02	-04	03	02
1580. Socialization	01	-00	01	02	01	06	07	15*	06	00
1586. Achievement via Independence	-01	-02	-01	-02	02	-05	-02	-01	-07	05
No. of pairs: min.	239	232	225	221	119	120	52	51	75	68
max.	256	248	241	238	127	129	58	55	84	74

[a]See footnote, table 5-13.

weight, are differentially reported for nearly all the identical-twin pairs in the sample, as compared to the 10%–20% of differing pairs on many of the other variables. In addition, associations with these variables have been reported in a number of previous twin studies.

The first of these two variables, birth order, does not appear to relate systematically to any of our personality and ability measures. The second, birth weight, shows a replicated relationship with the CPI Dominance scale (the twin heavier at birth scores higher in dominance at adolescence). It also shows marginal relationships with self-rating variables "stubborn" and "calm," high CPI Self-Acceptance, interpersonal difficulties with father, and NMSQT Mathematics score. Most of these relationships can plausibly be seen as associated with dominance.

A relationship between birth weight and dominance in identical-twin pairs has been observed in several previous investigations. Shields (1962, p. 85) reports such an association for English twins, as do Tienari (1966, p. 101) in Finland and Koch (1966, p. 34) in the United States. These authors also note a tendency for birth weight differences to persist as differences in size and strength in childhood and are inclined to interpret the dominance differences as arising out of early interaction of the pair. Partanen, Bruun, and Markkanen (1966, p. 114) found that birth weight was associated with physical but not social dominance (in the same Finnish adult male twin sample Tienari used).

Another relationship that has been reported for birth weight in identical twins is with intelligence. Babson et al. (1964), in 6 out of 7 differing pairs, Willerman and Churchill (1967), in 23 out of 25, and Scarr (1969a), in 16 out of 21, found the twin who was heavier at birth to be higher in IQ as measured in childhood. In a large English sample of 857 pairs, Record, McKeown, and Edwards (1970) found an association between birth weight and scores on the verbal-reasoning test of the Eleven-plus examination, but it was appreciable only for the 13% of their pairs who had fairly large differences in birth weight. By contrast, Tienari's adult sample shows little association between birth weight and IQ for 76 identical pairs differing in both birth weight and IQ—in only 40 cases was the heavier at birth the more intelligent (Tienari 1966, p. 103). Nor did Shields find differences in birth weight to be associated with differences in intelligence test scores in his sample (1962, p. 113); again, most of his twins were adult when tested. Any association in our own adolescent sample is also very weak: for Vocabulary, probably the purest measure of intelligence among the subtests, the correlation is close to zero, and it is quite low, though positive, for the other subtests. It is possible, then, that an association between birth weight and IQ differences is a developmentally transient phenomenon, largely disappearing by later ages.

Other personality associations of birth weight differences are not marked. While Matheny and Brown (1971) found associations between birth-weight differences and various behavioral differences in infant twins, such reports are less common for older twins. Tienari found his identical twins who were heavier at birth to be significantly different on only 1 out of 14 personality inventory scales in his study (low on aggression—1966, p. 101); Shields failed to find much association of birth weight with neuroticism or extraversion (1962, p. 113); and Scarr did not find relationships between birth weight and any of her measures of activity, introversion-extraversion, or curiosity (1969a, p. 251). On the whole, the present data do not disagree.

Birth order, although showing no important associations with personality and abilities for our twins, has shown up more strongly in some other studies. Tienari, for 125 identical-twin pairs, found the first-born to be significantly more often physically stronger in childhood, dominant in childhood, better in school achievement, a leader in youth, lower on an ambition questionnaire scale, higher in educational level, less reserved in the interview, and showing less disturbance on psychological tests (1966, p. 104). Some resemblance of this list to the correlates of birth weight will be noted—the two variables are associated in Tienari's data: the first-born was heavier in 72 of 109 pairs. Koch feels that the size difference is probably the variable affecting dominance. Tienari believes, however, that "awareness of being the first born twin may have some emotional bearing" (1966, p. 137). Scarr also found the first-born twin to be the heavier at birth in 33 of 54 cases in her data and in Willerman and Churchill's—however, it was the birth-weight difference and not the birth-order difference that appeared to be associated with IQ (1969a, p. 254). Record, McKeown, and Edwards (1970) did not find birth order to be associated with ability in their twin sample. Likewise, Matheny and Brown (1971) found many more associations of birth weight than birth order with behavior in infant twins. As we have seen, our own data tend also to support birth weight as the more important of the two variables.

The remaining three developmental variables in table 5–15—age of walking, being toilet trained, and learning to swim—show only marginal relationships with ability and personality measures at adolescence. Earlier walking is possibly related to the CPI Dominance scale; earlier toilet training to CPI Socialization, good relationships with mother, and self-rating as outgoing; and earlier swimming to self-rating as carefree and energetic and to good performance on the NMSQT Mathematics subtest. Only the last of these relationships would seem to present much mystery, and, if pressed, one could again interpret this in terms of masculine identification. But, since none of these results holds up significantly across subsamples, it is probably inappropriate to dwell on them further.

What general conclusions can be drawn from the analyses reported in tables 5–13 through 5–15? First, we have found exactly four replicated relationships— between "Did better work in grade school" and three of the NMSQT subtests and between heavier birth weight and CPI Dominance. And even in these cases the correlations are small, suggesting that little of the total variation in these traits can be accounted for by these variables—at least by differences in them within the range of those that occur between identical twins brought up together in U.S. middle-class homes. While we have found suggestions of a number of other relationships in our data, most of them fairly plausible, statistical prudence does not permit us to take these too seriously, except insofar as they may be substantiated in other investigations.

Thus, this analysis, like the others that have preceded it in this chapter, suggests that relationships between measures of early environment and adolescent measures of personality and abilities can, indeed, be demonstrated but that these relationships tend to be very weak. We will return again to this topic in our final chapter.

Chapter 6

Some Special Analyses

In the present chapter we present some special analyses undertaken to exploit various additional aspects of the data. In the first of these we will consider some of the questionnaire items that asked the twins to report on the twin relationship itself. In the second we will consider the bearing of the data on a question with a long history of investigation—left- and right-handedness in twins. In a third section of the chapter we will report a number of analyses of twin covariation that explore twin resemblances in the *associations* among traits, as distinct from the traits themselves. Finally, we will examine the distributions of twin differences on a number of traits in an effort to shed light on possible forces of contrast acting to differentiate twins of a pair.

THE TWINSHIP

Most of the emphasis in the present study has been on twins as individuals who happen to have been born and reared in pairs. However, the questionnaire did have a number of items in which the twins were asked to look at themselves as twins and to make some judgments about their experiences as a pair or to make direct comparisons between themselves and their twin (1053 to 1091). These items were located at the end of the questionnaire, since we did not want to introduce a set toward such comparisons earlier.

The twins appeared to be generally contented with their twin status. In response to the item "If you could start life over, would you like to be a twin again?" the majority indicated that they would definitely or probably so choose (1090). The girls were a little more positive than the boys, with mean scores of 1.92 and 1.95 on a five-point scale for the two female groups, as against 2.23 and 2.23 for the males—a low score indicates a stronger preference. As is evident from these figures, there was no difference between the identicals and fraternals in overall liking for being a twin. On the item "How frequently do you and your twin quarrel or fight?" the male means were 2.22 and 2.23 and the female means 2.30 and 2.20 for the identicals and fraternals, respectively—a score of 2.00 meaning "sometimes" and a score of 3.00 meaning "rarely or never" (1084). Again there was little difference. Some writers have argued that identicals tend to have a better time of it as twins because they are more strongly identified with each other and less competitive than fraternals. However, neither the item on fighting nor the one on satisfaction with being a twin offers much support for this notion in the present twin sample. One interesting difference did, however, emerge: the identicals were more likely to *agree* on whether or not they found the twin condition satisfying—represented by an intraclass correlation of .58 for their ratings as against one of .39 for the fraternals. Apparently, since the overall ratings of satisfaction do not differ, there were more instances in the fraternal group in which one twin's satisfaction was obtained at the expense of the other.

The twins' own statements support the parents' reports (discussed in the

Table 6-1. "Which Twin" Items on Twin Questionnaire

Item	Difference[a]				Agreement				"He does"			
	Identical		Fraternal		Identical		Fraternal		Identical		Fraternal	
	I	II	I	II	I	II	I	II	I	II	I	II
1053. Has more friends	19	24	25	35	35	26	56	30	06	04	10	10
1054. Makes better grades	23	23	21	16	79	80	82	88	08	11	04	06
1055. Talks to strangers	54	47	46	53	45	56	61	54	23	15	22	27
1056. Wins at sports	38	40	46	35	47	51	59	68	20	18	18	15
1057. Reads faster	40	40	42	42	49	48	66	63	00	05	10	04
1058. Has more dates	32	30	28	31	56	63	73	74	17	17	19	25
1059. Gets up first	45	45	43	49	58	55	66	58	18	20	33	30
1060. Goes to sleep first	54	58	54	52	32	40	51	48	-14	-23	-15	-13
1061. Is a better artist	21	23	22	29	72	73	79	71	06	-05	-01	03
1062. Is a better musician	19	25	25	28	66	58	72	71	03	09	01	05
1063. Is a better writer	42	45	41	49	49	47	60	53	-03	00	-05	01
1064. Knows more science	28	31	34	37	63	57	66	62	06	07	04	01
1065. Better public speaker	42	34	48	41	37	55	50	58	21	16	18	17
1066. Gets elected	40	47	46	40	48	38	56	61	10	02	-04	06
1067. Is more religious	20	22	37	30	52	52	35	43	01	00	15	09
1068. Studies harder	35	36	35	34	52	59	71	70	00	04	-01	04
1069. Liked more by mother	15	17	30	21	44	35	21	48	-02	-01	-10	-08
1070. Liked more by father	19	14	29	23	29	42	27	39	-02	02	-04	-07
1071. Decides for the pair	36	31	47	40	23	41	28	37	13	15	13	17
1072. Decided as a child	28	35	43	43	31	22	43	28	00	02	06	04
1073. Wins arguments	37	32	35	38	15	20	32	22	-04	04	07	06
1074. Knows more jokes	26	28	44	34	39	37	46	57	05	06	15	12
1075. Gets angry easier	56	57	51	60	43	41	54	42	-31	-33	-17	-24
1076. Saves more money	31	40	32	38	67	56	71	62	05	12	11	01
1077. Gets sick oftener	37	34	37	30	36	50	56	60	-16	-16	-20	-08

[a]"Difference" = mean absolute pair difference; "agreement" = intraclass correlation between twins; "He does" = mean tendency to give higher rating to other twin. Decimal points omitted throughout.

preceding chapter) concerning such matters as dressing alike (1085), having common friends (1086), and spending time together (1089). The identicals rated their experience as more alike than the fraternals did on each of these three items. There was also a tendency toward a sex difference, with the girls more similar than the boys in both twin groups.

Among the items in the final portion of the questionnaire were a series in which each twin was asked to indicate whether he or his twin had more friends, got better grades in school, and so forth. In scoring these items, the ratings of the second twin were reversed so that a low score in either case means, for example, that twin 1 had more friends. Thus, a small difference in ratings would indicate agreement between the twins as to who had the most friends.

Table 6-1 shows two measures of twin agreement, as well as a measure of bias toward rating the self or the other twin higher on a particular characteristic. The first four columns of the table show the absolute amounts of disagreement between pair members. Such disagreements tend to be relatively small on items for which there is relatively clear objective reference (such as "Makes better grades in school") and relatively large on more subjective items (such as "Gets angry more easily"). Also, some items have few disagreements because they were mostly answered "both the same"—the item "Is more liked by your mother" is an example. There may be a slight tendency toward larger differences among the fraternals—the trend is in this direction for about two-thirds of the items—but the difference is not an impressive one.

The center columns of table 6-1 show agreement expressed by intraclass correlations between the pairs' ratings. This is agreement in a different sense—not just absolute similarity of ratings, but similarity relative to the distinctions being made. Here there is a tendency toward higher correlations (i.e., more agreement) among the fraternal twins. In other words, the fraternal pairs discriminate between themselves more consistently because they have larger differences to judge, even though the absolute discrepancies between a pair's ratings may be larger than in the case of identicals.

Note that these intraclass correlations can be interpreted as interjudge reliability coefficients. Thus, the reliabilities of these ratings range from lows of .25 or .35 (who usually wins arguments or makes decisions) to highs of .75 or .85 (who is the better artist or gets better grades). The rather low agreement on who makes the decisions suggests that the sharp role differentiation in this regard sometimes held to characterize twin pairs is not very conspicuous among the twins of our sample.

The final columns of the table suggest an interesting interpersonal phenomenon. A positive value indicates a tendency for both twins to attribute more of a particular characteristic to the other twin; a negative value, a tendency to attribute more of the characteristic to the self. While the majority of the differences are fairly small, on some items they are consistent in direction and appreciable in size. The larger of these differences suggest that each member of the pair is inclined to attribute to the other member a self-confidence and equanimity that he is all too aware of not possessing himself; for instance, his twin talks more freely to strangers, is a better public speaker, has more dates, makes decisions for the pair, wins at sports, and gets up earlier in the morning, whereas he himself gets angry easier, gets sick oftener, and goes to bed earlier at night. This phenomenon is what one would predict in a social world in which anxiety and inferiority feelings tend to be concealed from others—successfully, more often than not.

HANDEDNESS

The question of a possible genetic basis of left- or right-handedness has a rath-

Table 6-2. Tendency toward Left-Handedness in Identical and Fraternal
Males and Females in Random Subsamples I and II

| | Males | | Females | | Intraclass |
	Mean	N	Mean	N	correlation
Identicals I	1.40[a]	240	1.37	274	-.08
Identicals II	1.49	188	1.51	310	.12
Fraternals I	1.42	118	1.33	196	-.15
Fraternals II	1.37	150	1.38	190	.08
All twins	1.42	696	1.40	970	.01

[a]A scale value of 1 represents always right-handed, and scale values 2-5 represent increasing degrees of left-handed tendency. The standard errors of the means are in the range .06 to .09 for the twin subsamples and about .04 for the combined group. The standard errors of the intraclass correlations in the twin subsamples range from .06 to .08.

er disputatious history, into which we do not wish to enter in any detail here. The reader is referred to reviews and discussions by Collins (1970), Fuller and Thompson (1960), Koch (1966), Nagylaki and Levy (1973), and Zazzo (1960). Dahlberg (1926) summarizes the early history of the topic. Suffice it to say that family studies have often tended to suggest the hypothesis of recessive inheritance of left-handedness, usually involving a single gene plus some additional assumptions about variations in penetrance in the hetero- or homozygote (Merrell 1957; Trankell 1955). The data from twin studies have been more consistent with the notion that left-handedness is an occasional chance event (Collins 1970).

Item number 13 on the twin questionnaire asks for a self-rating of handedness on a five-point scale ranging from "I have always been right-handed" to "I am left-handed and tried, unsuccessfully, to switch." Table 6-2 shows the mean scores on this item for the various twin groups. It is evident from the table that there are no very dependable differences in tendency toward left-handedness associated with sex or zygosity among groups. The intraclass correlations for our sample hover around zero for both identical and fraternal twins—one twin's handedness can be predicted from population frequencies as accurately as from knowledge of the handedness of the other twin. This fact is further brought out in table 6-3, based this time upon the parental rating "Was left-handed" (142). As can be seen from the table, the observed values are very close to the values expected on the hypothesis that the pairing of handedness in twins occurs on a chance basis in both the fraternal and identical groups. Zazzo (1960, p. 123) made a similar analysis of the combined data of 10 studies, including his own, altogether involving 1,210 identical and 1,145 fraternal pairs, and came to a similar conclusion. Husén (1959, p. 87) reports data for 261 identical and 526 fraternal pairs, which also fit this pattern.

Table 6–3. Distribution of Handedness in Male and Female Identical- and Fraternal-Twin Pairs

Handedness	Observed				Expected[a]			
	IM	IF	FM	FF	IM	IF	FM	FF
R–R	162	218	104	157	164	225	103	149
R–L	50	73	31	39	49	67	31	44
L–L	5	6	1	1	4	5	2	3
Total	217	297	136	197	$\chi^2 = 5.08$, 7 df, $.70 > p > .50$			

[a]Expected values on the hypothesis that the handedness of twin pair members is independent and that the proportion of left-handers in each group equals the overall proportion of .1293.

In the preceding chapter we examined the association of handedness with a number of personality and ability characteristics in identical-twin pairs (see table 5–14) and found no replicated relationships, although there may have been a weak association between left-handedness and a self-rating of stubbornness. A similar analysis carried out with the fraternal twins yielded one replicated relationship—between left-handedness and poor relationships with mother—plus marginal associations of left-handedness with low scores on the NMSQT Social Studies subtest, poor relationships with other adults, and low CPI Dominance. There was no dependable relationship of handedness with stubbornness among the fraternals (point-biserial r's of .17 and –.13 in the two half-samples).

Koch (1966, p. 79) found an association between left-handedness in twins and ratings of resistance—which receives some support in our identical-twin sample but little from our fraternals. She also reports a positive relationship between left-handedness and dominance; our data (and Shields 1962) fail to support this. On the whole, it would seem that any personality and ability associations of handedness are weak enough to be explained in secondary terms, such as an acquisition of folk beliefs about left-handed people.

TWIN COVARIATION

A good deal of theoretical interest in analyzing trait intercorrelations in identical- and fraternal-twin groups has been expressed in recent years (for example, Kempthorne and Osborne 1961; Nichols 1964; Vandenberg 1965; Loehlin 1965; Partanen, Bruun, and Markkanen 1966; Bock and Vandenberg 1968; Roudabush 1968; Loehlin and Vandenberg 1968; Eaves 1973b; Eaves and Gale 1974). Parallel interests have developed in the context of animal work, with an inbred mouse strain playing the role of an expanded identical twinship (Meredith 1968; Hegmann and DeFries 1968, 1970).

The motivation underlying such analyses is the hope that they may provide a powerful tool for studying how genetic and environmental influences affect phenotypic traits. The basic reasoning runs something like this: It is unlikely that our convenient phenotypic trait measures are aligned in a simple one-to-one fashion with either the genetic or the environmental sources of influence upon them. If they are not, the effects of such influences should often show up more clearly on the associations among traits than on the measures of the individual traits themselves. Thus, two genetically independent traits might be correlated because they are subject to common environmental influences, or two traits that share no important environmental inputs might both be affected by a particular gene or genes ("pleiotropy"). A heritability analysis of a given trait can only indicate what proportion of the influences upon it are genetic in origin and what proportion are environmental. While this may be worth knowing, a similar heritability analysis of the correlations (or covariances) of that trait with other traits can, in principle, show which other traits genetic influences are shared with and which other traits environmental influences are shared with; this should give a much sharper insight into the nature of the trait in question.

As we shall see later, it may not always be quite this simple, but, clearly, intercorrelations are worth looking at. Let us begin with half a dozen trait self-ratings, arbitrarily selected to have means close to the center of the rating scale and to offer reasonably diverse coverage of personality.

Table 6-4 shows the intercorrelations of these ratings in identical- and fraternal-twin individuals, plus their cross-pair correlations—correlations between a given trait in one twin and the same trait or other traits in the other twin. The ordinary intercorrelations are in the correlation matrix marked "Total correlations," and the cross-pair correlations are in the matrix marked "Between pairs." This indicates that the latter represent the components of variation and covariation produced by influences common to both pair members and differing between twin pairs. The diagonal elements of the "Between pairs" matrix correspond essentially to the intraclass correlations between twins for these traits. The third pair of matrices in table 6-4, marked "Within pairs," represents the covariation between traits that occurs within twin pairs—that is, the covariation due to influences that are not shared, or not shared to the same degree, by the two pair members. To put it differently, if twin *pairs* who are more introverted tend also to be more stubborn, this will be reflected in the between-pair covariation; if the pair *member* who is more introverted tends also to be the more stubborn one, this will be reflected in the within-pair covariation. The within-pair matrix may be obtained, as here, by subtraction, or it may be calculated from the covariation of twin within-pair devia-

Table 6–4. Pattern of Intercorrelations of Selected Trait Self-Ratings in Identical- and Fraternal-Twin Groups, plus Within- and Between-Pair Components of the Correlations

Self-rating	Identicals						Fraternals					
	GI	In	Ca	Bo	PC	RT	GI	In	Ca	Bo	PC	RT
Total correlations[a]												
473. Give in easily (GI)	100	10	10	-04	05	02	100	02	18	03	06	06
474. Introverted (In)		100	-06	-28	02	01		100	-05	-33	09	-07
480. Carefree (Ca)			100	18	07	32			100	15	04	22
483. Bold (Bo)				100	05	21				100	-08	14
484. Politically conservative (PC)					100	06					100	03
500. Rarely tired (RT)						100						100
Between pairs												
473. Give in easily	18	00	05	-05	-02	01	06	-02	09	04	05	01
474. Introverted		32	03	-13	-03	-00		04	-02	-05	02	10
480. Carefree			20	09	-01	14			-02	09	07	04
483. Bold				26	02	07				05	-03	05
484. Politically conservative					39	-00					42	09
500. Rarely tired						28						10
Within pairs												
473. Give in easily	82	10	05	01	07	01	94	04	09	-01	01	05
474. Introverted		68	-09	-14	05	01		96	-03	-28	07	-17
480. Carefree			80	09	07	18			102	06	-03	18
483. Bold				74	03	14				95	-05	09
484. Politically conservative					61	06					58	-05
500. Rarely tired						72						90

[a]Total correlations are based on roughly 960 identical and 640 fraternal individuals and the component matrices on the corresponding 480 and 320 pairs. Decimal points omitted in this and the two succeeding tables.

tions (or pair differences) on the various traits. The diagonal of the within-pair matrix reflects, in addition to stable individual differences on the traits, any variance that may be present due to unreliability of measurement—presumably a fairly substantial amount for these single ratings.

The point of chief interest in table 6–4 is that all six matrices appear to show much the same general pattern of interrelationships. There are five correlations that are above .10 in both "total" matrices: the negative r between "introverted" and "bold"; and the positive r's between "carefree" and "rarely tired," "bold" and "rarely tired," "bold" and "carefree," and "give in easily" and "carefree." All five relationships persist in both the within- and between-pair matrices for both identical and fraternal twins, although the component of correlation between fraternal pairs tends to be fairly small.

A similar state of affairs may be seen for six selected "life goals" items in table 6–5. (The grounds for selection were the same as for the trait ratings—

Table 6-5. Pattern of Intercorrelations of Selected Life Goals in Identical- and Fraternal-Twin Groups, plus Within- and Between-Pair Components of the Correlations

Life goal	Identicals						Fraternals					
	WO	HO	BE	Re	RA	EA	WO	HO	BE	Re	RA	EA
				Total correlations[a]								
368. Being well off (WO)	100	-07	24	23	02	12	100	-13	10	26	-01	12
370. Helping others (HO)		100	08	04	28	15		100	12	-03	27	11
373. Being an expert (BE)			100	34	11	19			100	23	10	21
386. Recognition (Re)				100	11	23				100	04	22
397. Religious affairs (RA)					100	-03					100	08
400. Exciting activity (EA)						100						100
				Between pairs								
368. Being well off	31	-05	15	14	02	08	15	-04	03	02	-02	-02
370. Helping others		35	02	00	21	03		19	01	06	20	04
373. Being an expert			30	23	06	15			13	14	01	10
386. Recognition				33	08	14				13	03	-05
397. Religious affairs					61	-07					61	-02
400. Exciting activity						27						07
				Within pairs								
368. Being well off	69	-02	09	09	01	04	85	-09	07	23	01	14
370. Helping others		65	06	04	07	12		81	11	-09	08	06
373. Being an expert			70	11	04	04			87	10	09	10
386. Recognition				67	03	09				87	01	27
397. Religious affairs					39	04					39	09
400. Exciting activity						73						93

[a]Same sample as table 6-4.

good psychometric properties and a variety of content.) A response set tends to bias these correlations in a positive direction. However, eight of the ten positive correlations above .10 in both total-correlation matrices are positive in all four of the component matrices. And the only negative correlation appearing in both total-correlation matrices—that between the goal of being well-off financially and the goal of helping others who are in difficulty—is also negative in all four of the component matrices.

The same kind of analysis is presented for abilities in table 6-6. Here we have used the larger body of data available from the 1965 testing. In this case, the results are presented separately for two arbitrary halves of the total sample (obtained by taking alternate pairs), each half containing approximately 650 identical and 430 fraternal pairs. Correlations based on the two halves of the data are shown above and below the diagonal of each matrix (the diagonal elements for the upper half are shown). It will be observed that, with

Table 6–6. Pattern of Intercorrelations of NMSQT Subtests in Identical- and Fraternal-Twin Groups from the 1965 Twin Sample, plus Within- and Between-Pair Components of the Correlations

NMSQT subtest	Identicals					Fraternals				
	E	M	S	N	V	E	M	S	N	V
Total correlations[a]										
5. English (E)	100	47	63	54	70	100	54	67	60	72
6. Mathematics (M)	51	100	52	56	54	52	100	54	62	55
7. Social Studies (S)	62	53	100	66	75	66	54	100	68	77
8. Natural Science (N)	53	61	64	100	63	56	61	67	100	67
9. Vocabulary (V)	68	50	73	60	100	73	57	77	65	100
Between pairs										
5. English	73	44	58	49	66	50	33	44	32	49
6. Mathematics	47	71	47	50	49	37	53	35	39	38
7. Social Studies	56	49	69	58	70	44	38	52	40	52
8. Natural Science	48	57	56	65	58	34	40	43	45	41
9. Vocabulary	64	46	68	55	88	50	40	52	42	61
Within pairs										
5. English	27	04	06	06	04	50	21	23	28	23
6. Mathematics	05	29	05	05	04	16	47	19	23	18
7. Social Studies	06	04	31	08	06	22	16	48	28	25
8. Natural Science	05	03	08	35	05	22	21	25	55	26
9. Vocabulary	04	03	05	04	12	23	17	24	23	39

[a] Total correlations are based on roughly 1,300 identical and 860 fraternal individuals in each half-sample—one shown above and one below the diagonal; the component matrices are based on the corresponding 650 and 430 pairs.

these substantial *N*'s, agreement across the half-samples is good, although not perfect.

The major correlational pattern among the off-diagonal elements in each of the six matrices is clearly that of a single general factor, confirming the similarity we have found in our two preceding tables. There appears also to be some stable variation within the matrices; for example, the correlation of the Vocabulary subtest with English Usage and Social Studies tends to be relatively high, while its correlation with Mathematics tends to be lower. The pattern is quite faint in the within-pair identical-twin matrix, where all the correlations are small, but the four possible rank-order correlations between the off-diagonal elements of the within-pair identical-twin matrices and the corresponding elements of the within-pair fraternal-twin matrices have an average value of .58, suggesting that the pattern, though weak, is there.

In short, in all three kinds of data we tend to find the same correlational pattern in both total matrices and in all four component matrices.

Table 6–7. Number of Factors Extracted before Reaching Criterion from 26-Item Intercorrelation Matrices of Twin Sums and Twin Differences

Correlation matrix	Differences		Sums	
	Identical	Fraternal	Identical	Fraternal
26 trait self-rating items	8	8	7	7
26 OBI items	10	10	9	9
26 health items	9	11	8	9
26 twin-comparison items	10	10	9	9

Now, since we know that any correlations occurring within identical pairs cannot be due to common genetic influences on the traits, whereas correlations in the other three matrices may be expected to reflect both common genetic and common environmental influences, we may conclude that either (*a*) the covariation in all the matrices derives from the same source, namely, common environmental influences, or (*b*) the pattern of covariation due to genetic causes closely parallels that due to environmental causes. The fact that there is relatively more covariation between pairs for the identical twins would, on hypothesis (*b*), be explicable by the fact that all the genetic covariation occurs between pairs for the identicals and only about half of it between pairs for the fraternals. On hypothesis (*a*), the difference would presumably be attributed to greater similarity of identical-twin environments. We may note that Hegmann and DeFries (1970), commenting on a similar finding in inbred mouse data, arrive at a conclusion approximately equivalent to (*b*).

In any case, we do *not* find patterns of intercorrelation fitting a third alternative for which we had rather hoped—(*c*) that distinct and different intercorrelation patterns characterize the genetic and environmental sources of influence on phenotypic traits. There is also a fourth alternative that can be excluded, namely, (*d*) that the observed patterns of intercorrelation stem largely or entirely from genetic overlap among traits.

Essentially similar conclusions can be reached by a slightly less direct method from a series of four analyses summarized in table 6–7. Intercorrelation matrices of twin-pair sums and twin-pair differences were factor analyzed by the principal-axes method using a computer program that extracts factors in approximate order of magnitude until an eigenvalue of less than 1.00 is obtained—a conventional point for stopping factor extraction (Kaiser 1960). While the factor analyses were carried out in too exploratory and perfunctory a fashion to justify reporting their results in detail, the number of factors extracted by the program from each correlation matrix before the criterion was reached should give some indication of the structural complexity of the matrix. If the genes and environment are contributing separate dimensions of covariation to the correlation matrices, the matrix obtained by correlating identical-twin differences should tend to have fewer dimensions than the other three. As table 6–7 shows, this is not the case. Results are presented there for four rather arbitrarily chosen 26-item intercorrelation matrices. The self-rating matrix consisted simply of the first 26 self-rating items. The OBI matrix consisted of 26 of the first 29 items from that questionnaire (3 items with extremely high or low endorsement frequencies were omitted). The health matrix consisted of 26 of the 31 health items—again, omissions were on the basis of extreme endorsement frequency. The twin-comparison items consisted of the 25 "Which twin" items (1053 to 1077), plus the "Born first" item (1087).

The fact that the environmentally based matrices are of essentially the same dimensionality as those subject to both genetic and environmental influences is again consistent with either (a) all covariation environmental in origin or (b) a closely parallel structure of genetic and environmental covariation. The results tend again to be inconsistent with (c) major different genetic and environmental dimensions of covariation or (d) most of the covariation stemming from common genes.

One important qualification should be added, however. What our methods analyze is variation, and this is as true for correlations as for single traits. An invariant species characteristic will not be shown to be genetic by a within-species biometrical analysis, and the same applies to an invariant association between traits. Only as the strength of the association varies in different groups of individuals in conjunction with differences in genes or environments does a genetic analysis of the sort we are doing become meaningful. An association that is inherent in the measuring instrument rather than in what is measured may tend to have the invariant character that defeats sensible genetic analysis. A correlation between two scales that derives from item overlap would be an example. A more subtle case, which may well be arguable for some of the examples in the present chapter, would be an association inherent in language. If "shy" means the opposite of "bold," then one would expect to find a negative correlation between ratings on the two traits made by English-speaking raters, quite irrespective of what is being rated. And, therefore, one would not wish to draw substantive conclusions from the fact (say) that the identical twin of a pair who is rated more "shy" tends also to be rated as less "bold." The possibility of a structure inherent in the measurement process provides, then, another alternative, (e), to be added to our list, a hypothesis that, along with (a) and (b), is compatible with our empirical findings. Again, we will return to this matter in our final chapter.

DISTRIBUTION OF TWIN DIFFERENCES

Some writers have argued for the importance of assimilation and contrast effects in influencing twin differences in personality and abilities. Initially similar twins, according to this reasoning, would tend to identify with each other and over time become more similar, while initially dissimilar twins would tend to contrast themselves (and be contrasted by others) and hence over time become more dissimilar. At least part of the difference between identical- and fraternal-twin resemblance, in this view, could be the result of a greater proportion of assimilative pairs in the identical-twin group and a greater proportion of contrastive pairs in the fraternal-twin group.

A bit of empirical support has been adduced for such mechanisms. For example, Thurstone (see Anastasi 1958, p. 284) reported an excess of extremely different fraternal pairs in his twin sample, and Jinks and Fulker (1970, p. 333) interpret Shields's data on extraversion as suggesting the presence of an effect of competition or contrast among fraternal-twin pairs for that trait.

Now, if there are, indeed, powerful mechanisms of this type operating among twin pairs, one might expect this to have an effect on the distribution of twin differences. In general, the tendency should be toward bimodality, with an excess of small and large pair differences and a deficiency of those of intermediate size. Furthermore, the excess of small differences should be more marked in the identical-twin group, and the excess of large differences should be more marked in the fraternal group. For various reasons, it is unlikely that one would obtain sharply bimodal distributions, since the size of initial difference leading to contrast effects would doubtless vary and other factors affecting differences would be operating, as well, but, if mechanisms of assimilation and contrast are playing a major role in producing twin differences, one would anticipate at least some distortion of the distributions of differences away from simple normality.

We have examined this possibility for several ability and personality traits. Figure 1 shows the obtained distributions of absolute pair differences on the five NMSQT subtests for identical- and fraternal-twin pairs, compared to the theoretical distributions to be expected on the hypothesis of an underlying normal distribution.[1]

Figure 1 suggests that the obtained distributions of pair differences on the ability measures of our study are quite well predicted by the hypothesis of an underlying normal distribution of differences. The probability values given, based on a chi-square test of goodness of fit, suggest that in only two cases, both involving identical-twin pairs, can one conclude that the observed distribution departs significantly from the theoretical one. There is a suggestion among the identical-twin pairs of an assimilation effect, in that there appears to be a slight excess of zero differences and a modest deficiency of differences in the middle range. There is little evidence of a systematic excess of large differences for either group. Indeed, there is little evidence of *any* substantial departure from the a priori curves in the fraternal-twin group.

The curve showing the strongest assimilation effect for identical twins, Natural Science, represents an area in which mutual sharing of interests in some identical-twin pairs might plausibly lead to unusually similar performances on the test. Mathematics shows a similar pattern, although not to a

1. Each theoretical curve is fitted using one parameter, the standard deviation of the distribution of differences, calculated from the intraclass correlation and the standard deviation of scores by the relation $\sigma_d = \sigma_t \sqrt{2(1 - r_i)}$. Concerning the form of the distribution of absolute pair differences, see Jensen (1970). The dip at the zero end of the curve is due to the fact that every interval but this one is the sum of two intervals from the symmetrical unimodal distribution of signed differences.

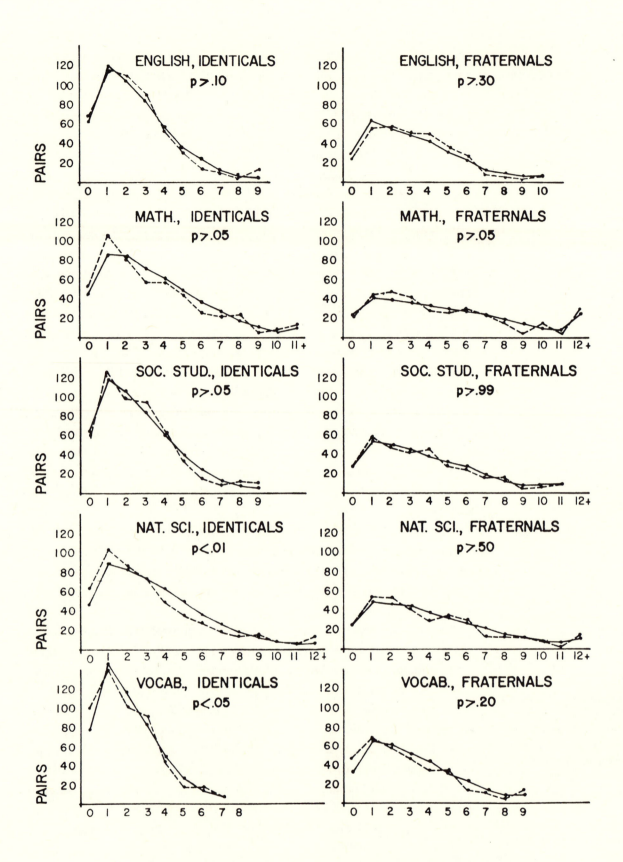

Figure 1. Distributions of absolute differences on NMSQT subscales for identical- and fraternal-twin pairs (theoretical, solid lines; observed, dotted lines).

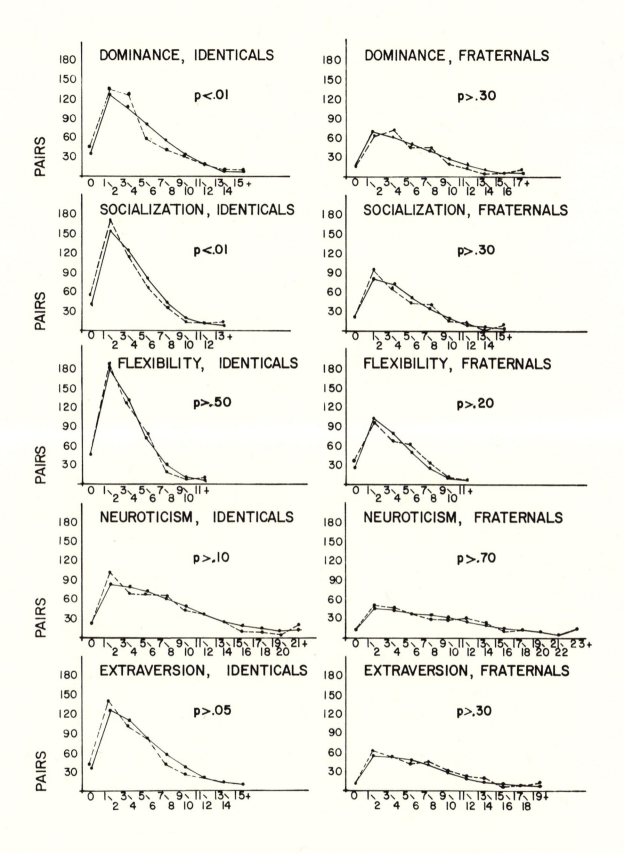

Figure 2. Distributions of absolute differences on selected CPI scales for identical- and fraternal-twin pairs (theoretical, solid lines; observed, dotted lines).

statistically significant degree. Vocabulary, which has the other significant chi-square, is less regular, although it does have an excess of zero differences and an overall deficiency in the range 1–5.

In short, for abilities we see some evidence in our data of an assimilation mechanism at work in the identical-twin group but little evidence of a contrast mechanism in either group.

What about personality? On theoretical grounds one might make a stronger case for contrast effects here, particularly for traits like dominance-submission or extraversion-introversion.

The evidence is presented in figure 2 for five selected CPI scales. These include the Dominance, Socialization, and Flexibility scales, plus two special a priori scales of items selected by H. J. Eysenck (personal communication) to represent the neuroticism and extraversion-introversion dimensions as he defines them.

In general, in the personality realm as in the ability realm, the distributions of absolute differences follow fairly closely the expectations based on the normal distribution. What exceptions there are (Dominance, Socialization) again indicate a slight excess of very small differences among the identicals, suggesting a possible operation of an assimilation mechanism in some pairs of that group. There is no evidence of a contrast mechanism among the fraternals. (There might, of course, be such a mechanism that would operate in a manner sufficiently uniform as to stretch out the entire distribution of differences without disturbing its normality; this would imply (a) the essential absence of fraternal pairs similar enough to give rise to assimilation effects and (b) a strictly linear relationship between the size of the initial difference and the amount of contrast—neither of which is a particularly attractive assumption.)

On the genetic side, it may be noted that the essential normality of the observed distributions of fraternal-twin differences tends to argue against any marked effect of single genes on these traits. A trait strongly influenced by a major gene might be expected to show a normal distribution of differences in the identical-twin group (due to random environmental effects) but a tendency toward bi- or trimodality of differences in the fraternal-twin group, due to gene segregation.

In brief, when both identical- and fraternal-twin differences are normally distributed, this suggests a multiplicity of independent causal factors for both the genes and the environment—and very nearly normal distributions are what we observe in the data.

Chapter 7

Heredity and Environment

In this final chapter we will attempt to pull together the various pieces of evidence reported in the preceding chapters and bring them to bear on the major theoretical issue underlying the research on which this book is based: what relative roles do heredity and environment play in the shaping of personality, ability, and interests?

We will begin by entering some disclaimers—but for our purposes not disabling ones. We remind our readers, first, that our sample is selected in at least three important respects: it consists of National Merit Scholarship test takers, it consists of questionnaire answerers, and it consists of twins. The first of these clearly restricts the sample materially in terms of ability, social class, and, no doubt, various personality, interest, and motivational variables; but equally clearly, considerable variation remains on such dimensions (as shown by the standard deviations in tables 2–2 and 2–4 in chapter 2). The further restriction—those testees who were willing to complete the mailed questionnaire battery—may in some respects have accentuated the above trends, but, again, the excellent level of response obtained, plus the direct evidence presented earlier, suggests that the individuals in our sample still vary widely enough in ability and personality for us to detect substantial relationships if they exist. Finally, the fact that the persons in our sample are twins has been examined at some length in chapter 3, with the general conclusion that as individuals the twins were generally like a comparison group of non-twins, although a few average differences were detectable.

The net effect of the kinds of selection we have discussed is that quantitively we would not expect estimates of heritability or other parameters based on our sample to be identical to those that would be found using a completely representative sample of U.S. adolescents. This is not too grave a problem. Any heritability estimate—or any mean or standard deviation—is an arbitrary figure referring to the particular population from which it is derived and the particular time at which the population is sampled. Insofar as we can estimate, even crudely, the kinds of selection involved in our sample, we can get some idea of how our figures might look in a wider population. However, where important elements are missing altogether in our sample, generalizations should be cautious. For example, we would recommend great care in extending our results to the black population of the United States. Very few blacks are represented in our data.

A second major restriction of our study is that it is largely based on self-report questionnaires. However, (a) we have employed a considerable variety of self-report techniques, ranging from the semiprojective "Problems of Young People" to the highly specific factual reports in the Objective Behavior Inventory, and (b) we do have a number of cross-checks from twin to twin and from parent to child to reassure us that our questionnaires are measuring more than random error or trivial response sets, and we have internal checks as well on the care with which our respondents carried out their tasks (see chapter 2).

So much, for the moment, for the caveats. Let us now move on to an examination of our findings and some of their possible theoretical implications. We will proceed by stating each empirical generalization briefly; afterwards, we will discuss their relevance to the heredity-environment issue. In the light of our preceding remarks, the reader should take the empirical generalizations as applying to the data of the present study, with probable—but somewhat more tenuous—implications beyond it.

SUMMARY OF THE EMPIRICAL FINDINGS

1. *The identical-twin pairs tended to be more alike than the fraternal-twin pairs in personality, ability, and interests.* This finding is, of course, hardly novel; it is amply supported in the previous literature reviewed in chapter 4.

2. *The degree of resemblance within pairs of twins, both identical and fraternal, tended to differ in different domains.* Table 7–1 summarizes results from several tables in chapter 4. In our data, as in preceding studies, the highest intraclass correlations are found for general ability, of the order .85 and .60, for identicals and fraternals, respectively. Special abilities run somewhat lower, at around .70 and .50, and personality inventory scales lower still, at around .50 and .30. Lowest of all are self-concepts, ideals, goals, and vocational interests, at around .35 and .15. Activities correlations run somewhat higher, at around .65 and .50.

3. *The differences between identical- and fraternal-twin correlations did not appear to be consistently greater for some traits than for others.* Chapter 4 reviewed the evidence, from both our own study and others in the literature, supporting this generalization. Our methods are not so precise that we can assert that there are *no* detectable differences, but the body of data we have surveyed is substantial enough so that it becomes difficult to defend the proposition that large and consistent trait-to-trait differences in the resemblance of identical- and fraternal-twin pairs are characteristic of traits in the personality and ability domain. (We did, however, find some evidence that political and social attitudes showed less differential twin resemblance—and thus, on a genetic hypothesis, lower heritability—than personality and ability traits.)

4. *Few, if any, consistent sex differences in twin correlations emerged in our data.* Most of our tables present results separately for males and females. While one can occasionally find possibly dependable sex differences, it is much more characteristically the case that the differences between male and female correlations are of the same general order of magnitude as those between random subsamples of the data. Furthermore, we have not found convincing evidence that identical and fraternal twins differ more for some traits in one sex than in the other—evidence that on a genetic model would imply sex differences in the heritability of different traits.

5. *According to their parents, the twins were treated very much alike as*

Table 7-1. Resemblance of Identical- and Fraternal-Twin Pairs in Various Personality, Ability, and Interest Domains

| | Typical intraclass correlations | | | |
| | Present study | | Previous studies | |
Trait domain	Identical	Fraternal	Identical	Fraternal
General ability	.86	.62	.85	.59
Special abilities	.74	.52	.67	.44
Personality inventory scales	.50	.28	.48	.28
Self-concept clusters	.34	.10	—	—
Ideals, goals, and vocational interests clusters	.37	.20	—	—
Activities clusters	.64	.49	—	—

children. When asked about their twin-rearing philosophy, more than eight times as many parents chose the alternative "We have tried to treat them exactly the same" as chose the alternative "We have tried to treat them differently." This general philosophy was amply borne out in the parents' reports of specific kinds of treatment and experience; only rarely, especially in the early years, was one twin reported as having received some kind of treatment or experience different from that of the other twin. This twin sample, as discussed in chapter 2, was probably to some degree selected for similarity of experience. In addition, parental memory is often faulty, and we can hardly claim that our questionnaire fully reflects the fine details of the differences in the twins' worlds. Nevertheless, we suspect that there is a law of least parental effort in twin rearing, which, in the absence of specific policy to the contrary, ensures that unless twins act differently they will get treated pretty much alike. And such contrary policy seems not to have been dominant in the period in which our twins were growing up.

Theoretically, one point of interest is that, despite this apparent high degree of similarity of early treatment, twin correlations on personality measures tend often to be quite low. This suggests that other, differentiating factors must be quite important.

6. *Identical twins had more similar early experience than fraternal twins.* Several kinds of evidence reviewed in chapters 5 and 6, both from the parents and from the twins themselves, plus data from other studies, agree in suggesting that members of identical-twin pairs are in fact treated more alike in many ways than are members of fraternal-twin pairs. Most probably, identical twins are treated more alike because they look and act more alike—at least, we found little evidence that parental beliefs about zygosity were important per se.

7. *There was some tendency toward correlation between differences in*

early experience and differences in personality, but these correlations were too low to be of any predictive value. Correlations between various measures of differential experience (dressing differently, playing apart, and so on) and a number of representative measures of personality, abilities, and interests tended to fluctuate around a typical level of +.05 or +.06. Using a composite of a variety of differential experience measures raised the typical correlation by only a point or two.

8. *The correlations between measures of differential early experience and measures of twin resemblance were of about the same size among identical and fraternal twins.* If the personality differences within pairs of identical twins are purely environmental in origin and if the differences within fraternal-twin pairs stem partly from the genes and partly from the environment, then one might expect to find the identical-twin differences more highly predictable from treatment differences than the fraternal-twin differences are. This was not the case; the median correlation between a composite measure of differential treatment and various personality measures was +.06 for identical twins and +.07 for fraternals.

9. *Identical-twin differences in early childhood were not highly predictive of differences observed in adolescence, and the few relationships observed tended to be fairly specific.* The identical twin who was reported as having done better work in elementary school tended to score higher on the NMSQT. The twin who was heavier at birth scored higher on the CPI Dominance scale—possibly by virtue of greater size and strength during childhood. Both findings suggest some degree of enduring influence of early environment on personality. (Retrospective rating bias might plausibly also be involved in the first case but seems less likely as an explanation in the second.) In a few other instances there was some degree of association—for example, closer to mother versus self-rated current good relations with mother—but not enough to permit a confident rejection of the hypothesis of chance association.

10. *Increased impact of the home environment did not tend to make twins more alike.* Estimates of the extent to which the home environment was actively impressed on the child (frequency and variety of discipline, parental demandingness, amount of family interaction) were essentially unrelated to personality, ability, and interest differences between the twins. Thus, there was little evidence that those homes in which parental values were actively imposed turned out a more standard product than did more permissive homes.

11. *Intercorrelation matrices in which genes and environment may be presumed to carry different weights did not differ substantially in structure.* The correlations among identical-twin differences on different traits must reflect either common environmental influences in the formation of those traits or a commonality that resides in the measurement process. Correlations derived from covariation within fraternal pairs or covariation between families for either kind of twin may reflect genetic commonality as well. Within the degree

of resolution provided by our methods, all four kinds of matrices appeared to be alike in their structure.

12. *Fraternal-twin differences on personality and ability measures were approximately normally distributed; identical twins showed an excess of small differences on some measures.* Interpersonal mechanisms of assimilation and contrast have often been postulated as operating between twins. Under a variety of assumptions one would expect such mechanisms to produce nonnormal distributions of twin pair differences. Major effects of single genes would also be expected to result in nonnormal distributions of fraternal-twin differences but not of identical-twin differences. The data suggest that some assimilation effects may occur among identical pairs, but there is little evidence of contrast effects for either type of twin or of major single-gene effects on the several personality and ability traits examined.

IMPLICATIONS OF THE FINDINGS

Let us now examine some of the implications of these empirical findings for the broad question of primary interest: what is the relative contribution of genes and environment to the development of personality, ability, and interests?

First, the consistently greater similarity of identical- than fraternal-twin pairs, under the conventional assumptions of the twin method, implies that the genes make an appreciable contribution to individual differences in these domains. However, if the conventional assumptions are invalid, this result could be interpreted as reflecting a greater similarity of the environments of identical-twin pairs. As we have seen, our data do indeed suggest that identical-twin pairs are subjected to environments that are in many respects more similar than those of fraternal pairs. But, in those same respects, variations in environmental similarity show negligible ability to predict personality resemblance *within* the two twin groups. Thus, either it is their greater genetic similarity that makes identical twins alike or it is environmental factors that are largely independent of such traditional ones as dressing alike, playing together, being treated alike by parents, and so forth.

Taking the genetic hypothesis for the moment, let us consider the implications of the curious uniformity of identical-fraternal differences both within and across trait domains. In chapter 4 we considered at some length the evidence, both from the present data and from previous studies in the literature, suggesting a rather remarkable absence of consistent tendencies for some traits to show larger differences between identical and fraternal correlations than others. The simplest way of estimating heritability from twin data is merely to double the difference between identical- and fraternal-twin correlations (Falconer 1960). If identical-fraternal differences in correlation fluctu-

1. Allowance for assortative mating and genetic dominance and epistasis would probably not affect the estimate much in the case of personality traits. A mild degree of positive assortative mating tends to prevail in this domain (Vandenberg 1972). Correcting for this would raise the heritability estimate slightly. But it is likely that this would be offset by at least some degree of nonadditivity in the genetic variance (i.e., dominance and epistatic effects), which would tend to bias heritability estimation in the opposite direction. Hence, the original .50 may not be too far off the mark. (For the benefit of readers unfamiliar with quantitative genetics: if the effect of a given gene on a trait depends on which particular other genes are present, genetic *dominance* or *epistasis* is said to exist, the former if the genes involved are at the same locus on the chromosome, the latter if they occur at different loci. These conditions may be collectively referred to as *nonadditivity*. *Assortative mating* is said to be present if the selection of who mates with whom in the population is related to the trait in question.)

In the case of ability traits, much higher levels of assortative mating may prevail—husband-wife correlations on the order of .40 or .50 for general intel-

ate randomly around a central tendency near .20, as our data suggest, this would imply heritabilities near .40. Plausible corrections for errors of measurement and diagnosis would raise this figure to slightly over .50[1], suggesting that the genes and environment carry roughly equal weight in accounting for individual variation in personality.

There is at least one theory which suggests that under long-term evolutionary conditions one might expect traits to tend toward roughly equal (and moderate) heritabilities. The theory derives from arguments outlined by Allen (1970). It holds that, if the heritability of a trait is low, gene mutations affecting the trait will tend to accumulate, increasing its genetic variance. Once the genetic variance becomes large enough relative to environmental variation so that the heritability of the trait is appreciable, stabilizing natural selection will begin to operate on the trait to slow and eventually to stop further increase in its genetic variability and hence to hold heritability at a stable level. If relevant environmental variation were to decrease, the trait heritability would temporarily rise, permitting selection to act more effectively on the genetic variation of the trait, bringing the genetic variation (and thus the heritability) back down again. Generally speaking, then, on this hypothesis all traits tend toward moderate levels of heritability because the genetic component of variation of any trait tends to increase until the process of natural selection can "see it" against the background of environmental variation present and hold it stable. This suggests that differences in the biological importance of difference traits will principally be reflected in the total amount of variation present, rather than in the relative proportions of this variation that are genetic and environmental. A critically important trait will show little variation among individuals and a trivial trait a lot, but their heritabilities will be about the same.

Such an argument also carries implications concerning the environmental influences on personality traits. For the described mechanism to work, the general level of environmental influence on any given trait must remain fairly constant on the scale of tens of thousands or hundreds of thousands of years on which human biological evolution takes place. The particular environmental mechanisms need not always be the same, but their general level of impact must remain reasonably constant. It seems plausible that some sorts of environmental influences—for example, prenatal factors or fundamental mother-infant emotional interactions—might better fit this criterion of long-term stability than others—such as practices in weaning or toilet training—whose wide degree of variation among contemporary peoples probably reflects an equally varied history through time.

Another perspective on the character of relevant environmental factors may be obtained by considering the different levels of twin correlation prevailing in different trait domains (cf. table 7-1). For identical twins, the genetic correlation is exactly the same—1.00—in each of the different domains. If the

Table 7–2. Correlations between Twin Environments in Various Domains Implied by the Typical Correlations of Table 7–1 (See Text for Calculation)

Trait domain	Present study	Previous studies
General ability	.73	.69
Special abilities	.54	.39
Personality inventory scales	.11	.13
Self-concept clusters	−.27	—
Ideals, goals, and vocational interests clusters	.05	—
Activities clusters	.49	—

ligence are commonly reported—and an appreciable amount of genetic dominance may also be present (cf. Jinks and Fulker 1970; but see also Eaves 1973a). Both assortative mating and genetic dominance may be less significant for special abilities, but one might still wish to be a bit cautious in generalizing the .50 figure into the ability domain. However, within that domain, as we have seen in chapter 4, there do not seem to be any more consistent trait-to-trait differences in heritability than in the case of personality traits.

2. A more complete analysis would take into account possible variations in the effects of gene-environment correlation and gene-environment interaction, but these are merged with the direct effects of the genes and the environment in twin data such as ours.

3. We could have used r_g = .5 and the observed fraternal-twin correlations; both methods give identical values for r_e. We may note that the results are not an artifact of differential reliability of measurement. Correcting the observed correlations for unreliability turns out to be algebraically equivalent to substituting the reliability coefficient for the 1 in the denominator in the expression for r_e. This will tend

proportion of genetic variance, the heritability, is approximately the same across domains, this implies that the variation in observed correlation must be due to changes in the environmental correlation between twins.[2]

We can, in fact, obtain rough quantitative estimates of the magnitude of the environmental correlations in the different domains. Under certain simple assumptions, the phenotypic (observed) correlation is the weighted sum of the genetic and environmental correlations:

$$r_p = h^2 r_g + (1 - h^2) r_e,$$

and, therefore,

$$r_e = \frac{r_p - h^2 r_g}{1 - h^2}.$$

If we estimate h^2 as $2(r_I - r_F)$ and use $r_g = 1$ and the observed identical-twin correlation as r_p, we can estimate the environmental correlation r_e in each of the trait domains in table 7–1. The results are given in table 7–2.[3]

The results are quite striking. Twins' environments show a substantial positive correlation in the case of abilities and activities. They show little or no correlation in the case of personality traits, ideals and goals, and vocational interests. They may even be negatively correlated for self-concepts. As far as personality and interests are concerned, then, it would appear that the relevant environments of a pair of twins are no more alike than those of two members of the population paired at random.

Can this possibly be true? It will be recalled that, according to the parent questionnaire, the twins of a pair were treated very much alike. And, indeed, many of the variables that psychologists have thought important for personality development—parents' child-rearing philosophies, atmosphere of the home, parental personalities, socioeconomic status, ages and sexes of siblings—are

Table 7-3. Intraclass Correlations on Personality Inventory Scales for Identical Twins Reared Together and Apart

to increase r_e, but the effect on low values of r_e will be small in absolute terms; so the contrasts in table 7-2 would tend to become even more marked if such corrections were made.

Scale	Condition of rearing		Pairs
	Apart	Together	
Neuroticism	.58	.56	19 & 50[a]
Neuroticism	.53	.38	42 & 43[b]
Extraversion	.61	.42	42 & 43[b]

[a]Newman, Freeman, and Holzinger 1937.
[b]Shields 1962.

correlated +1.00 in the case of twins reared in the same home. Nevertheless, other data suggest that our estimates of zero order or even negative r_e's in the personality realm may not be altogether absurd. The correlations on personality scales from the two extant studies of identical twins reared apart during substantial periods of their childhood are shown in table 7-3. Although the N's are small, the general tendency is clear: being reared apart in separate families does not make identical twins dissimilar in personality and being reared together in the same family does not make them more alike—it may even make them less alike. (In the case of general intelligence, the twins in these studies reared together were more similar than those reared apart, consistent with our finding of positive r_e's for abilities.)

Thus, a consistent—though perplexing—pattern is emerging from the data (and it is not purely idiosyncratic to our study). Environment carries substantial weight in determining personality—it appears to account for at least half the variance—but that environment is one for which twin pairs are correlated close to zero. Twins appear to be treated very much alike, but their correlations on personality measures are not high. The net effect of environment appears remarkably uniform across different traits and for the males and females, even though parental and social pressures must surely vary for different traits and between the sexes. Differences in the childhood treatment of twins are not very predictive of adolescent personality differences. Identical-twin differences—though necessarily environmental—are not better predicted from treatment differences than are fraternal-twin differences. Stronger attempts at parental influence do not result in more similar pairs of twins. Attempts to treat twins alike do not lead to greater similarity between them.

In short, in the personality domain we seem to see environmental effects that operate almost randomly with respect to the sorts of variables that psychologists (and other people) have traditionally deemed important in personality development.

What can be going on?

4. One additional possibility needs to be brought into consideration—that some of the phenomena suggesting "contrast effects" might be due instead to the presence of a large amount of epistasis among the genes affecting personality traits. A recent study by Lykken, Tellegen, and Thorkelson (1974) found high identical-twin correlations and low fraternal-twin correlations both for personality measures and for certain measures of electroencephalographic (EEG) frequencies. We can hardly suppose that twins have learned to contrast their EEG frequency spectra. But if these EEG patterns are highly dependent on the patterning of several genes—so that, when any one of the genes differs for the members of a twin pair, the whole pattern of EEG frequencies changes—then identical twins, who have identical genes, will have highly similar EEG patterns, but fraternal twins, who are quite likely to differ on at least one of the genes in the set, will show little average resemblance across pairs. If only a few genes are involved, such epistatic effects will produce nonnormal distributions of fraternal-twin differences—and there is evidence that this was the case for EEG spectra in the Lykken study. The authors do not report comparable data for their per-

One possibility that we have alluded to earlier is that there might exist effects of competition or contrast between members of twin pairs that are masking positive correlations that might otherwise be manifest. If a twin's reference point for self-definition is the other twin and if others around him are continually contrasting the pair members, it seems plausible that the two twins of a pair might often end up seeing themselves as much less similar in personality than they actually are. By such a mechanism, twins reared together might actually fill out a self-descriptive personality inventory in a less similar fashion than two twins reared apart, even though an observer might rate the twins reared together as more alike (there was a tendency of this sort in Shields's study). Such a mechanism would be consistent with the fact that in our study those measures most directly reflecting actual behaviors (NMSQT scales, activities) showed positive environmental correlations, whereas those most strongly dependent on judgments about the self showed low or negative r_e's.

While we find such a mechanism theoretically plausible, we are reluctant to place too much weight on it for several reasons: (a) to the extent that such a mechanism has its roots in parental and peer behavior, one would expect it to show some consistent pattern of differential effects across traits, sexes, and so forth, and such consistencies are not evident in our data; (b) on various assumptions, one would expect such a mechanism to produce nonnormal distributions of twin differences, but we did not find much evidence of such nonnormality; and (c) the extent to which twins tended to associate with each other was unpredictive of their personality differences, although one might expect such a contrast mechanism to be sensitive to this variable.[4]

If such contrastive factors are *not* playing a dominant role, it seems to us that one is thrown back on the view that the major, consistent directional factors in personality development are the genes and that the important environmental influences are highly variable situational inputs. This need not imply actual randomness in the environment, of course. If the ways in which environment affects personality are sufficiently complex, contingent, and subtle, they will appear random to such an analysis as ours.

One counterargument against this view is the fact that the correlation structure among personality variables can more readily be given a purely environmental than a purely genetic interpretation. However, it may be that this structure is more a product of the overlap in the way personality traits are defined and measured than of any basic structure within the individual.

In the end, we are left with three alternative ways of accounting for our data. The first holds that personality and interest dimensions as measured are about equally influenced by genes and environment but that the environmental contribution to the variance is largely random with respect to most of the variables that psychologists have conventionally emphasized as important in this domain. This interpretation has its greatest difficulty in accounting for

sonality measures. As we have noted, we did not find nonnormal distributions in our own data.

similar trait-intercorrelation patterns in various sources of trait covariance—although it can attribute these to measurement artifacts.

The second interpretation postulates negative environmental correlations due to contrast effects between twins as offsetting positive environmental correlations due to common environments, which leads to net correlations near zero. Such an interpretation has difficulties with the equal heritabilities across traits and sexes, the normal distributions of fraternal-twin differences, and the lack of influence of time spent together. However, it could coexist at a secondary level along with a primary interpretation of the first kind.

The third possible interpretation is that the genes have nothing directly to do with twin resemblance in personality and interests. While such a hypothesis is not logically excludable in the present study, the results we have presented suggest that if environment alone is to account for the data, it would have to be an environment with some strange properties indeed. It would have to be highly sensitive to the differences between identical and fraternal twins, yet this sensitivity must remain remarkably unresponsive to the differences between males and females or between one trait and another. It must be an environment that is almost uncorrelated with what the parents say the experiences of the children have been. It must lead to the same intertrait associations between families as within them. Finally, it must coexist with a rather different sort of environment affecting abilities. All in all, this seems a rather formidable set of requirements.

Our data have thus not yielded any final and conclusive answer to the heredity-environment question for personality, abilities, and interests. The data are generally consistent with a substantial influence of the genes in accounting for individual differences in these domains, but they imply a substantial influence of the environment as well—indeed, they do not altogether exclude a completely environmentalist position. The data do, it seems to us, have something important to say concerning this environment. And the upshot of what they say is that it operates in remarkably mysterious ways, given traditional views on personality and motivational development.

If we have made life more difficult for the authors of elementary textbooks on personality by stirring up these paradoxes, we apologize. We hope that more sharply focused research—ours or someone else's—will eventually resolve the paradoxes. There are many paths that such research might take. We will merely mention a few of the kinds of data that we looked for at one time or another in considering various hypotheses about our findings and that we discovered to be very limited or lacking altogether: personality data on adopted children and their natural and adoptive parents; personality data on maternally and paternally related half-siblings (important for an evaluation of prenatal environmental effects); personality data on siblings reared apart and unrelated persons reared together by adoption; and personality resemblances among ordinary family members—it is a paradoxical fact that there is now a great deal more such information available for twins than for ordinary brothers and sisters, normal parents and their children, or other relatives.

Finally, in exploring the relationships between personality and the environment in which it develops, we suspect that better means of assessing both will be critical. But we also suspect that improvement in measurement will go stepwise with improvement in understanding the phenomena involved. In the absence of some good ideas about what to measure, the most sophisticated psychometric methods are worthless.

And so in the end it comes back to the interplay between ideas and data. We have found our data richly provocative of hypotheses, some testable within the scope of this study, some awaiting further evidence of the kinds mentioned above, some only dimly suggesting lines of future investigation. We are confident that this process of research will continue and that it will eventually yield clear insight into today's puzzles and paradoxes about how the genes and environment act to shape the development of personality, abilities, and interests. We hope that our own results will have helped provoke such efforts.

Appendices

Appendix A

QUESTIONNAIRES

Questionnaires

Appendix A contains reproductions of the three main questionnaires used in the study: the questionnaire initially sent to the twins to diagnose zygosity, the main questionnaire sent separately to each twin, and the questionnaire filled out by a parent of the twins. In addition to the questionnaires reproduced in this appendix, each twin was sent a CPI booklet and answer sheet (Consulting Psychologists Press 1956).

The items in the questionnaire have been marked to correspond with the identifying numbers used in the text and in Appendix B.

The coding of items for purposes of analysis sometimes differed from the original booklet code used for recording the data on cards. When this is the case, it is also indicated in the booklet.

Preceding the questionnaires is a list of supplementary variables used in the study that do not appear directly in the questionnaires. These include such variables as sex and zygosity, the NMSQT, the scales from the California Psychological Inventory and the Holland Vocational Preference Inventory, and the various a priori composites derived from the parent questionnaire.

SUPPLEMENTARY VARIABLES

Twin Data

NUMBER	VARIABLE	SCORING
1	Pair identification number	
2	Sex	M = 1, F = 2
3	Zygosity	I = 1, F = 2
4	Confidence of diagnosis	1 to 4
5	NMSQT—English Usage	
6	NMSQT—Mathematics Usage	
7	NMSQT—Social Science Reading	Mean = 20
8	NMSQT—Natural Science Reading	SD = 5
9	NMSQT—Word Usage (Vocabulary)	
10	NMSQT—Selection Score (total)	Sum 5–9
	(11 to 1092: Twin Questionnaire items)	
1093–1572	CPI items 1–480	
1573	CPI—Dominance	
1574	CPI—Capacity for Status	
1575	CPI—Sociability	
1576	CPI—Social Presence	

NUMBER	VARIABLE	SCORING
1577	CPI—Self-Acceptance	
1578	CPI—Sense of Well-being	
1579	CPI—Responsibility	
1580	CPI—Socialization	
1581	CPI—Self-Control	
1582	CPI—Tolerance	
1583	CPI—Good Impression	
1584	CPI—Communality	
1585	CPI—Achievement via Conformance	
1586	CPI—Achievement via Independence	
1587	CPI—Intellectual Efficiency	
1588	CPI—Psychological-Mindedness	
1589	CPI—Flexibility	
1590	CPI—Femininity	
1591	CPI—Factor I: Emotional maturity	
1592	CPI—Factor II: Extraversion	
1593	CPI—Rigidity	
1594	CPI—Managerial	
1595	CPI—Acquiescence	
1596	CPI—Social Desirability	
1597	VPI—Realistic Orientation	
1598	VPI—Intellectual Orientation	
1599	VPI—Social Orientation	
1600	VPI—Conventional Orientation	
1601	VPI—Enterprising Orientation	
1602	VPI—Artistic Orientation	
1603	VPI—Masculinity-Femininity	
1604	VPI—Status	
1605	VPI—Control	
1606	VPI—Aggression	
1607	VPI—Infrequency	
1608	VPI—Total like (response set)	
1609	CPI—Eysenck neuroticism	
1610	CPI—Eysenck extraversion	

Parent Data

NUMBER	VARIABLE	SCORING
1–3	Same as twin data	
	(4 to 289: Parent Questionnaire items)	

NUMBER	VARIABLE	SCORING
290	Different treatment—infancy: 16, 20, 21, 22, 25, 28, 29, 33, 34, 36	No. of "1" or "2" responses
291	Different behavior—infancy: 19, 23, 24, 26, 30, 31, 32	No. of "1" or "2" responses
292	Different somatic problems—infancy: 12, 15, 17, 18, 35, 37, 38	No. of "1" or "2" responses
293	Different treatment—preschool: 41, 42, 46, 47, 50, 53, 54, 57, 59, 60, 72, 73, 76, 78, 79, 80	No. of "1" or "2" responses
294	Different behavior—preschool: 48, 49, 51, 52, 58, 62, 63, 64, 65, 67, 68, 69, 70, 71, 74, 75, 77	No. of "1" or "2" responses
295	Different treatment—childhood: 81, 83, 91, 92, 93, 98, 99, 103, 106, 109, 115, 116	No. of "1" or "2" responses
296	Different behavior—childhood: 82, 86, 88, 89, 90, 94, 95, 97, 101, 104, 105, 107, 108, 111	No. of "1" or "2" responses
297	Different treatment—adolescence: 118, 127, 128, 130, 132, 133, 135, 146, 147, 148, 149, 150, 151, 152, 153, 155, 157, 158	No. of "1" or "2" responses
298	Different behavior—adolescence: 117, 125, 129, 131, 134, 136, 137, 138, 139, 140, 141, 142, 156, 160	No. of "1" or "2" responses
299	Total different treatment: 290 + 293 + 295 + 297	
300	Total different behavior: 291 + 294 + 296 + 298	
301	Different current traits: 272–282	No. of "1" or "2" responses
302	Different current interests: 249–257	No. of "1" or "2" responses
303	Different current behavior: 258–263	No. of "1" or "2" responses
304	Different earlier treatment: 238, 239, 246, 247, 264, 265	No. of "1" or "2" responses
305	Did it first: 234, 236, 237, 248, 267–271	No. of "1" or "2" responses
306	Total current difference: sum of 301–303	
307	Childhood discipline: sum of 194–204	
308	Adolescent discipline: sum of 205–215	
309	Impact of home environment: (224 + 227) – (222 + 223 + 225 + 226 + 229 + 230) + a constant of 34	
310	Total home impact: sum of 307–309	

NUMBER	VARIABLE	SCORING
311	Disturbances: 177-179, 182-186	No. of "1" responses
312	Different treatment of twins: sum of 283-288	
313	Combined different treatment: 299 + 304 + 312	

NATIONAL MERIT SCHOLARSHIP CORPORATION

1580 Sherman Avenue, Evanston, Illinois   GReenleaf 5-2552

May, 1962

Dear Student:

We are writing to you because you indicated that you were a twin when you took the National Merit Scholarship Quali-fying Test last year. We are also writing to your twin brother or sister.

Our research department is doing a series of studies of factors influencing student development. You and your twin, by virtue of being twins, are in a unique position to contribute to these important studies.

We hope that you will help us by answering the questions in this brief questionnaire and returning it in the enclosed stamped envelope.

Your twin will receive a questionnaire just like this one. You should each answer the questions separately giving your own opinion. After completing the questions you may compare answers if you like but don't change any of your responses because of what your twin has said.

Thank you very much for your help.

Cordially,

John M. Stalnaker
John M. Stalnaker
President

Please check your name and
address on the envelope. If
there are any errors print your
correct name and address here.

_____

_____

_____

As you know, there are two kinds of twins: identical or one egg twins, which have
the same heredity, and fraternal or two egg twins, which have different heredity.
Most of the following questions are intended to help determine which kind you are.

_____

1. What is your hair color?_____Is your hair different in
    color, texture, or pattern of growth from that of your twin? In what way?

    _____

    _____

2. What is the color of your eyes?_____Is your eye color dif-
    ferent from that of your twin? In what way?

    _____

    _____

3. How tall are you?_____How much taller (or shorter) are you than
    your twin?

    _____

    _____

4. How much do you weigh?_____How much heavier (or lighter) are
    you than your twin?

    _____

    _____

5. If you know your blood type and Rh factor indicate them here_____

6. As a young child did your parents ever mistake you for your twin? (Check one.)

    _____Yes, frequently.
    _____Occasionally.
    _____Rarely or never.

7. Have your parents mistaken you for your twin recently? (Check one.)

    _____Yes, frequently.
    _____Occasionally.
    _____Rarely or never.

8. Have your teachers ever mistaken you for your twin? (Check one.)

    _____ Yes, frequently.
    _____ Occasionally.
    _____ Rarely or never.

9. Have close friends ever mistaken you for your twin? (Check one.)

    _____ Yes, frequently.
    _____ Occasionally.
    _____ Rarely or never.

10. Have casual friends ever mistaken you for your twin? (Check one.)

    _____ Yes, frequently.
    _____ Occasionally.
    _____ Rarely or never.

11. Do you know whether you are a fraternal or identical twin? (Check one.)

    _____ I know for sure that I am an identical twin.
    _____ I think I am an identical twin.
    _____ I know for sure that I am a fraternal twin.
    _____ I think I am a fraternal twin.
    _____ I don't know whether I am an identical or a fraternal twin.

12. If you know whether you are fraternal or identical, how do you know?
    (Indicate how and by whom it was determined?)

    _____

    _____

    _____

    _____

13. Have you had any major illnesses or accidents that your twin did not have?
    If yes, indicate the nature of the illness or accident and your age when
    it occurred.

    _____

    _____

    _____

    _____

    _____

14. Have you been separated from your twin for more than a month at a time? _____
    If yes, indicate where each of you was living, what you were doing, and your
    age at the time.

    _____

    _____

    _____

    _____

    _____

    _____

15. Have you had any other important experiences which your twin has not had?

    _____

    _____

    _____

    _____

    _____

    _____

16. Your responses to the above questions will be helpful in determining the fac-
    tors which influence students' scores on the National Merit Examination, and
    we greatly appreciate your cooperation. We now have another favor to ask you.
    We are conducting a large study of twins in which we would like for you and
    your twin to participate. If you agree we will send you a questionnaire which
    will take from two to three hours to complete. We think you will find this
    questionnaire interesting and when some results are available we will send
    you a newsletter describing the findings. Your help in this research will
    make a valuable contribution to knowledge about the factors which determine
    human behavior.

    Will you participate in the larger study? (Check one.)

    _____Yes, Please send the questionnaire.

    _____No, I do not want to participate.

    Thank you for completing this questionnaire. Please remember to mail it
    promptly.

NATIONAL MERIT SCHOLARSHIP CORPORATION

1580 Sherman Avenue, Evanston, Illinois   GReenleaf 5-2552

TWIN QUESTIONNAIRE

June 1963

INSTRUCTIONS: The analyses for a part of this research will be
performed by an electronic computer. For this
reason, it will facilitate the interpretation of
your responses if you follow certain standard
procedures in indicating your answers.

A. Most of the questions can be answered by drawing a circle around one or more numbers or letters.
Thus:

Are you a twin? (Circle one.)

Yes, I am a twin . . . . ①
No, but I have other brothers and sisters. . . 2
No, I am an only child 3

Have you done any of the following things?
(Circle one response for each item.)

Frequently
Occasionally
Not at all

Answered questionnaires like this   1   2   ③
Attended class. . . . . ① 2   3
Made good grades. . . . . 1 ② 3
Wished you had more money . . . . ① 2   3

NOTE: After each question there are instructions in parentheses
indicating how many numbers are to be circled. Please
follow these instructions closely.

If you make an error or decide to change your response, mark out the incorrect response like
this:

True False
I am over 21 years of age . . . . . . ⊠ ⑥

B. Some of the items contain boxes in which you are to write in numbers. Place a single digit in
each box. Do not put in fractions, but round to the nearest whole number. If the number you
are to write in is not large enough to use all the boxes, fill in the preceding zeros.

FOR EXAMPLE: The number "seven" would be indicated | 0 | 0 | 7 |

C. A few items have space to write in a response. Please write as clearly as possible.

D. Answer all of the items by yourself without consulting anyone. Do not change any of your
answers because of what your twin or anyone else has said. We want your own opinion.

Try to make your response as accurate as possible, but do not spend too much time on any one
item.

Thank you,

Robert C. Nichols

Robert C. Nichols
Study Director

Are your name and address correct?
(Please correct any errors.)
BE SURE YOU HAVE YOUR OWN QUESTION-
NAIRE AND NOT YOUR TWIN'S.

If the above address is not the best   Name _____
place to reach you one year from now
please indicate a better address here: Address _____
PLEASE PRINT.
    City and State _____

Please indicate here the name and
address of someone, living at a
different address from the one above,   Name _____
who will know where you are or could
forward a letter to you if you were   Address _____
not at the above address.
PLEASE PRINT.   City and State _____

_____

With your permission, we would like to get some impressions of you and your twin from your teachers
and fellow students. If you agree, we will write to two of your teachers and two of your fellow
students asking them to complete a brief questionnaire giving their impressions of you and your
twin. Their questionnaire will state that you are participating in a research project concerned
with the characteristics of twins. Their replies, like all of our data will be completely confidential and will be used in group comparisons for research purposes only. You and your twin may list
the same teachers and friends if you wish, or you may list different ones.

List two friends of your own age and sex who are familiar with both your and your twin's behavior
and experiences over the last year or so: PLEASE PRINT.

Name_____   Name_____

Address_____   Address_____

City and State_____   City and State_____

List two high school teachers who are familiar with both your and your twin's work in high school.
If you do not know the teacher's home address, give the name of the high school at which he teaches.
PLEASE PRINT.

        NOTE: If there are no teachers who know both you and
              your twin well, check here_____and leave blank.

Name_____   Name_____

Address_____   Address_____

City and State_____   City and State_____

_____

Please note the time _____. At the end of the questionnaire, we will ask how long it
took you to complete it.

~~1.~~ What is your sex? (Circle one.)

Male 1   (7)
Female 2

2. When did (will) you graduate from high school? (Circle one.)

011

Mid-term 1962-63. 1   (8)
Spring 1963 2
Summer 1963 3
Mid-term 1963-64. 4
Other (Circle and specify.)_____

~~3.~~ What will you be doing this fall? If you expect to be doing two things simultaneously, circle both. If you are considering two alternatives, circle only the more probable.

Student in college, high school or training course. 1   (9)
Working at a type of job which I expect to be my
   long-run career field. 2
Working at a job which will probably not be my
   long-run career field. 3
Military service. 4
Housewife 5
Other (Circle and specify.)_____ 6

~~4.~~ What college or school are you planning to attend next year? (If you will not be a student next fall, write in "None".)

_____ (10-13)
     Name of College   City and State

~~5.~~ What will be your future career or life work? (Be as specific as possible.)

_____ (14-15)

~~6.~~ What alternative career plans are you considering? _____ (16-17)

_____

7. What is the highest level of education you expect to complete? (Circle one.)

012

High school diploma. 1   (18)
Non-college training course (business school, nurse's training, etc.). . . . 2
College, but less than a bachelor's degree 3
Bachelor's degree or equivalent. 4
One or two years of graduate or professional study (M.A., M.B.A., etc.). . . 5
Doctor of Philosophy (Ph.D.) . . . . ⎫
Doctor of Medicine (M.D.) . . . . ⎬
Doctor of Dental Surgery (D.D.S.). . . . . ⎪
Bachelor of Laws (L.L.B.). . . . . ⎬ 6
Bachelor of Divinity (B.D.). ⎪
Other (Circle and specify.)_____ ⎭

8. Which hand do you favor? (Circle one.)

013

I have always been right handed. 1   (19)
I favored my left hand as a child, but am now right handed 2
I am left handed and tried, unsuccessfully, to switch. 5
I am left handed and have not seriously tried to switch. 4
I am ambidextrous. 3

9. What is your academic rank in your high school class?
(0001 is the highest rank, 0002 the next highest, etc.)

014 *transformed to percentile* *015*

I ranked number [percentile] in a class of [ ][ ][ ][ ]   (20-27)

How accurate is your report of high school rank? (Circle one.)

016
It is correct as reported to me by the school 1   (28)
It is an estimate calculated from grade average, percentile rank or some
   other measure of performance 2
It is a guess based on my general impression. 3
I have no idea of my high school rank and have left the item blank. 4

Is your rank in class as reported above a fair indication of your ability? (Circle one.)

017
It grossly under-represents my ability *1*   (29)
It slightly under-represents my ability. *2*
It is a fair representation of my ability. *3*
It slightly over-represents my ability *4*
It grossly over-represents my ability. *5*

---

10. Which of the following best describe the community which you think of as your home
town during high school days? (Circle one.)   *018 019*

Farm or open country. *1* (30) *1*
Suburb in a metropolitan area of--
                    more than 2 million population. *7*
                    500,000 to 2 million. *6*   *2*
                    100,000 to 499,999. . . . . *5*
                    less than 100,000 . . . . *4*
Central city in a metropolitan area or city of--
                    more than 2 million population. *7*
                    500,000 to 2 million. *6*
                    100,000 to 499,999. . . . . *5*   *3*
                    50,000 to 99,999. . . . . *4*
                    10,000 to 49,999. . . . . *3*
                    less than 10,000. . . . . *2*

---

11. How much do you smoke? (Circle all that apply.)

020
I have never smoked. *1* (31)
I used to smoke but stopped. *2*
I smoke only occasionally or under special circumstances *2*

I smoke from 1 to 19 cigarettes a day. *3*
I smoke from 20 to 39 cigarettes a day *4*
I smoke 40 or more cigarettes a day. *4*

I smoke from 1 to 3 cigars a day *3*
I smoke from 4 to 6 cigars a day *4*
I smoke 7 or more cigars a day *4*

I smoke from 1 to 3 pipefuls of tobacco a day. *3*
I smoke from 4 to 6 pipefuls of tobacco a day. *4*
I smoke 7 or more pipefuls of tobacco a day. *4*

---

12. If you smoke do you inhale the smoke into your lungs? (Circle one.)

021
I don't smoke. *1* (32)
I rarely or never inhale *2*
I sometimes inhale *3*
I usually inhale *4*

-4-

13. In an average week during the past school year, how much time did you spend in each of the following activities? Indicate time when you were <u>attending school</u>--do not include vacation time. Fill in the boxes with two digits indicating the average number of hours spent in each activity during a typical <u>seven-day</u> period. Indicate time to the nearest hour. Do not write in fractional hours.

(33-68)

FOR EXAMPLE:

If you spend about 8 hours a night sleeping, you sleep 7 x 8 hours a week, which you would indicate: . . . . | 5 | 6 |

No. of Hrs.   No. of Hrs.

022
Studying for school assignments . . . [|]   *032* Daydreaming. . . . . [|]

Attending class . . . . [|]   Personal care (bathing, fixing hair, putting on make-up, etc.) . . . . [|]

Reading for pleasure. . . . . [|]   Attending club or organizational activities (meetings pledge-duties, etc.) . . . . [|]

025
Talking informally with others. . . . [|]   *035* Participating in musical, dramatic or artistic activities . . . . [|]

Watching TV . . . . [|]

Attending movies and plays. . . . . . [|]   Working on other projects or hobbies not directly related to course work or a job . . . . [|]

Watching sports events. . . . . . . [|]

Sleeping. . . . . [|]   Fooling around, wasting time [|]

030
Working for a salary, hourly wage or commission . . . . [|]   Playing games (cards, chess, etc.) . . . . [|]

Working on your own private business enterprise . . . . [|]   *039* Participating in sports and practice sessions. . . . [|]

---

14. What is your racial background? (circle one.)
040
    White. 1 (69)
    Negro. 2
    Oriental 3
    Other (Circle and specify.)_____ 4

In which religion were you reared? (Circle one.)
041
    Protestant (Circle and specify.)_____ 1 (70)
    Roman Catholic 2
    Jewish 3
    Other (Circle and specify.)_____ 4
    None 5

What is your present religious preference? (Circle one.)
042
    Protestant (Circle and specify.)_____ 1 (71)
    Roman Catholic 2
    Jewish 3
    Other (Circle and specify.)_____ 4
    None 5

-5-

15. Below is a list of things that students sometimes do. Indicate which of these things you have done during the past year (since this time last year.) If you have engaged in an activity regularly with a frequency appropriate for the activity, circle the number under "Frequently." If you have engaged in an activity <u>one or more</u> times, but not frequently, circle the number under "Occasionally." If you have not engaged in the activity during the past year, circle the number under "Not at all." (Circle one for each item.)

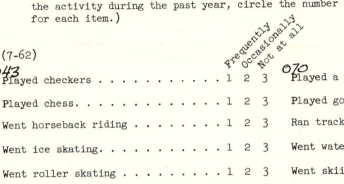

(7-62)

	Frequently	Occasionally	Not at all
043 Played checkers	1	2	3
Played chess	1	2	3
Went horseback riding	1	2	3
Went ice skating	1	2	3
Went roller skating	1	2	3
Picked-up a date in a bar, restaurant or similar place	1	2	3
Made minor repairs around the house	1	2	3
050 Took cough syrup	1	2	3
Cared for tropical fish or goldfish	1	2	3
Cared for other pet animals	1	2	3
Prayed (not including grace before meals)	1	2	3
Said grace before meals	1	2	3
Discussed how to make money with friends	1	2	3
Listened to modern (progressive) jazz	1	2	3
Listened to New Orleans' (Dixieland) jazz	1	2	3
Listened to folk music	1	2	3
Rode a motorcycle	1	2	3
060 Went to a party	1	2	3
Gambled with cards	1	2	3
Gambled with dice	1	2	3
Discussed school subjects with friends	1	2	3
Drove a car over 80 M.P.H.	1	2	3
Sold a used textbook	1	2	3
Went to sleep in class	1	2	3
Shot a gun	1	2	3
Borrowed money	1	2	3
Used "Man-Tan," "Tan-O-Rama," "Q.T." or similar products	1	2	3

	Frequently	Occasionally	Not at all
070 Played a practical joke on someone	1	2	3
Played golf	1	2	3
Ran track (dashes, hurdles, distance, etc.)	1	2	3
Went water skiing or surf board riding	1	2	3
Went skiing	1	2	3
Participated in crew events (sculls, pairs, fours, etc.)	1	2	3
Stayed up all night	1	2	3
Attended a public lecture (not for a course)	1	2	3
Drank wine	1	2	3
Gave a public recital (vocal, instrumental, etc.)	1	2	3
080 Gave a prepared talk to fifteen or more people	1	2	3
Listened to the radio	1	2	3
Performed magic or card tricks	1	2	3
Made wisecracks in class	1	2	3
Played a piano or other instrument while others were singing	1	2	3
Lent money to a friend	1	2	3
Bought a folk music record	1	2	3
Drank whisky, gin or other hard liquor	1	2	3
Made entries in a diary or journal	1	2	3
Hazed underclassmen	1	2	3
090 Worked on a scrap book	1	2	3
Knitted	1	2	3
Made an article of clothing	1	2	3
Went social (ballroom) dancing	1	2	3
Lied about your age	1	2	3
Polished your toenails	1	2	3
096 Played Tic-Tac-Toe, Hangman's Noose, or similar games in class	1	2	3

(7-63)

097

Frequently / Occasionally / Not at all — 1 2 3

Studied with another person 4 5 6

Took dancing lessons. 4 5 6

Took No-Doz or other stay-awake pills 4 5 6

100
Repaired or worked on a car 4 5 6

Changed clothes during the day
(exclude gym or athletics). 4 5 6

Baby sat. 4 5 6

Performed pledge duties 4 5 6

Took a sleeping pill. 4 5 6

Sang in a church choir. 4 5 6

Sang in a school choir. 4 5 6

Sang in a small ensemble (trio,
quartet, etc.). 4 5 6

Took golf lessons 4 5 6

Bought a popular or jazz record . . . 4 5 6

110
Took horseback riding lessons 4 5 6

Cooked a complete meal. 4 5 6

Cleaned and dusted your room. 4 5 6

Daydreamed in class 4 5 6

Worked backstage on a play. 4 5 6

Did voluntary work for a hospital or
service organization (Red Cross,
Heart Fund, etc.) 4 5 6

Arranged a date for a friend. . . . 4 5 6

Attended athletic events. 4 5 6

Worked on a number painting 4 5 6

Made bets on a game or other event
(not cards or dice) 4 5 6

120
Played charades 4 5 6

Attended a burlesque show 4 5 6

Went to a party with a date 4 5 6

Went to an overnight or week-end
party 4 5 6

x

124

Frequently / Occasionally / Not at all — 1 2 3

Went square dancing. 4 5 6

Cared for a potted plant 4 5 6

Argued with a teacher in class 4 5 6

Bought a paper-back book 4 5 6

Bought a classical or semi-classical
record 4 5 6

Chewed gum 4 5 6

130
Bit your fingernails 4 5 6

Rode in a sports car 4 5 6

Went sightseeing 4 5 6

Practiced on a musical instrument. . . . 4 5 6

Took a nap or rest during the day. . . . 4 5 6

Talked in a language other than English. 4 5 6

Conducted a choir, band or orchestra . . . 4 5 6

Took voice lessons 4 5 6

Crocheted. 4 5 6

Picked-up a hitch-hiker. 4 5 6

140
Tutored someone for money. 4 5 6

Tutored someone for free 4 5 6

Wrote articles for a school paper, yearbook or similar publication. 4 5 6

Went to a night club with a floor show . . 4 5 6

Took photographs 4 5 6

Built or flew a model airplane 4 5 6

Took Metrecal or similar dietary formula . 4 5 6

Participated in a student demonstration
(strike, water-fight, etc.). 4 5 6

Attended an orchestra concert. 4 5 6

Attended a formal dance. 4 5 6

150
Read magazines at a newsstand without
buying any 4 5 6

Worked for a club or organization. . . . 4 5 6

x

(7-52)

Frequently Occasionally Not at all
1 2 3 9

152 Played football (touch or tackle) . . 7 8 9

Bowled. 7 8 9

Went to the movies. 7 8 9

Developed pictures (darkroom work). . 7 8 9

Attended a professional stage play. . 7 8 9

Solicited advertising for a school paper, yearbook or similar publication. 7 8 9

Went swimming 7 8 9

Participated in field events (shot put, javelin, high jump, etc.). . . . 7 8 9

160 Saw a foreign movie 7 8 9

Rode a bicycle. 7 8 9

Attended a horse race 7 8 9

Played tennis 7 8 9

Took tranquilizing pills. 7 8 9

Attended a student stage play 7 8 9

Drove a car 7 8 9

Went boating. 7 8 9

Washed dishes 7 8 9

Worked crossword puzzles. 7 8 9

170 Ate lunch or dinner alone 7 8 9

Watched TV. 7 8 9

Put up decorations for a party. . . . 7 8 9

Attended a ballet performance 7 8 9

Overslept and missed a class or appointment 7 8 9

Visited a person in a hospital. . . . 7 8 9

Obtained a book or journal from the library 7 8 9

Read The Bible. 7 8 9

Danced the twist. 7 8 9

Frequently Occasionally Not at all
1 2 3 9

Took vitamins. 7 8 9

180 Participated in a drag race. 7 8 9

Attended a professional prize fight or wrestling match. 7 8 9

Flew in an airplane. 7 8 9

Attended a fashion show. 7 8 9

Visited a museum 7 8 9

Played baseball or softball. 7 8 9

Went on a camping trip 7 8 9

Voted in a student election. 7 8 9

Went hunting 7 8 9

Discussed religion with friends. 7 8 9

190 Took a laxative. 7 8 9

Talked for over thirty minutes at a time on the telephone 7 8 9

Called a teacher by his first name 7 8 9

Participated in a wedding (usher, bridesmaid, etc.). 7 8 9

Bought stamps for a stamp collection . . . 7 8 9

Cut class. 7 8 9

Twirled a baton. 7 8 9

Wrote letters to friends your own age. . . 7 8 9

Went window shopping 7 8 9

Drank in a bar 7 8 9

200 Took aspirin 7 8 9

Painted a picture (oil, watercolor, pastel, etc.). 7 8 9

Played cards (bridge, pinochle, etc.). . . 7 8 9

Told jokes 7 8 9

Listened to records in a store without buying 7 8 9

205 Played in a dance or jazz band 7 8 9

x

x

(7-57)

206
Ate Chinese food. 1 2 3

Swore in the presence of your parents 1 2 3

Swore in the presence of girls your
own age 1 2 3

Swore in the presence of boys your
own age 1 2 3

210
Was consulted for help or advice by
someone with a personal problem . . . 1 2 3

Took anti-acids (Bromo-Seltzer, Roll-
Aids, etc.) 1 2 3

Lay awake for an hour or more trying
to go to sleep. 1 2 3

Had a nightmare 1 2 3

Went without breakfast. 1 2 3

Went without lunch. 1 2 3

Went without dinner 1 2 3

Wrote a letter to a "pen-pal" whom
you have never met in person. 1 2 3

Did an imitation or impersonation of
another person. 1 2 3

Complained about service in a
restaurant. 1 2 3

214
Cribbed a paper or had someone ghost-
write one for you 1 2 3

Drank black coffee (no cream or
sugar). 1 2 3

Attended a church or service of a
religion other than your own. 1 2 3

Placed a long distance call of over
500 miles 1 2 3

Went on a double date 1 2 3

Wrote a "love-letter" 1 2 3

Purposely ditched a date. 1 2 3

Wrote a "Letter-to-the-Editor". . . . 1 2 3

Had a hangover. 1 2 3

Played a slot machine 1 2 3

230
Let work for a class pile up until just
before a test. 1 2 3

Read poetry that was not required reading. 1 2 3

Wrote poetry on your own initiative. . . . 1 2 3

Discussed sexual matters with your mother. 1 2 3

Discussed sexual matters with your father. 1 2 3

Discussed sexual matters with a male
friend 1 2 3

Discussed sexual matters with a female
friend 1 2 3

Borrowed clothing from a friend. 1 2 3

Wore glasses 1 2 3

Used a thermometer to take your
temperature. 1 2 3

240
Attended a religious revival meeting . . . 1 2 3

Looked something up in an encyclopedia . . 1 2 3

Bought or sold corporate stocks. 1 2 3

Baked a cake or pie from scratch (no
mixes) 1 2 3

Wore sun glasses after dark. 1 2 3

Awakened in the middle of the night and
was unable to go back to sleep 1 2 3

Ate a steak cooked rare. 1 2 3

Was "stood-up" by a date 1 2 3

Reported someone to the authorities for
some form of misbehavior 1 2 3

Entered a speech or debate contest 1 2 3

250
Had your back rubbed 1 2 3

"Bird-dogged" (stole another person's
date). 1 2 3

Had your date "bird-dogged" by someone
else 1 2 3

Had a drink before breakfast or instead
of breakfast 1 2 3

254
Produced a work of art (not for a
course). 1 2 3

(7-70)

Frequently / Occasionally / Not at all
1 2 3

255
Had a quarrel with your mother. . . . 4 | 5 6

Had a quarrel with your father. . . . 4 | 5 6

Had a quarrel with your brother or sister. . . . . 4 | 5 6

Had a quarrel with a male friend. . . 4 | 5 6

Had a quarrel with a female friend. . 4 | 5 6

260
Visited a friend's home overnight . . 4 | 5 6

Visited a relative's home overnight . 4 5 6

Had a friend visit your home overnight 4 5 6

Started a conversation with strangers 4 5 6

Went to the movies alone. 4 5 6

Tried on clothes in a store without buying anything 4 5 6

Pushed a stalled car (other than your own) 4 5 6

Listened to classical or semi-classical music 4 5 6

Smoked a cigarette or cigar before breakfast 4 5 6

Played a pinball machine. 4 5 6

270
Went skin diving. 4 5 6

Attended an art exhibition. 4 5 6

Played polo (indoor or outdoor) . . . 4 5 6

Went skeet or trapshooting. 4 5 6

Hitch-hiked 4 5 6

Acted in a play 4 5 6

Tried to hypnotize someone. 4 5 6

Taught Sunday school. 4 5 6

Attended Sunday school. 4 5 6

Attended church 4 5 6

280
Cried 4 5 6

Played basketball 4 5 6

Mended clothing 4 5 6

Discussed sports with friends 4 5 6

Blushed 4 5 6

Had a blind date. 4 5 6

Frequently / Occasionally / Not at all
1 2 3

286
Kissed your mother . . . . 4 | 5 6

Kissed your father . . . . : . 4 5 6

Wore formal clothing (evening gown, tuxedo, dinner jacket, etc.) 4 5 6

Told a "dirty joke" to male friends. . . 4 | 5 6

290
Told a "dirty joke" to female friends. . 4 | 5 6

Hit or slapped a boy of your own age . . . 4 | 5 6

Hit or slapped a girl of your own age. . . 4 5 6

Was hit or slapped by a boy of your own age. 4 5 6

Was hit or slapped by a girl of your own age. 4 5 6

Lent clothing to a friend. 4 5 6

Played Monopoly, Scrabble, or similar games. 4 5 6

Drew pictures or doodles in a notebook during class 4 5 6

Participated in a science contest or talent search. 4 5 6

Played sick to avoid taking an examination or other unpleasant duty 4 5 6

300
Played in a concert orchestra. 4 5 6

Lifted weights 4 5 6

Played table tennis or ping-pong 4 5 6

Worked on Hi-Fi or radio equipment 4 5 6

Dined by candle light. 4 5 6

Participated in a debate or speech contest 4 5 6

Played soccer. 4 5 6

Played in a marching band. 4 5 6

Lost your temper 4 5 6

Went fishing 4 5 6

310
Asked questions in class 4 5 6

Led a cheering section 4 5 6

Became intoxicated 4 5 6

Played solitaire 4 5 6

Collected insect specimens 4 5 6

Ate candy. 4 5 6

316
Drank beer 4 5 6

x   x

317

	Frequently	Occasionally	Not at all

Rode on a roller coaster, ferris wheel, merry go round, or similar ride. 1 2 3 7 8 9

As a check on accuracy of recording make no response at all to this item. 7 8 9

Studied with the radio, record player or TV on 7 8 9

320

Had a porter or red cap carry a suit-case for you. 7 8 9

Paid someone to polish your shoes. . . .   7 8 9

Cut your own hair. 7 8 9

Started a false rumor. 7 8 9

Voted for someone you knew nothing about   7 8 9

Spent an hour at a time daydreaming. . .   7 8 9

Smashed a vase or other object as an expression of anger or frustration . . .   7 8 9

Gave a tip of more than 15% of the check to a waiter, taxi driver, etc. 7 8 9

Gave a tip to a washroom attendant . . .   7 8 9

Read in bed before going to sleep. . . .   7 8 9

330

Fainted 7 8 9

Rode a horse. 7 8 9

Obtained the autograph of a famous person   7 8 9

Mixed a cocktail consisting of three or more ingredients (not including ice). .   7 8 9

Carried a good luck charm (like a rabbit's foot or four leaf clover). . .   7 8 9

Dove from a diving board or tower more than six feet above the water 7 8 9

Jumped in a parachute 7 8 9

Drank five or more cups of coffee a day   7 8 9

Drank four or more cokes or other soft drinks a day. 7 8 9

Ate two or more candy bars a day. . . .   7 8 9

340

Had a quarrel with your twin. 7 8 9

341

	Frequently	Occasionally	Not at all

Slept more than 12 hours at a time . . .   1 2 3 7 8 9

Recopied notes to make them neat 7 8 9

Stayed away from a party or dance in order to finish some work. 7 8 9

Tried to convince someone to change his (her) religious beliefs. 7 8 9

Tried to convince someone to change his (her) political or social beliefs. . . .   7 8 9

Practiced decorative or unusual hand-writing. 7 8 9

Took a bubble bath 7 8 9

Read the editorial page of a newspaper .   7 8 9

Made a new friend. 7 8 9

350

Made your own bed. 7 8 9

Washed dishes. 7 8 9

Took a long walk alone 7 8 9

Wrote a letter to a congressman. 7 8 9

Rode in a taxi 7 8 9

Took exercises 7 8 9

Turned down an invitation for a date . .   7 8 9

Stayed out on a date after 2 AM. 7 8 9

Read the Stock Market quotations 7 8 9

Visited a doctor for a physical exam or general check up. 7 8 9

360

Fed a stray dog or cat 7 8 9

Washed and/or polished a car 7 8 9

Ate breakfast in bed (not as a patient).   7 8 9

Looked up a word in the dictionary . . .   7 8 9

Chewed on a pencil 7 8 9

Confused people by pretending to be your twin. 7 8 9

366

Was sick in bed for one or more days . .   7 8 9

16. People have many different goals in life, some of the more common of which are listed below. Indicate the importance which you place on the following kinds of accomplishments, aspirations, and goals. (Circle one in each row.)

CD _____ (1-6)

	Essential (something I must achieve)	Very Important to achieve (but not essential)	Somewhat Important to achieve	Of little or no importance
367				
Becoming happy and content.	1	2	3	4 (7-41)
Being well-off financially.	1	2	3	4
Inventing or developing a useful product or device.	1	2	3	4
Helping others who are in difficulty.	1	2	3	4
Becoming accomplished in one of the performing arts (acting, dancing, etc.).	1	2	3	4
372				
Developing a meaningful philosophy of life. . .	1	2	3	4
Becoming an authority on a special subject in my field.	1	2	3	4
Doing something which will make my parents proud of me	1	2	3	4
Becoming an outstanding athlete	1	2	3	4
Making sacrifices for the sake of the happiness of others	1	2	3	4
377				
Becoming a community leader	1	2	3	4
Becoming influential in public affairs.	1	2	3	4
Becoming a mature and well-adjusted person. . .	1	2	3	4
Following a formal religious code	1	2	3	4
Having the time and means to relax and enjoy life.	1	2	3	4
382				
Making a theoretical contribution to science. .	1	2	3	4
Making a technical contribution to science. . .	1	2	3	4
Writing good fiction (poems, novels, short stories, etc.).	1	2	3	4
Being well read	1	2	3	4
Obtaining awards or recognition	1	2	3	4
387				
Never being obligated to people	1	2	3	4
Keeping in good physical condition.	1	2	3	4
Producing good artistic work (painting, sculpture, decorating, etc.).	1	2	3	4
Becoming an accomplished musician (performer or composer).	1	2	3	4
Becoming an expert in finance and commerce. . .	1	2	3	4
392				
Keeping up to date with political affairs . . .	1	2	3	4
Being well-liked.	1	2	3	4
Being a good husband or wife.	1	2	3	4
Being a good parent	1	2	3	4
Finding a real purpose in life.	1	2	3	4
397				
Being active in religious affairs	1	2	3	4
Having executive responsibility for the work of others	1	2	3	4
Avoiding hard work.	1	2	3	4
Engaging in exciting and stimulating activities	1	2	3	4
Being successful in a business of my own. . . .	1	2	3	4 x (42)

401

17. Which of the following statements best describes your religious belief? (Circle one.)

402

I believe in a personal God, a supreme being, who knows my thoughts and hears my prayers. 1 (43)

I believe in a supreme being who created and controls the universe, but I am not sure that individual people can communicate with Him 2

I am not sure whether or not there is a God, but I tend to think that there is. 3

I am not sure whether or not there is a God, but I tend to think that there is not. 4

I believe that there is no God. 5

I don't know what I believe 6

Other (Circle and specify.) _____ 7

18. An issue which has been the subject of public debate recently is the speed with which integration of the races, particularly Negroes and Whites, should take place in this country. Which of the statements below comes closest to your personal opinion? (Circle one.)

403

<u>All</u> discrimination among people on the basis of race is unfair and should be stopped immediately, even though this probably would change many current social institutions 1 (44)

The elimination of <u>all</u> discrimination among people on the basis of race should be our goal, but we should proceed slowly enough to allow people to make adjustments to the changes that would occur 2

Basic legal rights should be provided to all races, but beyond this, people should be able to limit their associations to members of their own race if they want to. 3

There are great differences between the races and there is no reason why these differences should not be used as the basis for certain civil rights such as voting privileges, educational opportunities, etc. 4

I have no particular feeling one way or the other 5

Other (Circle and specify.) _____
_____ 6

19. Another issue which has been the subject of public debate recently is the role of the federal government in providing for the needs of the people. Which of the statements below comes closest to your personal opinion? (Circle one.)

404

The federal government should do for the people <u>only</u> what they cannot possibly do for themselves. This includes such <u>matters</u> as international relations, national defense and the like. All other functions are better left to local governments or private enterprise 6 *1* (45)

The federal government can bring benefits to the people in many ways and should enter fields such as old age security, regulation of agri-culture, stimulation of the economy and the like, but <u>only if</u> local governments and private enterprise have failed to do an adequate job. . . 7 *2*

The federal government is responsible for the welfare of the people and should expand its activities in such areas as education, health, generation of power, etc., even though there are already local or private programs in existence 8 *3*

I have no strong feeling one way or the other 9

Other (Circle and specify.) _____ 0

20. What is your current marital or dating status? (Circle one.)

405

Married (children or expecting)   1   (46)
Married (no children)   2
Engaged   3
Pinned or going steady.   4
Usually date the same person.   5
Usually date different persons.   6
Do not date at all.   7

---

21. What is the frequency of your dates? Indicate the average number of dates of each type
that you have per month. Round to the nearest whole number. If less than one every two
months, write in "00." (If married, indicate the number of times you and your spouse go
out together to these events.)

(47-52)

Casual coke, *406*   ☐☐   Informal dates *407*   ☐☐   Formal dates *408*   ☐☐
coffee or   to movies, stu-   to dances and
study dates   dent gatherings,   big parties
(No. per month)   etc.   (No. per month)
    (No. per month)

---

22. Have you done any of the following things during the past year (since this time last year)?
If you have done a thing one or more times during the year, circle the number under "Yes;"
if not, circle the number under "No." (Circle one for each item.)

1G _____ (1-6)   (7-60)

	YES	NO
409	1	2
Gained more than ten pounds in weight . .	1	2
Lost more than ten pounds in weight . . .	1	2
Flunked a course.	1	2
Took a course over and above requirements	1	2
Went on a diet.	1	2
Became pinned or engaged.	1	2
Broke-up with a girlfriend.	1	2
Broke-up with a boyfriend	1	2
Donated money to a charity.	1	2
Worked for the election of a political party or candidate	1	2
Contributed money to a political party or candidate	1	2
Proposed marriage to someone.	1	2
Received a marriage proposal.	1	2
Got a ticket for a traffic violation. . .	1	2
Was arrested or got a ticket for something other than a traffic violation	1	2
Went on the wagon (swore off drinking). .	1	2
Signed a petition	1	2
Customized an automobile.	1	2
Read one or more non-fiction books that were not required reading.	1	2
Painted a room or house	1	2
Got a tatoo	1	2
Had a check bounce.	1	2
Set-up a schedule with specific times for various activities	1	2
Went to a carnival, amusement park or circus	1	2
Had psychotherapy	1	2
Made your own Christmas cards	1	2
Grew a beard.	1	2
Bleached or dyed your hair.	1	2
436		

437	YES	NO
Wore a wig.	1	2
Had a change in your glasses prescription	1	2
Dropped a course.	1	2
Changed your long-term career plans . . .	1	2
Fell in love.	1	2
Fell out of love.	1	2
Visited a foreign country	1	2
Was in an auto accident, but was not driving.	1	2
Had an auto accident while driving. . .	1	2
Read one or more novels that were not required	1	2
Went on a vacation trip with friends your own age	1	2
Was fired from a job.	1	2
Donated blood	1	2
Repeated a course because of low grades	1	2
Wrote a paper or report of ten or more pages.	1	2
Wrote a paper or report of thirty or more pages	1	2
Visited the dentist	1	2
Read the biography of a famous person .	1	2
Went to the basement or got under a table or bed to escape possible damage from a storm.	1	2
Changed your hair style	1	2
Seriously considered changing your first name	1	2
Seriously considered changing your last name.	1	2
Contemplated suicide.	1	2
Had a deep spiritual experience	1	2
460		

x   x

-14-

23. Below are a number of dimensions along which people can vary. Please rate yourself on each dimension as honestly as you can. The words or phrases describe each end of the scale. If one of a pair of words is descriptive of you, circle the number near that end. If neither is descriptive of you, or if both apply equally, circle one of the numbers near the center. Many of the traits depend on the situation, of course, but try to rate yourself as you usually are. (Circle one in each row.)

	Very	Fairly	Slightly	Neither or Both	Slightly	Fairly	Very	
461 Religious	1	2	3	4	5	6	7	Non-religious (7-53)
Good-looking	1	2	3	4	5	6	7	Unattractive
Happy	1	2	3	4	5	6	7	Unhappy
Satisfied with self	1	2	3	4	5	6	7	Dissatisfied with self
Considerate	1	2	3	4	5	6	7	Inconsiderate
Well-adjusted	1	2	3	4	5	6	7	Maladjusted
Dependable	1	2	3	4	5	6	7	Undependable
Ambitious	1	2	3	4	5	6	7	Unambitious
Optimistic	1	2	3	4	5	6	7	Pessimistic
High-strung	1	2	3	4	5	6	7	Calm
471 Responsible	1	2	3	4	5	6	7	Irresponsible
Lazy	1	2	3	4	5	6	7	Energetic
Stubborn	1	2	3	4	5	6	7	Give in easily
Extravert	1	2	3	4	5	6	7	Introvert
Critical of others	1	2	3	4	5	6	7	Uncritical of others
Talkative	1	2	3	4	5	6	7	Quiet
Like responsibility	1	2	3	4	5	6	7	Try to avoid responsibility
Messy	1	2	3	4	5	6	7	Neat
Easily angered	1	2	3	4	5	6	7	Good-natured
Worried	1	2	3	4	5	6	7	Carefree
481 Have many friends	1	2	3	4	5	6	7	Have few friends
Conforming	1	2	3	4	5	6	7	Non-conforming
Timid	1	2	3	4	5	6	7	Bold
Politically liberal	1	2	3	4	5	6	7	Politically conservative
Careless	1	2	3	4	5	6	7	Careful
Self-confident	1	2	3	4	5	6	7	Lacking in self-confidence
Patient	1	2	3	4	5	6	7	Impatient
Successful	1	2	3	4	5	6	7	Unsuccessful
Persistent	1	2	3	4	5	6	7	Give up easily
Friendly	1	2	3	4	5	6	7	Unfriendly
491 Original	1	2	3	4	5	6	7	Unoriginal
Strong	1	2	3	4	5	6	7	Weak
Popular	1	2	3	4	5	6	7	Unpopular
Kind	1	2	3	4	5	6	7	Cruel
Hard worker	1	2	3	4	5	6	7	Take it easy
Rugged	1	2	3	4	5	6	7	Delicate
Prefer to work alone	1	2	3	4	5	6	7	Prefer to work with others
Leader	1	2	3	4	5	6	7	Follower
Good sense of humor	1	2	3	4	5	6	7	Poor sense of humor
500 Often tired	1	2	3	4	5	6	7	Rarely tired
Great difficulty getting up in the morning	1	2	3	4	5	6	7	Little difficulty getting up in the morning
Masculine	1	2	3	4	5	6	7	Feminine
Confident	1	2	3	4	5	6	7	Unsure
Practical	1	2	3	4	5	6	7	Impractical
Shy	1	2	3	4	5	6	7	Outgoing
Sophisticated	1	2	3	4	5	6	7	Unsophisticated
501 Work best at night	1	2	3	4	5	6	7	Work best in the morning

24. Below are the same traits on which you rated yourself before. This time indicate how you <u>would</u> <u>like</u> <u>to</u> <u>be</u> on each trait. Remember, this time it does not matter how you are, just indicate how you would like to be. (Circle one in each row.)

Very / Fairly / Slightly / Neither or Both / Slightly / Fairly / Very

									(7-53)
508	Religious	1	2	3	4	5	6	7	Non-religious
	Good-looking	1	2	3	4	5	6	7	Unattractive
	Happy	1	2	3	4	5	6	7	Unhappy
	Satisfied with self	1	2	3	4	5	6	7	Dissatisfied with self
	Considerate	1	2	3	4	5	6	7	Inconsiderate
	Well-adjusted	1	2	3	4	5	6	7	Maladjusted
	Dependable	1	2	3	4	5	6	7	Undependable
	Ambitious	1	2	3	4	5	6	7	Unambitious
	Optimistic	1	2	3	4	5	6	7	Pessimistic
	High-strung	1	2	3	4	5	6	7	Calm
518	Responsible	1	2	3	4	5	6	7	Irresponsible
	Lazy	1	2	3	4	5	6	7	Energetic
	Stubborn	1	2	3	4	5	6	7	Give in easily
	Extravert	1	2	3	4	5	6	7	Introvert
	Critical of others	1	2	3	4	5	6	7	Uncritical of others
	Talkative	1	2	3	4	5	6	7	Quiet
	Like responsibility	1	2	3	4	5	6	7	Try to avoid responsibility
	Messy	1	2	3	4	5	6	7	Neat
	Easily angered	1	2	3	4	5	6	7	Good-natured
	Worried	1	2	3	4	5	6	7	Carefree
528	Have many friends	1	2	3	4	5	6	7	Have few friends
	Conforming	1	2	3	4	5	6	7	Non-conforming
	Timid	1	2	3	4	5	6	7	Bold
	Politically liberal	1	2	3	4	5	6	7	Politically conservative
	Careless	1	2	3	4	5	6	7	Careful
	Self-confident	1	2	3	4	5	6	7	Lacking in self-confidence
	Patient	1	2	3	4	5	6	7	Impatient
	Successful	1	2	3	4	5	6	7	Unsuccessful
	Persistent	1	2	3	4	5	6	7	Give up easily
	Friendly	1	2	3	4	5	6	7	Unfriendly
538	Original	1	2	3	4	5	6	7	Unoriginal
	Strong	1	2	3	4	5	6	7	Weak
	Popular	1	2	3	4	5	6	7	Unpopular
	Kind	1	2	3	4	5	6	7	Cruel
	Hard worker	1	2	3	4	5	6	7	Take it easy
	Rugged	1	2	3	4	5	6	7	Delicate
	Prefer to work alone	1	2	3	4	5	6	7	Prefer to work with others
	Leader	1	2	3	4	5	6	7	Follower
	Good sense of humor	1	2	3	4	5	6	7	Poor sense of humor
547	Often tired	1	2	3	4	5	6	7	Rarely tired
	Great difficulty getting up in the morning	1	2	3	4	5	6	7	Little difficulty getting up in the morning
	Masculine	1	2	3	4	5	6	7	Feminine
	Confident	1	2	3	4	5	6	7	Unsure
	Practical	1	2	3	4	5	6	7	Impractical
	Shy	1	2	3	4	5	6	7	Outgoing
	Sophisticated	1	2	3	4	5	6	7	Unsophisticated
554	Work best at night	1	2	3	4	5	6	7	Work best in the morning

x (54)

25. There is a lot of talk these days about the problems of young people starting out in the world. What, as you see it, are the major problems of young people graduating from high school today? (Circle one for each item.)

4B _____ (1-6)   (64-75)   5B _____ (1-6)   64-73)

Column headers (left): A major problem / Somewhat of a problem / Not much of a problem
Column headers (right): A major problem / Somewhat of a problem / Not much of a problem

555
Choosing a career . . . . 1 2 3   **566** Finding a suitable husband or wife 4 5 6

Getting along with their parents. . . . . 1 2 3   Having their ideas accepted by
                                                        older people 4 5 6

Obtaining money to get started in a
   business or profession . . . . 1 2 3   Finding a suitable job in these
                                                        days of unemployment. 4 5 6

Finding a meaning or purpose in life in
   these days of mass culture . . . . . 1 2 3   Adjusting to the possibility of
                                                        atomic war. 4 5 6

Worry over international tensions and
   uncertainty in the world . . . . . . 1 2 3   **570** Making an adequate adjustment to
                                                        relationships with the opposite
560   sex 4 5 6
Keeping up with events in this time of
   rapidly expanding knowledge. 1 2 3

Personal conflict and tension reflecting   Finding something to interest them
   our "Age of Anxiety" . . . .   and keep them occupied. 4 5 6
                                       1 2 3

Adjusting to the demands and responsibi-   Lack of a feeling of being a part of
   lities of adult status . . . . 1 2 3   our society. The feeling of being
                                                     a "lost generation" 4 5 6

Conflict about religious beliefs . . . . 1 2 3   Adjusting moral attitudes to the
                                                        behavior expected by the culture. . . 4 5 6
Disruption of plans by military service . 1 2 3

Financing a college education . . . . . . 1 2 3   **574** Gaining admission to a good college. . . 4 5 6
                                              x   x

26. Which of the following things do you have in your home? If an item is now in your home, circle
    the number under "Yes" if not, circle the number under "No." (Circle one for each item.)

2G _____ (1-6)   (7-49)

575	YES	NO		**595**	YES	NO
Carpentry tools (hand)	3	4		A telescope.	3	4
Power tools.	3	4		Farm equipment.	3	4
Library of more than 200 books	3	4		Chemical laboratory equipment.	3	4
One or more musical instruments.	3	4		Electronic laboratory equipment	3	4
Some art supplies or equipment	3	4		Botany or zoology laboratory equipment .	3	4
Sports equipment	3	4		A tape recorder.	3	4
A sewing machine	3	4		A movie or slide projector	3	4
Photographic equipment	3	4		Leather working tools.	3	4
A photographic dark room	3	4		A typewriter.	3	4
Fishing or hunting equipment	3	4		An encyclopedia set.	3	4
A collection of classical records. . . .	3	4		Automotive tools or work shop.	3	4
A Hi-Fi or Stereo set.	3	4		An unabridged dictionary	3	4
Reproductions of famous paintings. . . .	3	4		Five or more magazine subscriptions. . .	3	4
Examples of original art work (paintings,				A world atlas.	3	4
sculpture, ceramics, etc.).	3	4		Books in a foreign language.	3	4
A foreign cook book.	3	4		A stop watch.	3	4
A motor boat or sail boat.	3	4		A tent or sleeping bag	3	4
A motorcycle or motorbike.	3	4		A barometer.	3	4
A flower or vegetable garden	3	4		An FM radio.	3	4
A pet dog or cat	3	4		Two or more cars	3	4
Other animal pets.	3	4		A television set	3	4
594				**615**		

27. Which of the following adjectives do you consider to be descriptive of yourself? Circle the number beside any adjective that you might use in describing yourself to someone else. Your behavior will vary with the situation, of course, so circle the numbers beside adjectives which might apply to you frequently, even though they are not appropriate all the time. Work rapidly, putting down your first thoughts.

All coded 1 for circled, 2 for not

616
Absent-minded 1 (7)
Adaptable 2
Aggressive. 3
Alert 4
Aloof 5
Ambitious 6
Anxious 7
Apathetic 8
Argumentative 9

625
Artistic. 1 (8)
Assertive 2
Attractive. 3
Boastful. 4
Businesslike. 5
Calm. 6
Capable 7
Carefree. 8
Careless. 9

634
Cautious. 1 (9)
Cheerful. 2
Clear-thinking. 3
Clever. 4
Complaining 5
Confident 6
Conforming. 7
Confused. 8
Conscientious 9

643
Conventional. 1 (10)
Cooperative 2
Critical of others. 3
Curious 4
Cynical 5
Defensive 6
Deliberate. 7
Dependable. 8
Dependent 9

652
Determined. 1 (11)
Disorderly. 2
Dissatisfied. 3
Distractible. 4
Dominant. 5
Dull. 6
Easy-going. 7
Efficient 8
Egotistical 9

661
Emotional 1 (12)
Energetic 2
Enthusiastic. 3
Excitable 4
Fearful 5
Feminine. 6
Forceful. 7
Forgetful 8

668

670
Frank 1 (13)
Friendly. 2
Generous. 3
Good-looking. 4
Good-natured. 5
Helpful 6
High-strung 7
Honest. 8
Hostile 9

678
Humorous. 1 (14)
Idealistic. 2
Imaginative 3
Immature. 4
Impatient 5
Impulsive 6
Independent 7
Industrious 8
Ingenious 9

687
Inhibited 1 (15)
Insightful. 2
Intelligent 3
Irresponsible 4
Irritable 5
Jolly 6
Kind. 7
Lazy. 8
Leisurely 9

696
Logical 1 (16)
Loyal 2
Maladjusted 3
Mannerly. 4
Masculine 5
Mature. 6
Meek. 7
Messy 8
Methodical. 9

705
Mild. 1 (17)
Mischievous 2
Modest. 3
Moody 4
Naive 5
Nervous 6
Obliging. 7
Opinionated 8
Original. 9

714
Outgoing. 1 (18)
Outspoken 2
Patient 3
Persistent. 4
Pleasant. 5
Polished. 6
Practical 7
Preoccupied 8

721

723
Quarrelsome 1 (19)
Quiet 2
Realistic 3
Reasonable. 4
Rebellious. 5
Reckless. 6
Relaxed 7
Reliable. 8
Resentful 9

731
Reserved. 1 (20)
Resourceful 2
Responsible 3
Restless. 4
Rude. 5
Sarcastic 6
Self-centered 7
Self-confident. 8
Sensitive 9

740
Serious 1 (21)
Shrewd. 2
Shy 3
Sincere 4
Slow. 5
Snobbish. 6
Sociable. 7
Sophisticated 8
Stable. 9

749
Stubborn. 1 (22)
Submissive. 2
Suggestible 3
Suspicious. 4
Tactful 5
Talkative 6
Temperamental 7
Tense 8
Thorough. 9

758
Thoughtful. 1 (23)
Timid 2
Unambitious 3
Unassuming. 4
Unconventional. 5
Undependable. 6
Unemotional 7
Uninhibited 8
Versatile 9

767
Warm. 1 (24)
Well-adjusted 2
Well thought of 3
Whiny 4
Wholesome 5
Withdrawn 6
Witty 7
Worrying. 8

774

x (25)

28. How many times have you visited your physician during the past year? (Circle one.)

775

If this was mostly for some routine
treatment, such as allergy shots,
explain here: _____

_____

None.	1 (26)
1 - 3	2
4 - 6	3
7 - 9	4
10 - 12	5
13 - 15	6
16 or more.	7

29. How much time have you spent as a patient in the hospital or infirmary during the past year?
    (Circle one.)

776

None.	6 *1*	(27)
Between 1 and 5 days.	7 *2*	
Between 6 and 10 days	8 *3*	
More than 10 days	9 *4*	

30. Compared with most people your age, how would you describe your physical health? (Circle one.)

777

Much better.	6 *1*	(28)
A little better.	7 *2*	
About the same	8 *3*	
A little worse	9 *4*	
Much worse	0 *5*	

31. Have you had any of the following during the past year? (Circle one response for each item.)

(29-59)

778

	Frequently or severely	Occasionally or mildly	Not at all
Common cold	1	2	3
Nausea.	1	2	3
Allergy	1	2	3
Automobile accident	1	2	3
Other accident resulting in injury. . . .	1	2	3
Epilepsy.	1	2	3
Hemorrhoids	1	2	3
Excessive fatigue	1	2	3
Headaches	1	2	3
Insomnia.	1	2	3
Asthma.	1	2	3
Stomach ulcers.	1	2	3
Loneliness.	1	2	3
Shortness of breath	1	2	3
Sweating palms so that your hands were damp or clammy	1	2	3

792

793

	Frequently or severely	Occasionally or mildly	Not at all
Hay fever	1 *2* *3* 5 6		
Nervous breakdown	4	5	6
High blood pressure	4	5	6
Homesickness.	4	5	6
Constipation.	4	5	6
Diarrhea.	4	5	6
Loss of appetite.	4	5	6
Dizziness	4	5	6
Skin rashes	4	5	6
Muscle twitches or trembling . . .	4	5	6
Back pains.	4	5	6
Menstrual dysfunction	4	5	6
Indigestion	4	5	6
Acne.	4	5	6
Heart pounding or beating hard. . .	4	5	6
Hiccups	4	5	6

808

x (60)

32. Have you ever consulted a professional person (minister, doctor, lawyer, psychiatrist, etc.)
    about a personal problem?

809

Yes. . .	8 *1*	(61)
No . . .	9 *2*	

If Yes--

When? _____

Over how long a period? _____

What was the profession of the person you consulted _____

What was the nature of the problem? _____

_____

Do you think you were helped? _____ In what way? _____

-19-

33. Which of the following do you have displayed in your room? (Circle all that apply.)

810 *1 = circled 2 = not*

The walls are blank (parental or apartment rules)........	1	(62)
The walls are blank (by choice)..	2	
Pennants................	3	
Pin-ups................	4	
Maps.................	5	
A mobile..............	6	
Quotations and mottoes.......	7	
Scientific models.........	8	
Religious articles........	9	
Diplomas..............	0	
Scholarship trophies........	x	

820

821

Calendars or schedules........	1	(63)
Abstract paintings..........	2	
Other paintings or drawings.....	3	
Photographs of friends........	4	
Sculpture..............	5	
Jokes................	6	
Medals...............	7	
Biological charts.........	8	
Flags................	9	
Sports trophies..........	0	
Sports equipment.........	x	
Other (Circle and specify.) _____	v	

832

34. During the past year how well did you get along with the following people?
(Circle one in each row.)

833

	Very Well	Fairly Well	Just "so-so"	Fairly Poor	Very Poorly	
Boys your own age..........	1	2	3	4	5	(64-69)
Girls your own age........	1	2	3	4	5	
Your mother.............	1	2	3	4	5	
Your father.............	1	2	3	4	5	
Your teachers...........	1	2	3	4	5	
Other adults...........	1	2	3	4	5	

838

35. This is an inventory of your feelings and attitudes about many kinds of work. Show the occupations which <u>interest</u> or <u>appeal</u> to you by circling the number in the "Yes" column opposite that occupation. Circle the number in the "No" column for the occupations you <u>dislike</u> or find <u>uninteresting</u>. (Circle one for each item.)

3G _____ (1-6)   (7-56)   *1   2*

839

	YES	NO
Aviator.................	5	6
Private investigator........	5	6
YMCA secretary............	5	6
Detective..............	5	6
Post office clerk........	5	6
Route salesman...........	5	6
Electronic technician......	5	6
Humorist..............	5	6
Photographer...........	5	6
Interplanetary scientist.....	5	6
Airplance mechanic.........	5	6
Meteorologist...........	5	6

851

	YES	NO
Foreign missionary........	5	6
Bookkeeper.............	5	6
Speculator.............	5	6
Poet................	5	6
Deep sea diver..........	5	6
Newspaper editor.........	5	6
Nursery school teacher......	5	6
Lawyer...............	5	6
Fish and wildlife specialist.....	5	6
Biologist.............	5	6
High school teacher........	5	6
Quality control expert........	5	6

862

863

	YES	NO
Buyer.................	5	6
Symphony conductor........	5	6
Wrecker (building)........	5	6
Narcotics inspector........	5	6
Elementary school teacher......	5	6
School principal.........	5	6
Power Station operator.......	5	6
Astronomer............	5	6
Juvenile delinquency expert......	5	6
Budget reviewer..........	5	6
Stock and bond salesman.......	5	6
Musician.............	5	6

875

	YES	NO
Prize fighter...........	5	6
Diplomat.............	5	6
Experimental laboratory engineer...	5	6
Crane operator..........	5	6
Master plumber.........	5	6
Aeronautical design engineer.....	5	6
Speech therapist........	5	6
Traffic manager.........	5	6
Manufacturer's representative.....	5	6
Author..............	5	6
Fireman.............	5	6
Army general..........	5	6

886

x

x

88

	Yes	No
Interior Decorator	7	8
Novelist.	7	8
Power Shovel Operator	7	8
Anthropologist.	7	8
Marriage Counselor.	7	8
Statistician.	7	8
Television Producer	7	8
Commercial Artist	7	8
Wild Animal Trainer	7	8
U.N. Official	7	8
Sculptor.	7	8
Automobile Mechanic	7	8

89

	Yes	No
Surveyor.	7	8
Zoologist	7	8
Physical Education Teacher.	7	8
Court Stenographer.	7	8
Hotel Manager	7	8
Free Lance Writer	7	8
Stunt Man (Motion Picture).	7	8
Criminal Lawyer	7	8
Professional Athlete.	7	8
Carpenter	7	8
Construction Inspector.	7	8
Chemist	7	8

91

	Yes	No
Playground Director	7	8
Bank Teller	7	8
Business Executive.	7	8
Musical Arranger.	7	8
Jockey.	7	8
Ventriloquist	7	8
Army Officer.	7	8
Banker.	7	8
Radio Operator.	7	8
Independent Research Scientist.	7	8
Clinical Psychologist	7	8
Tax Expert.	7	8

92

	Yes	No
Restaurant Worker	7	8
Art Dealer.	7	8
Motorcycle Driver	7	8
Police Judge.	7	8
Referee (Sporting Events)	7	8
Truck Gardener.	7	8
Filling Station Attendent	7	8
Writer of Scientific or Technical Articles.	7	8
Social Science Teacher.	7	8
Inventory Controller.	7	8
Master of Ceremonies.	7	8
Dramatic Coach.	7	8

93

	Yes	No
Blaster (Dynamiter)	7	8
Mind Reader	7	8
English Teacher	7	8
Sales Manager	7	8
Tree Surgeon.	7	8
Editor of a Scientific Journal.	7	8
Director of Welfare Agency.	7	8
IBM Equipment Operator.	7	8

94   x

943

	Yes	No
Traveling Salesman	9	0
Concert Singer	9	0
F.B.I. Agent	9	0
Prosecuting Attorney	9	0
Factory Foreman.	9	0
College Professor.	9	0
Tool Designer.	9	0
Geologist	9	0
Asst. City School Superintendent	9	0
Financial Analyst.	9	0
Real Estate Salesman	9	0
Composer	9	0

955

	Yes	No
Mountain Climber	9	0
Congressional Investigator	9	0
Portrait Artist.	9	0
Machinist.	9	0
Locomotive Engineer.	9	0
Botanist	9	0
Personal Counselor	9	0
Cost Estimator	9	0
Industrial Relations Consultant.	9	0
Stage Director	9	0
Explorer	9	0
Supreme Court Judge.	9	0

967

	Yes	No
Draftsman.	9	0
Judge.	9	0
Photoengraver.	9	0
Scientific Research Worker	9	0
Psychiatric Case Worker.	9	0
Pay Roll Clerk.	9	0
Sports Promoter.	9	0
Playwright	9	0
Test Pilot	9	0
Criminologist.	9	0
Children's Clothing Designer	9	0
Truck Driver	9	0

979

	Yes	No
Electrician.	9	0
Physicist.	9	0
Vocational Counselor	9	0
Bank Examiner.	9	0
Political Campaign Manager	9	0
Cartoonist	9	0
Racing Car Driver.	9	0
Book Censor.	9	0
Social Worker.	9	0
Locksmith.	9	0
Funeral Director	9	0
Counter-Intelligence Man	9	0

991

	Yes	No
Architect.	9	0
Shipping and Receiving Clerk	9	0
Criminal Psychologist.	9	0
Insurance Clerk.	9	0
Barber	9	0
Bill Collector	9	0
Ward Attendant	9	0
Masseur.	9	0

998   x

36. Below are a number of honors which high school students might achieve. Circle the number beside those accomplishments which you have achieved during high school.

999 *1 = circled 2 = not*

Wrote an independent paper on a scientific topic which received the highest possible mark in my school. 1 (7)

1000
Did an independent, scientific experiment (not a course assignement) 2

Was a member of a student honorary scientific society. 3

Invented a patentable device. 4

Had a paper published in a scientific journal. 5

Built a piece of equipment or laboratory apparatus on my own (not course work). 6

Participated in a scientific contest or talent search. 7

Participated in a National Science Foundation summer program for high school students at: 1 (8)

_____ Name of College

Placed first, second or third in a:
National science contest 2
Regional or state science contest. . . 3
City or county science contest 4
School Science contest 5

1011
Won a prize for any other scientific work or study. 6

Placed first, second or third in a:
National speech or debate contest. . . 7
Regional or state speech or debate contest 1 (9)
City or county speech or debate contest 2
School speech or debate contest. . . . 3
Had a leading role in one or more plays . 4
Had minor roles in one or more plays. . . 5

Wrote a play. 6
Directed a play 7

1020
Appeared on radio or TV as a performer. . 1 (10)

Read for a part in a high school or church play. 2

Read for a part in a play which was not sponsored by my school or church . . . 3

Organized a school political group or campaign.. 4
Organized my own business or service. . . 5
Received a Junior Achievement award . . . 6

1026
Composed music which has been given at least one public performance 7

1027
Performed with a professional orchestra 1 (11)

Played in a school musical organization 2

Played a musical instrument. 3

1030
Played in a dance or jazz band for wages 4

Organized your own dance or jazz band. 5

Received a rating of "Good" or "Excellent" in a:
National music contest. 6
Regional or state music contest . . 7
City or county music contest. . . . 1 (12)
School music contest. 2

Organized a singing group. 3

1037
Directed (publicly) a band or orchestra 4

Exhibited a work of art (painting, sculpture, etc.) at:
A national art show 5
A regional or state art show. . . . 6
A city or county art show 7
A school art show 1 (13)

Won a prize or award for an artistic creation (painting, sculpture, etc.) at:
A national art show 2
A regional or state art show. . . . 3
A city or county art show 4
A school art show 5

1046
Won a prize or award for a work published in a public newspaper or magazine 6

Edited a school paper or literary magazine. 7

Won a literary award for creative writing 1 (14)

Had poems, stories, essays or articles published in a school publication 2

Wrote an original, but unpublished piece of creative writing on my own (not as part of a course). 3

Published one or more issues of my own newspaper 4

1052
Had poems, stories or articles published in a public newspaper or magazine (not school) 5

37. In the items listed below please compare yourself with your twin and indicate whether each statement is more true of you or more true of your twin. (Circle one for each item.)

note: coding reversed for Twin 2

		I am (or do)	Both the same	My twin is (or does)	
	Which twin:				
1053	Has more friends	1	2	3	(15-39)
	Makes better grades in school.	1	2	3	
	Does more talking when the two of you meet a new person.	1	2	3	
	Usually wins in athletic contests between you? (tennis, bowling, etc.)	1	2	3	
	Reads faster	1	2	3	
1058	Has more dates.	1	2	3	
	Usually gets up first in the morning	1	2	3	
	Usually goes to sleep first at night	1	2	3	
	Is the better artist (painting, drawing, etc.)	1	2	3	
	Is the better musician (singing, playing an instrument, etc.)	1	2	3	
1063	Is the better writer (stories, essays, etc.)	1	2	3	
	Knows more about science	1	2	3	
	Is better at public speaking	1	2	3	
	Is more likely to be elected the leader of a group to which both belong.	1	2	3	
	Is more religious.	1	2	3	
1068	Studies harder	1	2	3	
	Is more liked by your mother	1	2	3	
	Is more liked by your father	1	2	3	
	Usually decides what you are going to do when you are together.	1	2	3	
	Used to decide what you were going to play, etc. when you were children.	1	2	3	
1073	Usually wins arguments between you	1	2	3	
	Knows more jokes	1	2	3	
	Gets angry more easily	1	2	3	
	Saves more money	1	2	3	
	Gets sick more frequently.	1	2	3	

38. Which of the following things do you and your twin usually do together? (Circle one for each item.)

		Usually do together	No usual pattern	Usually do separately	
1078	Eat lunch.	1	2	3	(40-45)
	Study.	1	2	3	
	Go to the movies	1	2	3	
	Go out on dates.	1	2	3	
	Work on hobbies.	1	2	3	
	Read books	1	2	3	(46) X̄

39. How frequently do you and your twin quarrel or fight? (Circle one.)

1084

We are usually fighting	1 (47)
We sometimes fight.	2
We rarely or never fight.	3

-23-

40. Do you and your twin dress alike? (Circle one.)

1085

		(48)
We always dress alike.	5	**1**
We usually dress alike	6	**2**
We sometimes dress alike	7	**3**
We rarely or never dress alike	8	**4**

---

41. Do you and your twin have the same or different friends? (Circle one.)

1086

All my friends are also my twin's friends. 1   (49)
Most of my friends are also my twin's friends. 2
Some of my friends are also my twin's friends. 3
Few or none of my friends are also my twin's friends 4

---

42. Which twin was born first? (Circle one.)

1087

			Twin 1	**Twin 2**
I was.	1	(50)	**1**	**3**
My twin was.	2		**3**	**1**
I don't know	3		**2**	**2**

---

43. What was the longest period of time that you have been separated from your twin? (Circle one.)

1088

One day or less. 1   (51)
Two or three days. 2
Four to six days 3
One or two weeks 4
Two weeks to one month 5
More than one month. 6

---

44. How often are you and your twin together? (Circle one.)

1089

Almost always (more than 90% of the time) 1   (52)
Usually (75% to 90% of the time). 2
Often (50% to 75% of the time). 3
Sometimes (25% to 50% of the time). 4
Rarely (less than 25% of the time). 5

---

45. If you could start life over, would you like to be a twin again? (Circle one.)

1090

I would definitely choose to be a twin. 1   (53)
I would probably choose to be a twin. 2
I wouldn't care one way or the other. 3
I would probably choose not to be a twin. 4
I would definitely choose not to be a twin. 5

---

46. Do you and your twin share many things or do you each have your own possessions? (Circle one.)

1091

We share almost all our possessions 1   (54)
We share many things but each have some individual possessions. . . 2
We generally have our own possessions, but share some things. . . . 3
We have our own possessions and share very little 4

(55-57)

How long did it take you to answer the questions in this booklet? ☐ Hours, ☐☐ minutes

1092

changed to minutes

NATIONAL MERIT SCHOLARSHIP CORPORATION

1580 Sherman Avenue, Evanston, Illinois   GReenleaf 5-2552

PARENT QUESTIONNAIRE

June 1963

Dear Parent:

Your twins have volunteered to participate in a research project concerned with the similarities and differences of twins. The study is being conducted by the National Merit Scholarship Corporation. For this project it is necessary to know about the early life experiences and behavior of the twins who are serving as research subjects. It is particularly important to know about any differences in the life experiences of the twins. We will greatly appreciate your help in completing the items in this booklet. It will take from thirty minutes to an hour of your time.

Please answer the questions as frankly and accurately as you can. Your answers will be absolutely confidential and will be used in group comparisons for research purposes only. Scores for individual students will not be reported nor will any participant's name be revealed.

Thank you for your cooperation.

Sincerely,

John M. Stalnaker

John M. Stalnaker
President

INSTRUCTIONS: The analyses for a part of this research will be performed by an electronic computer. For this reason, it will facilitate the interpretation of your responses if you follow certain standard procedures in indicating your answers.

A.   Most of the questions can be answered by drawing a circle around one or more numbers or letters. Thus:

Which of the following are true of you? (Circle one for each item.)

	True	False
I am a parent of twins	①	2
I have no children	1	②

If you make an error or decide to change your response, mark out the incorrect response like this:

	True	False
I am over 21 years of age . . .	①	✗

B.   IMPORTANT: Many of the items require that you indicate what was true for one particular child. In these items the children are referred to as "Twin one" and "Twin two". The children which you should consider as "Twin one" and "Twin two" are as follows:

Twin one is: _____   Twin two is: _____

It is very important that you have the right child in mind in responding to the items. If in doubt refer back here to check. If it will help you to write in the names of the twins for those items which refer to "Twin one" and "Twin two" please feel free to do so.

Your Name _____ Date _____

1. What is your relationship to the twins for whom you are completing this questionnaire? (Circle one.)

   004

Mother.	1	(7)
Father.	2
Stepmother.	3
Stepfather.	4
Guardian (Circle and explain.)_____	5
Other (Circle and specify.)_____	6

2. How well did you know the twins as children? (Circle one.)

   005

   If you knew the twins only casually
   or not at all, do not complete the
   questionnaire. If there is no one
   available who knew them well, check
   here _____ and return the questionnaire
   blank.

   Very well. 7   *1*   (8)
   Fairly well. 8   *2*
   Casually 9
   Not at all 0

3. What is the current status of the family? (Circle all that apply.)

   006

   [If the twins are not living
   with the true parents, answer
   the following five questions
   in regard to those now acting
   as the parents.]

True mother deceased	1	*2*	(9)
True father deceased	2	*2*
Parents together	3	*1*
Parents separated, but not divorced. . .	4	*2*
Parents divorced	5	*2*
Mother remarried	6	*2*
Father remarried	7	*2*

~~4~~. What is the father's occupation? (If duties are not clear from the job title,
   please give details.)   (10-11)

~~5~~. What is the mother's occupation? (If duties are not clear from the job title,
   please give details.)   (12-13)

6. What are the parents' ages? (Write in age at the last birthday.) If deceased,
   write in the age which would have been attained if still living.

   007   Mother. . . [|]   (14-15)

   008   Father. . . [|]   (16-17)

7. What is each parent's highest educational attainment?
   (Circle one in each column.)

	009 Mother	*010* Father	
8th grade or less.	1	1	(18-19)
Part high school	2	2
High school graduate	3	3
Part college or junior college . .	4	4
College graduate	5	5
Graduate or professional degree beyond the bachelor's degree . .	6	6

8. What is the family's income? Indicate total family income before taxes.
   (Circle one.)

   011

Less than $5,000 per year . . .	1	(20)
$5,000 to $7,499.	2
$7,500 to $9,999.	3
$10,000 to $14,999.	4
$15,000 to $19,999.	5
$20,000 to $24,999.	6
$25,000 and over.	7

9. Below are listed a number of things that children can do and things that can happen to them at various ages. Note that the statements are divided into groups according to the ages at which they apply. Think of your twins as they were during the particular age level. When you have the age clearly in mind, indicate whether or not each of the statements was true of one or the other or both twins at <u>this age</u>. If a statement is true for both twins, circle the number under both. If it is true for only one, then circle the number for that twin; if it is true for neither twin, circle the number under neither. You may find it helpful to write the names of "Twin one" and "Twin two" above the respective columns. (Circle one for each item.)

NOTE: Parents of Girls: We have occasionally used the pronouns "he" and "his". Whenever this occurs, please translate to "she" and "her". We apologize for this, but we couldn't think of any better alternative.

INFANCY (Birth to Two Years)

IMPORTANT: See instructions on front of booklet for explanation of who is "Twin one" and who is "Twin two"

(7-18) Twin one only / Twin two only / Both twins / Neither twin

1K _____ (1-6) (19-31) Twin one only / Twin two only / Both twins / Neither twin

012
Had colic frequently 1 2 3 4

Learned to walk early (before 10 months) 1 2 3 4

Learned to walk late (after 20 months) 1 2 3 4

Had one or more serious illnesses (Circle and specify.) _____ 1 2 3 4

_____

Was usually rocked and held when he cried. 1 2 3 4

There were complications at birth (anoxia, blood disorders, etc.) (Circle and specify.) _____ 1 2 3 4

_____

Wore corrective shoes or leg braces for one month or longer 1 2 3 4

Was easily awakened by noise around the house 1 2 3 4

020
Was usually left to cry alone when just crying for attention 1 2 3 4

Was cared for by his father at least half of the time when he cried at night 1 2 3 4

Was often allowed to run about the house without clothes 1 2 3 4

Could amuse himself for several hours playing alone 1 2 3 4

024
Was a calm, peaceful child and easy to take care of 1 2 3 4

Was breast fed for two months or longer. 1 2 3 4

Cried a lot 1 2 3 4

Was toilet trained before 18 months of age. 1 2 3 4

Was played with frequently by his mother or some other adult . . . 1 2 3 4

Was fed on a regular schedule rather than when he seemed hungry . . . 1 2 3 4

030
Soon learned to sleep through the night and awoke only in unusual circumstances. 1 2 3 4

Often cried when put to bed and cried himself to sleep 1 2 3 4

Was generally fun to care for as an infant. 1 2 3 4

Was allowed to play freely around the house most of the time rather than being kept in a play pen or crib 1 2 3 4

Used a pacifier to suck on for one year or longer 1 2 3 4

Could not eat certain foods or formulas because of allergic reactions. 1 2 3 4

036
Took a bottle to bed most nights . 1 2 3 4

(32-49)   Twin one only / Twin two only / Both twins / Neither twin   (7-25)   Twin one only / Twin two only / Both twins / Neither twin

037
Was a premature child (____ months) . 1 2 3 4

Frequently had diarrhea 1 2 3 4

039
Wore diapers until he trained himself (no special toilet training
procedure was used) **1 2 3 4**
5 6 7 8

PRE-SCHOOL (Two to Six Years)

040
Learned to read before starting
the first grade 1 2 3 4

Was read a bedtime story almost
every night 1 2 3 4

Attended Sunday school or church
fairly regularly 1 2 3 4

Learned poems, stories or songs
which he would recite for family
and friends 1 2 3 4

Showed signs of sibling rivalry to
the birth of a brother or sister
(demanding attention, regression,
emotional upset, etc.) 1 2 3 4

045
Learned a child's prayer which he
said before meals or before
going to bed 1 2 3 4

Was taught such things as numbers,
the alphabet, telling time, etc.
at home before entering kindergarten or first grade 1 2 3 4

Attended kindergarten before
entering first grade 1 2 3 4

Sometimes wet the bed after the
third birthday 1 2 3 4

Had one or more fairly severe fears
(ghosts, the dark, certain
animals, etc.) 1 2 3 4

050
Was made to clean up the messes he
made in playing around the house . 1 2 3 4

Had occasional temper tantrums . . . 1 2 3 4

Was finicky about food and was hard
to please at meals 1 2 3 4

Usually slept in a room by himself . 1 2 3 4

Usually slept in a bed by himself . 1 2 3 4

Had frequent skin rashes 1 2 3 4

056
Had frequent chest congestion and
wheezing 5 6 7 8

Was encouraged to fight back when
attacked by other children 5 6 7 8

Was easy to train (to keep clean,
to respect property, etc.) 5 6 7 8

Attended nursery school 5 6 7 8

060
Did not have any serious illnesses . 5 6 7 8

Demonstrated some unusual talent
before entering school (e.g., music,
dancing, singing, mathematics, etc.)
(Circle and specify.) _____

_____ 5 6 7 8

Was frequently destructive (marred
furniture, marked walls, broke
things, etc.) 5 6 7 8

Was a very affectionate child . . . 5 6 7 8

Demanded a great deal of attention
from adults 5 6 7 8

065
Often followed his mother around,
hanging on her skirts 5 6 7 8

Had a pet dog or cat 5 6 7 8

Was shy around strangers 5 6 7 8

Occasionally had night terrors
(awoke frightened at night) . . . 5 6 7 8

Liked to show-off in front of guests 5 6 7 8

070
Sucked his thumb 5 6 7 8

Had one or more imaginary companions 5 6 7 8

Had birthday parties which several
children his own age attended . . . 5 6 7 8

073
Was taught to speak a language other
than English 5 6 7 8

Twin one only
Twin two only
Both twins
Neither twin

074

Would cry when his parents went out
and left him with a baby sitter .   1 2 3 4 / 5 6 7 8

Would often fight with other
children without provocation. . . .   5 6 7 8

Pajamas covering the hands, bitter
substances, or other devices were
used one or more times to prevent
thumb-sucking 5 6 7 8

Did not like to be dirty. 5 6 7 8

078

Was frequently cared for by the
father while the mother went out   1 2 3 4 / 5 6 7 8

Was left one or more times with
relatives, friends or at home with
a sitter while the parents took
a vacation of one week or longer.   5 6 7 8

080

Had a definite bed time and was made
to go to bed whether he wanted to
or not. 5 6 7 8

CHILDHOOD (Six to Twelve Years)

081

Attended Sunday school or church
fairly regularly. 5 6 7 8

Was very active and always running,
jumping or playing some active
game. 5 6 7 8

Was taken by his parents to visit a
zoo (don't include school trips).   5 6 7 8

Was often picked-on or teased by
other children. 5 6 7 8

085

Picked out most of the clothes that
were bought for him 5 6 7 8

Was often disobedient 5 6 7 8

Had speech correction or training to
correct a speech defect 5 6 7 8

Stuttered or stammered. 5 6 7 8

Was finicky about food and was hard
to please at meals. 5 6 7 8

090

Walked in his sleep 5 6 7 8

Was often away from home all day
playing, without his parents knowing where he was or what he was
doing 5 6 7 8

Had a definite bed time and was made
to go to bed whether he wanted
to or not 5 6 7 8

Helped care for a younger brother
or sister 5 6 7 8

Usually obeyed parent's instructions.   5 6 7 8

095

Wanted to quit school one or more
times 5 6 7 8

Had friends over for lunch or dinner   5 6 7 8

Spent a great deal of his time at
home reading. 5 6 7 8

Was taken on a camping trip or other
outing one or more times by his
father. 5 6 7 8

Was a member of the Cub or Brownie
Scouts. 5 6 7 8

100

Took private dancing lessons 5 6 7 8

Had a quick temper 5 6 7 8

Often asked his parents for suggestions of things to do. 5 6 7 8

Had regular jobs around the house
that were his responsibility. . .   5 6 7 8

Ran away from home one or more times   5 6 7 8

105

Bit his fingernails. 5 6 7 8

Was given a regular allowance which
he could spend as he wished . . .   5 6 7 8

Had occasional temper tantrums . . .   5 6 7 8

Had one or more fairly severe fears
(ghosts, the dark, certain
animals, etc.). 5 6 7 8

109

Was taken on family vacations of a
week or more (not including
visits to see relatives). 5 6 7 8

Twin one only
Twin two only
Both twins
Neither twin

110
Would often be so busy playing that he would skip meals entirely, or just grab a bite and run. . . . .   1 2 3 4   9 0 x y

Did not enjoy attending school. . . .   9 0 x y

Had friends over to spend the night .   9 0 x y

Had a personality conflict or other non-academic difficulty with a teacher which required a visit to the school by the parents. . .   9 0 x y

Twin one only
Twin two only
Both twins
Neither twin

114
One or more of his grade school teachers was invited to dinner or to be a guest in the home. . .   1 2 3 4   9 0 x y

Missed an extensive amount of school work in one or more years due to travel, illness or other reasons . . . .   9 0 x y

116
Had rules which governed the time spent watching TV and/or the programs seen . . . .   9 - 0 x y

---

ADOLESCENCE (Twelve to Eighteen Years)

117
Spent a great deal of his time at home reading. . . . .   9 0 x y

Attended church or Sunday school regularly . . . .   9 0 x y

Had serious discussions with parents about sex . . . .   9 0 x y

120
Brought friends home to play or study once a week or more on the average . . . .   9 0 x y

Frequently disagreed openly with parents . . . .   9 0 x y

Often talked over personal problems with parents . . . . . .   9 0 x y

Took sleeping pills for insomnia one or more times . . . .   9 0 x y

Was jealous of another child (brother sister, girl or boy friend) . . .   9 0 x y

125
Bit his fingernails . . . .   9 0 x y

Had an automobile accident with more than $50.00 total damage. . . . .   9 0 x y

Was given money or other tangible reward for good grades in school.   9 0 x y

Parents have tried to influence his occupational choice . . . . .   9 0 x y

Refused to eat three or more commonly served foods. . . . .   9 0 x y

130
Had a definite curfew or time when he was to come home on weekend nights. . . . .   9 0 x y

Walked in his sleep one or more times . . . .   9 0 x y

Had rules which governed the time spent watching TV and/or the programs seen . . . .   9 0 x y

Belonged to the Boy Scouts or Girl Scouts. . . . .   9 0 x y

Often expressed emotion outwardly by yelling, cursing, slamming doors, etc. . . . .   9 0 x y

135
Was never allowed to drink alcoholic beverages . . . .   9 0 x y

Liked to spend time alone . . . . .   9 0 x y

Had a sweet tooth--seemed to like sweets a great deal . . . .   9 0 x y

Often took a nap during the day . .   9 0 x y

Had sensitive feelings and was easily hurt . . . .   9 0 x y

140
Resembled the mother more in personality than the father. . . . . .   9 0 x y

Resembled the father more in personality than the mother. . . . . .   9 0 x y

142
Was left-handed . . . .   9 0 x y

(40-48)

143

	1	2	3	4
Was often the first one in the house to get up in the morning .	9	0	x	y
Went out on the average of three or more nights a week.	9	0	x	y
145 Was punished or criticized at a rate of one or more times a month for staying out too late .	9	0	x	y
Parents objected to his association with one or more of his boy-friends.	9	0	x	y
Parents objected to his association with one or more of his girl-friends.	9	0	x	y
Was not permitted to read certain books.	9	0	x	y
Was frequently allowed to take the family car for a drive with friends	9	0	x	y
150 Made his own bed.	9	0	x	y
Had definite chores or duties at home which were his responsibility. .	9	0	x	y

(49-57)

152

	1	2	3	4
Wore braces to straighten his teeth	9	0	x	y
Parents required that he spend a specified amount of time each week studying	9	0	x	y
Had a personality conflict or other non-academic difficulty which required a visit to school by the parents.	9	0	x	y
155 Was not permitted to go out on school nights under ordinary circumstances.	9	0	x	y
Was a light sleeper	9	0	x	y
Was not allowed to smoke.	9	0	x	y
Had a room of his own	9	0	x	y
One or more of his high school or junior high teachers was invited to dinner or to be a guest in the home	9	0	x	y
160 Wanted to quit school one or more times and had to be persuaded to continue	9	0	x	y

10. Which of the following things were true of your home when your twins were young? (From birth to six years.) If an item was true of the twin's home during this age period, circle the number under "True;" if not, circle the number under "False." (Circle one for each item.)

161 (58-65)

	True	False
	1	2
The whole family gathered regularly for meals.	x	y
The father took a good deal of responsibility for the care of the twins.	x	y
A nurse or housekeeper took a good deal of responsibility for the care of the twins.	x	y
The mother had no other responsibility than the care of the home and family	x	y
165 The family lived in the home of grand-parents or other relatives	x	y
There was good agreement between the parents concerning child-rearing practices.	x	y
One or more of the twin's grand-parents lived in the same town . . .	x	y
There was a grandparent or older person living in the home for one year or longer	x	y

169 (66-73)

	True	False
	1	2
The father had a job which often required him to be away from home at night	9	0
170 The family usually said grace or a prayer before meals	9	0
The family lived in a house of their own	9	0
The family lived in an apartment building.	9	0
The mother was mainly responsible for punishing the twins when they were bad	9	0
The father was mainly responsible for punishing the twins when they were bad	9	0
There was a lot of fighting and competitiveness between the twins	9	0
176 The parents had many of their friends and relatives visit the house for dinner or parties . .	9	0

11. At what ages were the following things true of the twins. Circle the ages at which each item occurred. "O" indicates from birth to one year, "1" indicates the year in which the twins were one year old, etc. (Circle as many ages as apply for each item. If the event in a particular item did not occur at all, circle the letter "x" at the end of the row.)

FOR EXAMPLE: If the father was away from home for three years when the twins were ages six through eight and again for a year when the twins were ten, you would indicate it thus: CL_____ (1-6) (7-42)

Father was absent from home.

0 1 2 3 4 5 (6 7 8) 9 (10) 11 12 13 14 15 16 17 18 x

171

The twins were cared for by a nurse or baby sitter during the day.

0 1 2 3 4 5 6 7 8 9 10 11 12 13 14 15 16 17 18 x

Mother was absent from home for six months or more during the year.

0 1 2 3 4 5 6 7 8 9 10 11 12 13 14 15 16 17 18 x

Father was absent from home for six months or more during the year.

0 1 2 3 4 5 6 7 8 9 10 11 12 13 14 15 16 17 18 x

The child was hospitalized one or more times during the year. (Exclude birth.)

180

Twin one   0 1 2 3 4 5 6 7 8 9 10 11 12 13 14 15 16 17 18 x
Twin two   0 1 2 3 4 5 6 7 8 9 10 11 12 13 14 15 16 17 18 x

The family moved from one town to another.

0 1 2 3 4 5 6 7 8 9 10 11 12 13 14 15 16 17 18 x

The family moved from one house or apartment to another in the same town.

0 1 2 3 4 5 6 7 8 9 10 11 12 13 14 15 16 17 18 x

A parent was incapacitated by a serious illness for six months or more during the year.

0 1 2 3 4 5 6 7 8 9 10 11 12 13 14 15 16 17 18 x

185

A parent died.

0 1 2 3 4 5 6 7 8 9 10 11 12 13 14 15 16 17 18 x

A grandparent, aunt or uncle who was close to the twins died.

0 1 2 3 4 5 6 7 8 9 10 11 12 13 14 15 16 17 18 x

Went away to boarding school or military school for six months or more during the year.

Twin one   0 1 2 3 4 5 6 7 8 9 10 11 12 13 14 15 16 17 18 x
Twin two   0 1 2 3 4 5 6 7 8 9 10 11 12 13 14 15 16 17 18 x

Attended summer camp for one week or more.

190

Twin one   0 1 2 3 4 5 6 7 8 9 10 11 12 13 14 15 16 17 18 x
Twin two   0 1 2 3 4 5 6 7 8 9 10 11 12 13 14 15 16 17 18 x

Took private piano, voice or other music lessons. (Do not include music instruction in school.)

Twin one   0 1 2 3 4 5 6 7 8 9 10 11 12 13 14 15 16 17 18 x
Twin two   0 1 2 3 4 5 6 7 8 9 10 11 12 13 14 15 16 17 18 x

The twins were separated for more than six months during the year.

193

0 1 2 3 4 5 6 7 8 9 10 11 12 13 14 15 16 17 18 x

12. Parents use many different forms of discipline to train their children. Some of the more common ones are listed below. Indicate to what extent each was used in the training of the twins, both as young children (before six) and as older children (after six). Try to indicate how the twins were actually treated rather than what now seems correct. (Circle one number in each row as young children and one number in each row as older children or adolescents.)

194-204

205-215

	YOUNG CHILDREN			OLDER CHILDREN AND ADOLESCENTS		
	Never used	Occasion-ally used	Frequent-ly used	Never used	Occasion-ally used	Frequent-ly used
194, 205 Spanking.	1	2	3	4	5	6 (43-53)
Withdrawal of privileges (movies, TV, reduced allowance, etc.). . .	1	2	3	4	5	6
Temporary restriction of activities (sat on a chair, sent to room, etc.).	1	2	3	4	5	6
Extra duty (wash dishes, clean. house, etc.).	1	2	3	4	5	6
Tangible reward for good behavior (money, candy, etc.).	1	2	3	4	5	6
Verbal scolding (labeling as bad boy or girl, bawling out, etc.) .	1	2	3	4	5	6
200, 211 Reasoning (explain reasons why certain behavior is or is not desirable).	1	2	3	4	5	6
Rejection, withdrawal of love . .	1	2	3	4	5	6
Praise for good behavior.	1	2	3	4	5	6
Comparison with friends or siblings.	1	2	3	4	5	6
204, 215 Threat of severe punishment (death, desertion, incarceration)	1	2	3	4	5	6

13. How strict was the discipline of the twins?

216

Very strict.	1 (54)
Strict	2
Firm	3
Somewhat easy-going or permissive. .	4
Very easy-going or permissive. . . .	5

14. How consistent was the discipline of the twins? Could they always count on the same response from the parents for a given action or did it vary from time to time?

217

Always very consistent	1 (55)
Usually consistent	2
Often inconsistent	3
Usually inconsistent	4

15. To what extent were they threatened with punishment that was not actually carried out?

218

Threats of punishment always followed through. . . .	1 (56)
Threats of punishment usually followed through . . .	2
Threats of punishment sometimes followed through . .	3
Threats of punishment rarely followed through. . . .	4

16. Parents usually follow fairly definite patterns in raising their children. Below are listed some of the ways in which these patterns can differ. Please indicate the general patterns that were actually followed in raising the twins. If the twins were treated more like the statement on one side of the page than the other, circle one of the numbers on that side. If neither statement is particularly descriptive or if both apply equally, circle one of the numbers in the middle. The headings "Very," "Fairly," etc. refer to the degree to which a statement is descriptive   (Circle one in each row.)

(57-71)

Very / Fairly / Slightly / Neither or Both / Slightly / Fairly / Very

219

Left statement	1	2	3	4	5	6	7	Right statement
Mother takes responsibility for raising the twins.	1	2	3	4	5	6	7	Father takes responsibility for raising the twins.
Punishment for misbehavior is the main method of control.	1	2	3	4	5	6	7	Praise for good behavior is the main method of control.
Parents give the twins as many things as they can afford.	1	2	3	4	5	6	7	Parents restrict the twins' possessions.
There is a lot of contact between parents and child. Do many things together.	1	2	3	4	5	6	7	Parents and child pursue their interests independently with little contact or interaction.
Parents attempt to train the twins to give up baby ways as soon as possible (early toilet training, early weaning, prevention of thumb sucking, etc.)	1	2	3	4	5	6	7	Parents let the twins develop in their own way, at their own speed.

224

Left statement	1	2	3	4	5	6	7	Right statement
Home is calm, quiet and peaceful.	1	2	3	4	5	6	7	Home is lively, with lots of excitement and many things going on.
Mother is overtly demonstrative of love for the twins with much hugging, kissing and expression of affection.	1	2	3	4	5	6	7	Mother is not overtly demonstrative of love for the twins.
Father is overtly demonstrative of love for the twins with much hugging, kissing and expression of affection.	1	2	3	4	5	6	7	Father is not overtly demonstrative of love for the twins.
Parents let the twins do whatever they want to.	1	2	3	4	5	6	7	Parents actively direct the behavior and interests of the twins.
Parents attempt to make the twins as independent and self-sufficient as possible, and let them work their own way out of difficulties.	1	2	3	4	5	6	7	Parents try to shelter the twins from unnecessary stress and smooth the way as much as possible.

229

Left statement	1	2	3	4	5	6	7	Right statement
Parents want the twins to do well in whatever they undertake and push them to work and try hard in order to achieve to the maximum of their ability.	1	2	3	4	5	6	7	Parents leave it up to the twins to determine how much they undertake and how hard they work.
Parents set many rules and regulations for the twins to live by.	1	2	3	4	5	6	7	Parents let the twins set their own limits.
Mother is stricter with the twins than the father.	1	2	3	4	5	6	7	Father is stricter with the twins than the mother.
Mother has much love and affection for the twins.	1	2	3	4	5	6	7	Mother has little love and affection for the twins.
Father has much love and affection for the twins.	1	2	3	4	5	6	7	Father has little love and affection for the twins.

233

17. The following items are concerned with differences between the twins. Indicate for which twin each statement is most appropriate. (See instructions on front of booklet for explanation of "Twin one" and "Twin two.") (Circle one for each item.)

CM _____ (1-6)

Twin one / Twin two / Neither twin / I don't know

234 (7-30)

Which twin:

Was born first. 1 2 3 4

Weighed more at birth 1 2 3 4

Learned to walk first 1 2 3 4

Was toilet trained first. 1 2 3 4

Received more attention from the
     mother 1 2 3 4

Received more attention from the
     father 1 2 3 4

240 Did better work in grade school
     (1st to 6th grades). 1 2 3 4

Was more friendly as a young child. .   1 2 3 4

Had a better appetite as a young
     child. 1 2 3 4

Was closer to the mother. 1 2 3 4

Was closer to the father. 1 2 3 4

245 Had more minor illnesses as a child .   1 2 3 4

Had stricter discipline as a child. .   1 2 3 4

Had stricter discipline as an
     adolescent 1 2 3 4

Had a date first. 1 2 3 4

Is more interested in art 1 2 3 4

250 Is more interested in business. . . .   1 2 3 4

Is more interested in mechanics . . .   1 2 3 4

Is more interested in science 1 2 3 4

Is more interested in politics. . . .   1 2 3 4

Is more interested in dramatics . . .   1 2 3 4

255 Is more interested in athletics . . .   1 2 3 4

Is more interested in helping others.   1 2 3 4

Is more interested in religion. . . .   1 2 3 4

(31-55)

Twin one / Twin two / Neither twin / I don't know

258 Studies harder 1 2 3 4

Reads more 1 2 3 4

260 Watches TV more. 1 2 3 4

Sleeps more. 1 2 3 4

Has saved more money 1 2 3 4

Has more dates 1 2 3 4

Was spanked more often as a child.   1 2 3 4

265 Was rocked and held more often as
     a child 1 2 3 4

Cried more as a child. 1 2 3 4

Learned to swim first. 1 2 3 4

Learned to ride a bicycle first. .   1 2 3 4

Learned to drive a car first . . .   1 2 3 4

270 Started menstruation first
     (for boys leave blank). 1 2 3 4

Voice changed first
     (for girls leave blank) 1 2 3 4

Usually decides what the two of
     them will do together 1 2 3 4

Is more dependable 1 2 3 4

Is more curious. 1 2 3 4

275 Is more imaginative. 1 2 3 4

Is more original 1 2 3 4

Is more outgoing 1 2 3 4

Is more self-confident 1 2 3 4

Is more sensitive. 1 2 3 4

Is more talkative. 1 2 3 4

Is shyer 1 2 3 4

282 Is more temperamental. 1 2 3 4

18. Were the twins dressed alike? (Circle one.)

283

Almost always 1
Part of the time. . . . 2   (56)
Rarely or never 3

-11-

19. As children (ages 6 to 12) did the twins tend to play together or separately? (Circle one.)

284

They were almost always together. 1   (57)
They were usually together but sometimes played apart . . 2
They usually played apart but sometimes were together . . 3
They almost never played together 4

---

20. As adolescents (ages 12 to 18) did the twins tend to spend their time together? (Circle one.)

285

They were almost always together. 1   (58)
They were usually together but sometimes apart. 2
They usually were apart but sometimes together. 3
They were almost never together 4

---

21. Did the twins have the same teacher in school? (Circle one.)

286

Usually had the same teacher. 1   (59)
Sometimes the same, sometimes different 2
Usually had different teachers. 3

---

22. Did the twins sleep in the same or separate rooms? (Circle one.)

287

Separate rooms most of their life . . . . 1 <i>4</i> (60)
Usually slept in separate rooms . . . . 2 <i>3</i>
Usually slept in the same room. . . . . 3 <i>2</i>
Slept in the same room most of their life . . . . 4 <i>1</i>

---

23. Many parents of twins try to treat both children exactly alike. Others make an effort to treat them differently. In raising the twins which of these methods have you followed? (Circle one.)

288

We have tried to treat them exactly the same. 1   (61)
We tended to treat them alike 2
We have tried to treat them differently . . . . 3 <i>5</i>
We tended to treat them differently . . . . 4 <i>4</i>
At times we treated them alike, at other times, differently . 5 <i>3</i>

---

24. As you know there are two kinds of twins: identical twins which have the same heredity, and fraternal twins which have different heredity. Which kind are your twins? (Circle one.)

289

I am certain they are identical twins 1   (62)
I think they are identical twins, but am not certain. 2
I don't know which kind they are. 3
I think they are fraternal twins, but am not certain. 4
I am certain they are fraternal twins 5

✗. What, in your opinion, are the most striking differences between the twins? _____

_____

_____

_____

_____

✗. What do you feel is the main cause of these differences? _____

_____

_____

_____

_____

Appendix B

Basic Data Tables

Appendix B consists of two lengthy tables. The first contains data from the twin questionnaire, and the second contains data from the parent questionnaire. The variables are as identified in Appendix A. For each one, several basic statistics are given. Binary (yes-no) variables are treated differently from the rest. For binary variables in the twin questionnaire, the intraclass correlations, number of pairs, and proportion of respondents saying "yes" are given for each of four groups: male identical twins, female identical twins, male fraternal twins, and female fraternal twins. The Objective Behavior Inventory items are treated as binary items in this table, with "frequently" and "occasionally" combined as "yes." For the remaining twin-questionnaire variables, the intraclass correlation, number of pairs, and mean are given for each group, and the combined within-groups standard deviation is given. In general, if either twin was missing a score on an item, neither twin was used for that item; the *N*'s reflect the pairs actually included.

The parent-questionnaire items are somewhat more varied in form, but analogous statistics are reported for each.

The data tape from which these tables was constructed was missing 11 twin pairs; therefore, the *N*'s and means will not always agree exactly with those reported elsewhere in the book.

Intraclass correlations based on extreme splits (proportions of a given response close to 0.0 or 1.0) are included in the tables but should not be taken seriously—their values are highly unreliable and often bizarre. For example, low negative intraclass correlations will result if, say, only three or four individuals give a particular response and happen not to be paired up with one another. Where there is *no* variation on a variable, the intraclass correlation is undefined; it is reported as zero in the tables.

TWIN DATA FOR ALL VARIABLES

NOTE--FOR BINARY VARIABLES, PERCENT AGREEING IS GIVEN INSTEAD OF MEAN

VAR.	INTRACLASS R				PAIRS				MEAN OR PERCENT				SD
NO.	IM	IF	FM	FF	IM	IF	FM	FF	IM	IF	FM	FF	NS

SEX AND ZYGOSITY

2	0.00	0.00	0.00	0.00	216	293	135	195	1.00	2.00	1.00	2.00	0.00
3	0.00	0.00	0.00	0.00	216	293	135	195	1.00	1.00	2.00	2.00	0.00
4	1.00	1.00	1.00	1.00	216	293	135	195	2.60	2.56	2.15	2.21	.71

NMSQT

5	.72	.78	.65	.50	216	293	135	195	18.68	20.09	19.63	20.19	4.63
6	.74	.71	.41	.46	216	293	135	195	22.98	19.54	23.51	19.89	6.05
7	.75	.79	.44	.57	216	293	135	195	21.11	20.22	21.43	19.89	4.85
8	.70	.65	.52	.53	216	293	135	195	21.22	19.76	21.81	19.20	5.61
9	.85	.87	.61	.66	216	293	135	195	20.82	21.00	21.36	20.79	4.79
10	.87	.88	.60	.66	216	293	135	195	104.81	99.62	107.75	99.97	21.85

MISCELLANEOUS BACKGROUND INFORMATION

11	.36	.59	.41	.44	204	282	129	191	2.19	2.19	2.16	2.13	.42
12	.64	.66	.38	.56	202	289	127	186	4.72	3.85	4.72	3.89	1.19
13	.07	.01	-.07	-.01	214	292	134	193	1.44	1.45	1.39	1.35	.98
14	.71	.84	.64	.51	147	204	88	132	77.50	81.68	76.71	79.36	18.30
15	.82	.84	.97	1.00	156	213	92	144	294.07	249.41	263.83	248.43	261.63
16	.67	.79	.33	.72	190	272	121	179	1.93	1.93	1.87	1.84	1.17
17	.39	.32	.30	.18	161	219	100	137	2.45	2.76	2.51	2.79	.57
18	.90	.92	.84	.93	208	271	130	175	3.78	3.71	3.70	3.61	2.08
19	.79	.80	.64	.84	208	271	130	175	2.23	2.17	2.28	2.17	.79
20	.64	.78	.55	.54	210	287	128	190	1.50	1.41	1.62	1.47	.72
21	.55	.75	.49	.48	201	283	132	184	1.63	1.62	1.87	1.72	1.15

TIME DIARY

22	.45	.58	.35	.42	210	286	128	191	17.70	19.17	17.08	18.45	9.88
23	.13	.37	.15	.47	211	288	130	190	32.29	33.18	31.20	32.15	8.61
24	.11	.28	.03	.28	209	285	129	192	5.80	6.10	5.39	5.48	5.75
25	.41	.44	.10	.38	201	275	126	175	15.39	15.79	14.10	15.97	12.48

TWIN DATA (CONT.)

VAR. NO.	INTRACLASS R				PAIRS				MEAN OR PERCENT				SD NG
	IM	IF	FM	FF	IM	IF	FM	FF	IM	IF	FM	FF	
26	.38	.57	.32	.42	207	284	131	192	10.14	9.55	8.69	8.76	8.81
27	.01	.43	.13	.47	201	281	128	186	2.48	2.57	2.04	2.47	3.62
28	.19	.52	.52	.46	203	276	129	181	4.75	3.26	3.84	3.41	4.97
29	.34	.26	.02	.19	211	287	132	191	53.41	53.11	53.10	54.07	9.55
30	.37	.50	.40	.70	191	269	123	181	9.34	4.54	7.47	5.57	11.51
31	.04	.33	.09	.02	187	255	113	173	1.11	.61	.54	.45	4.21
32	.04	.19	-.00	.51	198	275	123	182	3.51	4.15	3.39	4.44	5.52
33	.13	.20	-.03	.22	208	286	129	188	6.12	10.04	5.78	9.56	6.92
34	.08	.40	.08	.45	196	279	127	184	3.32	4.51	3.62	4.75	5.63
35	.24	.53	.28	.41	194	264	122	182	3.18	4.22	3.33	3.69	6.47
36	.10	.38	.04	.14	197	271	127	180	4.21	3.74	3.54	3.65	6.05
37	.08	.49	.07	.38	199	278	123	185	8.80	7.89	8.43	8.16	8.79
38	.02	.42	.21	.29	197	271	124	178	2.59	2.12	1.78	1.92	4.29
39	.47	.52	.37	.32	202	269	128	180	9.25	3.76	8.38	4.12	6.79

RELIGION AND RACE

VAR. NO.	INTRACLASS R				PAIRS				MEAN OR PERCENT				SD NG
40	1.00	.92	1.00	.90	214	293	134	194	1.01	1.05	1.01	1.03	.20
41	.80	.89	.63	.94	214	292	134	192	1.70	1.64	1.44	1.62	.90
42	.73	.75	.42	.67	212	291	134	192	1.81	1.71	1.69	1.65	1.04

OBJECTIVE BEHAVIOR INVENTORY

VAR. NO.	INTRACLASS R				PAIRS				MEAN OR PERCENT			
43	.40	.40	.21	.35	215	292	135	195	53	56	49	45
44	.61	.66	.32	.46	215	292	135	195	57	22	56	21
45	.62	.65	.43	.50	215	291	134	195	31	40	27	43
46	.71	.65	.49	.57	215	292	135	195	35	44	44	53
47	.58	.55	.49	.48	214	292	134	195	31	28	31	31
48	.25	.41	.15	.45	213	292	135	193	10	2	10	5
49	.34	.21	.10	.27	214	290	134	192	94	79	91	82
50	.38	.49	.16	.34	214	292	135	193	49	51	50	54
51	.41	.47	.27	.58	215	290	135	194	15	16	11	18
52	.74	.65	.63	.64	213	290	134	194	69	76	66	73
53	.56	.54	.44	.40	214	292	135	195	89	96	90	94
54	.58	.72	.44	.65	214	292	134	191	71	78	81	80
55	.29	.25	.04	.13	215	292	135	193	89	86	90	87
56	.19	.37	.14	.30	215	291	135	195	75	77	74	79
57	.23	.28	.15	.17	215	292	135	195	65	66	71	66
58	.38	.25	.27	.25	215	292	135	195	88	91	91	92
59	.17	.49	.29	.31	214	292	134	195	16	11	18	13
60	.42	.35	.30	-.02	214	291	135	194	95	98	96	98
61	.53	.51	.31	.42	215	292	135	195	49	19	44	15
62	.37	.27	.43	.23	215	292	134	195	13	4	12	2

TWIN DATA (CONT.)

VAR. NO.	INTRACLASS R				PAIRS				MEAN OR PERCENT				SD
	IM	IF	FM	FF	IM	IF	FM	FF	IM	IF	FM	FF	NS
63	-.00	-.01	-.01	0.00	215	291	134	195	100	99	99	100	
64	.57	.51	.49	.28	215	291	134	195	46	17	49	18	
65	.70	.88	.62	.74	215	292	135	193	26	28	25	26	
66	.33	.50	.32	.24	215	291	135	193	33	22	31	26	
67	.52	.53	.45	.41	215	291	135	194	63	24	65	26	
68	.19	.26	.23	.11	214	292	134	193	74	80	73	82	
69	.34	.48	.33	.44	213	292	134	193	15	20	13	22	
70	.33	.42	.28	.23	214	290	134	195	84	74	83	75	
71	.53	.55	.58	.40	214	290	135	195	41	26	36	24	
72	.51	.55	.32	.50	214	289	135	194	52	22	50	22	
73	.61	.64	.50	.65	215	291	134	195	35	31	40	35	
74	.50	.65	.31	.69	214	291	133	195	12	12	13	18	
75	.35	.18	.25	.34	213	289	129	190	17	14	21	14	
76	.36	.51	.31	.38	214	292	134	195	55	61	60	54	
77	.30	.47	.20	.24	215	288	133	194	40	43	42	42	
78	.55	.60	.40	.56	212	292	134	195	47	49	41	47	
79	.29	.40	.21	.30	215	289	134	194	25	29	26	30	
80	.30	.26	.25	.22	215	292	135	195	81	82	76	80	
81	-.00	0.00	-.01	-.01	213	292	135	195	100	100	99	99	
82	.28	.36	.21	.23	214	291	134	194	23	19	26	14	
83	.31	.42	.25	.33	215	291	135	194	73	49	76	57	
84	.43	.54	.45	.41	214	292	134	193	15	32	24	33	
85	.09	.18	-.04	.03	215	292	134	195	94	92	96	91	
86	.53	.60	.30	.60	215	292	134	194	27	28	24	29	
87	.44	.55	.45	.54	212	292	135	195	31	30	35	34	
88	.11	.50	.11	.24	215	292	135	195	8	30	5	31	
89	.29	.46	.15	.21	215	283	135	190	47	30	44	31	
90	.46	.45	.29	.30	215	291	135	194	27	54	19	56	
91	-.01	.58	-.02	.37	213	290	135	194	1	30	2	35	
92	-.02	.54	-.01	.40	215	290	134	194	2	62	1	72	
93	.39	.44	.05	.35	214	289	135	190	57	61	57	62	
94	.30	.48	.29	.44	215	292	135	194	21	18	21	16	
95	-.01	.45	-.01	.45	214	290	135	194	1	46	1	47	
96	.21	.32	.12	.20	215	291	135	193	59	60	55	56	
97	.25	.29	.12	.05	215	291	135	194	94	97	90	95	
98	.51	.33	.13	.37	215	291	135	194	8	13	6	9	
99	.49	.28	.34	.47	215	292	135	195	13	5	9	11	
100	.52	.26	.31	.36	215	291	135	194	60	13	63	11	
101	.14	.24	.15	.09	215	292	135	195	88	92	88	93	
102	.62	.60	.51	.46	215	292	135	194	47	84	37	87	
103	.31	.37	.04	.39	212	282	133	190	21	27	20	28	
104	.37	.08	.27	.50	214	292	135	195	7	7	5	10	
105	.68	.71	.53	.65	215	291	135	195	24	38	24	42	
106	.71	.75	.49	.61	214	292	134	194	18	34	20	43	
107	.65	.55	.35	.53	215	292	135	195	18	25	19	28	
108	.15	.61	.48	.42	215	291	135	195	5	7	4	7	
109	.57	.48	.43	.40	215	291	135	194	47	50	44	51	

TWIN DATA (CONT.)

VAR. NO.	INTRACLASS R				PAIRS				MEAN OR PERCENT				S)
	IM	IF	FM	FF	IM	IF	FM	FF	IM	IF	FM	FF	N'3
110	.39	.34	.66	.26	215	292	135	195	1	5	1	4	
111	.32	.35	.35	.32	215	292	135	195	52	85	47	86	
112	.45	.66	.29	-.00	215	291	135	195	86	99	82	99	
113	.24	.34	.10	.22	215	291	135	195	85	88	83	93	
114	.37	.57	.29	.40	214	292	135	195	31	35	27	41	
115	.29	.52	.13	.30	215	292	135	194	20	44	27	39	
116	.42	.55	.38	.47	215	291	135	193	42	43	42	51	
117	.33	.38	-.03	-.03	215	292	135	195	96	95	97	97	
118	.24	.52	.12	.33	215	292	133	195	15	24	11	26	
119	.45	.21	.43	.14	215	291	135	195	49	22	41	22	
120	.48	.36	.44	.42	214	289	134	194	31	47	26	46	
121	.63	-.01	.43	.59	215	292	135	195	10	1	9	3	
122	.49	.63	.47	.42	215	290	134	195	76	77	78	84	
123	.31	.47	.26	.32	213	291	135	194	21	53	33	53	
124	.57	.47	.58	.49	215	292	135	195	15	20	17	19	
125	.20	.47	.24	.21	215	290	134	194	19	44	23	41	
126	.23	.40	.19	.23	215	290	135	194	67	46	75	52	
127	.33	.59	.38	.44	213	292	134	195	81	81	81	78	
128	.33	.50	.13	.48	215	291	135	195	24	27	27	23	
129	.37	.32	.08	-.04	215	292	135	195	93	96	91	96	
130	.34	.35	.17	.15	215	292	135	195	54	53	53	53	
131	.36	.54	.30	.50	215	292	135	195	59	54	63	53	
132	.30	.36	.36	.18	215	291	135	195	77	82	78	87	
133	.56	.62	.40	.50	215	292	135	195	33	45	40	44	
134	.21	.39	.09	.20	215	292	134	195	80	86	76	85	
135	.49	.56	.32	.34	214	292	135	194	56	67	51	65	
136	.30	.36	.40	.32	215	292	135	195	7	8	11	8	
137	-.03	.50	-.01	.56	215	292	135	195	3	4	1	6	
138	.20	.49	-.03	.20	214	290	132	195	4	10	3	12	
139	.59	.54	.45	.37	215	292	135	194	39	10	41	11	
140	.35	.48	.35	-.02	215	292	135	195	4	3	6	2	
141	.31	.52	.12	.27	212	291	134	194	35	31	34	25	
142	.46	.47	.25	.48	215	292	135	194	32	41	32	52	
143	.60	.50	.42	.54	215	292	135	195	15	17	13	19	
144	.32	.40	.21	.38	215	292	135	195	69	80	68	82	
145	.11	-.02	.20	.49	215	292	135	195	15	2	16	2	
146	.55	.54	.17	.43	213	292	135	195	7	11	4	15	
147	.28	.30	.13	.51	215	291	135	193	28	17	27	17	
148	.41	.49	.42	.41	215	292	135	195	46	51	52	52	
149	.56	.64	.41	.63	213	292	135	195	74	75	76	76	
150	.42	.40	.32	.23	215	292	135	195	55	45	57	45	
151	.40	.38	.22	.30	215	292	135	194	69	86	77	86	
152	.41	.42	.24	.35	215	290	134	195	88	26	87	24	
153	.51	.60	.51	.36	215	291	134	195	81	76	85	84	
154	.45	.49	.43	.68	215	289	134	195	94	99	95	95	
155	.63	.66	.12	.44	215	291	133	195	9	3	11	7	
156	.46	.50	.34	.38	215	291	131	195	34	45	37	45	

TWIN DATA (CONT.)

VAR. NO.	INTRACLASS R				PAIRS				MEAN OR PERCENT				SD NS
	IM	IF	FM	FF	IM	IF	FM	FF	IM	IF	FM	FF	
157	.48	.58	.40	.44	215	291	133	194	29	37	29	40	
158	.56	.62	.22	.57	214	289	134	195	90	91	92	91	
159	.39	.43	.23	.45	215	291	134	194	35	9	31	8	
160	.43	.43	.32	.44	212	288	134	195	43	38	45	39	
161	.44	.51	.19	.51	215	291	134	195	73	75	73	75	
162	.66	.52	.36	.59	212	291	134	195	8	9	6	10	
163	.64	.66	.46	.57	215	290	134	195	53	53	51	55	
164	.26	.19	-.03	.54	215	290	134	195	3	8	3	7	
165	.30	.44	.26	.19	214	291	134	194	81	89	83	90	
166	.88	.64	.57	.51	215	290	134	195	91	86	91	87	
167	.50	.44	.32	.50	215	291	134	195	59	58	65	63	
168	.35	.66	.20	-.00	215	291	134	195	86	99	82	99	
169	.27	.38	.22	.30	215	291	134	194	43	60	40	57	
170	.30	.27	.11	.18	215	289	134	195	82	77	85	77	
171	-.01	.21	.11	.30	215	291	134	195	99	98	95	95	
172	.39	.54	.27	.25	215	291	134	195	58	77	59	76	
173	.43	.48	.65	.18	215	291	133	195	2	12	3	5	
174	.34	.21	.19	.41	215	291	134	195	22	13	21	12	
175	.58	.55	.28	.52	214	290	134	194	70	80	71	78	
176	.03	.33	.11	-.03	215	291	134	194	95	97	95	97	
177	.34	.52	.31	.47	215	291	134	195	63	73	67	77	
178	.39	.56	.55	.26	215	291	134	194	71	85	66	89	
179	.62	.56	.55	.52	215	291	134	195	57	57	55	58	
180	.53	.38	.37	.40	215	290	134	195	20	7	23	8	
181	.55	.35	.47	.27	215	291	134	195	8	2	6	2	
182	.51	.49	.49	.51	215	290	134	194	17	15	19	13	
183	.37	.56	.60	.55	214	291	134	195	10	53	7	49	
184	.45	.51	.28	.41	215	291	134	194	63	59	65	60	
185	.43	.48	.32	.28	215	291	132	195	90	65	87	69	
186	.54	.61	.55	.51	215	291	133	195	43	26	47	25	
187	.11	-.01	.13	-.02	215	291	134	195	97	99	96	98	
188	.72	.54	.56	.47	215	291	133	195	36	7	39	11	
189	.15	.41	.05	.07	215	291	133	195	87	92	87	95	
190	.32	.35	.27	.38	215	290	134	194	17	22	12	27	
191	.49	.46	.21	.41	214	291	133	195	62	76	58	81	
192	.23	.39	.23	.30	214	291	134	194	37	23	35	28	
193	.69	.65	.42	.68	215	290	133	195	16	23	18	23	
194	.25	.26	.34	.11	215	291	134	195	9	4	9	4	
195	.41	.41	.24	.40	215	291	134	195	25	22	31	20	
196	.11	.43	.22	.50	214	290	133	194	6	21	6	20	
197	.42	.39	.20	.25	215	290	134	194	67	91	65	92	
198	.27	.18	.20	.36	215	290	134	195	56	94	53	94	
199	.58	.47	.49	.42	214	290	134	195	15	6	13	8	
200	.21	.46	.08	.31	214	291	134	194	90	95	91	97	
201	.24	.39	.10	.26	214	289	134	194	20	32	11	34	
202	.29	.47	.26	.34	215	291	133	195	83	80	81	82	
203	.09	.29	-.02	.22	213	290	134	193	96	92	98	96	

TWIN DATA (CONT.)

VAR. NO.	INTRACLASS R				PAIRS				MEAN OR PERCENT				SD NG
	IM	IF	FM	FF	IM	IF	FM	FF	IM	IF	FM	FF	
204	.37	.46	.24	.38	215	291	134	195	30	29	25	24	
205	.56	.44	.49	.70	213	291	133	194	9	2	15	4	
206	.48	.61	.35	.50	215	290	134	195	52	57	50	59	
207	.51	.64	.40	.56	214	292	133	195	43	37	37	43	
208	.52	.57	.35	.39	215	292	133	195	41	52	43	63	
209	.55	.49	.31	.41	215	291	134	193	81	26	87	35	
210	.28	.22	.05	.09	215	292	134	195	68	83	71	84	
211	.20	.35	.05	.34	215	292	134	195	26	23	22	27	
212	.26	.31	.15	.17	215	292	134	195	80	84	78	81	
213	.26	.41	.03	.00	215	292	134	195	42	57	47	53	
214	.38	.39	.35	.42	215	292	134	195	68	79	68	74	
215	.35	.31	.23	.25	215	292	134	195	59	68	62	66	
216	.32	.31	.27	.31	215	291	134	195	33	40	35	36	
217	.16	.47	.13	.31	215	292	134	195	10	25	6	28	
218	.23	.31	.20	.21	215	292	134	194	65	52	62	59	
219	.14	.35	.27	.23	215	292	134	195	47	49	50	52	
220	.21	.20	.09	.10	213	290	133	195	12	7	14	6	
221	.34	.50	.19	.11	214	292	134	195	28	34	38	37	
222	.37	.54	.50	.42	214	291	134	194	38	50	47	53	
223	.38	.40	.28	.17	215	290	134	194	13	16	18	14	
224	.67	.63	.29	.32	214	292	134	194	79	80	77	88	
225	.38	.37	.25	.27	214	290	134	194	38	35	35	40	
226	.22	.20	.29	.14	213	290	134	192	11	14	12	23	
227	.35	.65	.33	.29	215	292	134	195	8	6	6	7	
228	.52	.56	.18	.33	215	292	133	195	14	5	15	9	
229	.18	.34	.40	.41	215	292	134	195	12	11	10	11	
230	.33	.41	-.01	.12	215	292	134	195	71	65	71	65	
231	.40	.46	.15	.29	215	292	134	195	57	73	58	70	
232	.17	.30	.09	.11	213	291	134	193	27	34	26	32	
233	.41	.44	.41	.21	215	292	132	195	26	65	23	64	
234	.48	.52	.56	.26	215	289	132	192	29	14	27	12	
235	.35	.47	.13	.45	215	291	132	195	78	38	77	45	
236	.28	.42	.17	.35	215	292	132	195	40	81	37	85	
237	.48	.45	.42	.43	214	292	134	194	31	48	27	44	
238	.59	.67	.18	.18	215	292	133	195	51	59	53	60	
239	.36	.50	.20	.28	215	292	134	195	62	62	62	63	
240	.59	.70	.50	.57	215	292	132	193	19	22	21	23	
241	-.01	-.00	-.02	.32	215	291	134	194	99	100	98	98	
242	.46	.28	.46	.49	215	291	134	194	11	5	7	6	
243	.28	.54	-.03	.32	215	292	134	195	13	55	14	61	
244	.46	.39	.15	.19	214	292	133	191	18	17	14	18	
245	.17	.26	.03	.12	215	292	134	194	36	60	41	59	
246	.25	.42	.24	.23	215	292	134	195	46	47	47	47	
247	.20	.18	-.08	.31	214	292	133	195	9	9	7	11	
248	.29	.09	.15	.09	215	291	134	195	10	7	15	7	
249	.36	.41	.21	.39	215	290	133	195	22	14	22	16	
250	.26	.38	.14	.34	214	291	134	195	64	71	60	74	

TWIN DATA (CONT.)

VAR. NO.	INTRACLASS R				PAIRS				MEAN OR PERCENT				SD
	IM	IF	FM	FF	IM	IF	FM	FF	IM	IF	FM	FF	MG
251	.20	.30	.19	.12	215	292	134	195	7	6	9	8	
252	.07	.20	.20	-.07	214	291	134	193	7	7	10	6	
253	-.03	.32	-.06	-.02	215	292	134	195	3	2	6	2	
254	.24	.29	.05	.19	214	292	133	195	18	27	15	26	
255	.43	.40	.25	.08	215	292	135	194	86	86	83	91	
256	.57	.52	.47	.46	215	290	135	191	72	71	73	74	
257	.33	.32	.19	-.03	214	292	133	194	95	98	97	97	
258	.27	.51	.14	.30	215	291	134	194	73	61	71	62	
259	.34	.44	.21	.28	215	292	135	194	56	63	54	66	
260	.47	.62	.30	.40	213	292	135	194	46	76	52	84	
261	.48	.53	.42	.44	215	291	135	194	59	57	54	61	
262	.61	.60	.45	.46	215	292	135	193	48	74	52	82	
263	.30	.28	.15	-.01	215	292	135	194	88	79	86	85	
264	.43	.36	.38	.35	214	290	135	192	33	8	28	8	
265	.40	.40	.23	.16	215	292	135	192	38	85	38	84	
266	.38	.37	.40	.33	215	290	135	194	74	24	73	30	
267	.31	.41	.26	.12	215	292	135	193	77	78	76	81	
268	.53	.58	.48	.45	215	292	135	194	11	9	17	13	
269	.39	.41	.36	.37	215	292	135	194	52	21	52	20	
270	.43	.49	.54	-.01	215	292	135	194	7	2	9	1	
271	.26	.39	.29	.35	215	291	135	194	33	49	36	49	
272	.16	-.00	-.02	.39	214	292	135	194	3	0	2	1	
273	.55	.39	.34	-.01	214	291	135	194	8	1	9	1	
274	.56	.30	.52	.42	215	292	135	194	42	5	44	5	
275	.37	.48	.53	.44	215	292	135	194	28	34	33	37	
276	.38	.45	.10	.23	215	292	135	194	9	8	9	7	
277	.75	.69	.34	.59	215	291	135	193	10	22	11	27	
278	.80	.76	.73	.83	214	291	135	193	46	45	48	50	
279	.58	.61	.65	.54	215	292	135	193	91	93	96	93	
280	.30	.34	.19	.28	215	292	135	194	44	95	38	97	
281	.47	.60	.07	.42	215	292	135	194	86	65	88	69	
282	.30	.12	.10	.01	215	291	135	194	32	91	33	93	
283	.38	.30	.19	.39	214	292	135	194	94	90	94	88	
284	.18	.39	.21	.35	214	292	135	194	84	90	84	92	
285	.25	.42	.13	.24	215	291	135	193	27	36	27	43	
286	.60	.69	.52	.49	214	289	135	192	72	85	72	83	
287	.47	.67	.47	.55	214	288	134	189	22	76	17	72	
288	.51	.60	.31	.51	215	289	135	194	70	81	71	81	
289	.35	.56	.34	.37	215	288	135	194	83	23	85	28	
290	.38	.55	.33	.42	215	289	135	194	35	52	37	66	
291	.22	.34	.27	.34	214	289	135	194	53	29	51	35	
292	.06	.23	.14	.10	215	289	135	194	7	16	7	14	
293	.22	.25	.09	.10	215	291	135	194	47	13	47	14	
294	.24	.27	.07	.15	215	290	135	194	23	15	22	14	
295	.50	.41	.40	.40	215	289	135	194	40	55	38	56	
296	.33	.39	.42	.34	215	291	135	194	72	78	74	82	
297	.28	.26	.29	-.08	215	290	135	193	81	91	80	92	

TWIN DATA (CONT.)

VAR. NO.	INTRACLASS R				PAIRS				MEAN OR PERCENT				SD NG
	IM	IF	FM	FF	IM	IF	FM	FF	IM	IF	FM	FF	
298	.50	.39	.25	.36	214	290	135	194	30	19	29	23	
299	.26	.30	.15	.18	215	291	135	193	18	20	19	17	
300	.50	.59	.31	.40	215	291	135	194	11	8	16	7	
301	.42	.39	.36	.39	213	290	135	194	69	8	69	9	
302	.26	.42	.45	.40	215	290	135	194	82	72	80	73	
303	.37	.06	.22	.07	215	291	133	194	23	4	26	5	
304	.38	.49	.27	.26	214	290	135	194	32	41	35	37	
305	.33	.44	.07	.47	214	291	134	194	22	15	25	19	
306	.43	.44	.31	.37	215	291	135	194	28	14	29	14	
307	.69	.78	.59	.55	215	291	135	194	15	14	21	14	
308	.22	.10	.01	.23	214	290	134	194	87	94	88	94	
309	.54	.42	.41	.47	215	291	135	194	50	32	57	32	
310	.27	.41	.19	.18	215	291	135	192	98	98	97	97	
311	.27	.47	.19	.32	215	291	135	194	16	24	19	27	
312	.52	.49	.37	.40	215	290	135	194	14	8	20	11	
313	.46	.55	.35	.40	215	290	135	194	49	62	52	61	
314	.28	.33	-.07	.28	215	291	135	194	8	8	7	8	
315	-.02	.66	.11	-.02	215	291	135	194	98	99	95	98	
316	.60	.63	.57	.53	215	289	135	194	43	29	41	27	
317	.51	.44	.24	.30	215	292	135	195	71	84	78	83	
318	-.50	-.27	-.33	-.33	3	7	2	2	67	21	25	25	
319	.45	.23	.34	-.00	215	290	135	194	84	90	86	87	
320	.38	.47	.25	.33	215	292	134	195	12	28	15	27	
321	.36	.25	.35	-.04	215	292	135	195	24	3	19	4	
322	.42	.49	.12	.27	215	292	135	194	11	62	10	65	
323	.28	.29	.05	.20	215	291	134	195	9	4	10	6	
324	.28	.33	.11	.17	215	291	135	195	32	32	27	27	
325	.17	.26	.00	.30	215	292	135	194	25	37	21	34	
326	.32	.33	-.06	.06	214	292	135	195	12	6	17	5	
327	.42	.39	.35	.18	215	292	135	195	46	27	40	28	
328	.48	.35	.22	.15	215	291	135	195	7	10	6	9	
329	.39	.54	.41	.17	215	292	135	195	85	91	83	92	
330	.31	.25	.07	.07	215	291	135	194	5	14	6	12	
331	.60	.60	.30	.48	214	292	135	195	35	41	32	46	
332	.24	.56	.19	.43	215	292	135	195	17	21	14	21	
333	.35	.37	.04	.33	215	292	135	195	9	6	7	6	
334	.23	.29	.15	.15	214	292	134	195	18	19	16	18	
335	.51	.37	.40	.28	215	292	135	195	53	22	59	25	
336	-.00	-.00	0.00	-.00	215	289	135	195	0	1	0	0	
337	.40	.46	.28	.16	214	291	135	195	10	11	14	10	
338	.34	.47	.29	.26	215	291	135	195	54	33	48	31	
339	.28	.47	.23	.26	215	291	135	195	64	54	59	57	
340	.47	.73	.48	.34	215	290	134	195	94	97	96	97	
341	.25	.28	.09	.15	215	289	135	195	48	43	46	42	
342	.21	.29	.24	.33	215	288	134	195	84	93	81	91	
343	.34	.34	.10	.22	215	288	135	192	64	60	62	58	
344	.22	.48	.26	.22	215	289	135	195	24	29	31	24	

TWIN DATA (CONT.)

VAR.	INTRACLASS R				PAIRS				MEAN OR PERCENT				SD
NO.	IM	IF	FM	FF	IM	IF	FM	FF	IM	IF	FM	FF	NG
345	.22	.36	.08	.25	215	289	135	194	54	44	56	44	
346	.24	.12	.15	.11	214	290	135	195	31	56	38	58	
347	.28	.49	.20	.26	215	290	135	195	8	63	6	71	
348	.20	.23	.11	.31	215	290	135	195	84	89	87	85	
349	.13	.28	-.02	-.01	215	291	135	195	97	99	98	99	
350	.45	-.00	.31	0.00	215	290	135	195	96	100	94	100	
351	.46	.33	.16	-.01	215	291	135	195	86	99	83	99	
352	.38	.38	.15	.30	214	290	135	195	70	66	70	74	
353	.22	.41	.09	.42	213	291	135	195	12	7	11	5	
354	.50	.56	.32	.49	215	291	135	194	46	54	41	54	
355	.34	.39	-.02	-.04	215	289	134	195	88	89	87	91	
356	.20	.45	.10	.36	213	290	135	195	42	67	46	69	
357	.55	.58	.33	.42	214	290	135	195	59	58	64	64	
358	.51	.52	.32	.30	215	291	135	195	46	35	47	29	
359	.45	.37	.42	.22	215	292	135	195	86	77	87	75	
360	.26	.38	.14	.37	213	291	135	195	34	46	33	37	
361	.45	.42	.22	.54	215	292	135	194	92	81	94	83	
362	.12	.25	-.03	.38	215	292	135	195	6	6	3	7	
363	-.00	-.00	0.00	-.01	215	292	134	195	100	100	100	99	
364	.33	.26	.15	.09	215	292	135	195	63	74	64	75	
365	.35	.39	.30	.50	214	291	135	195	71	72	15	22	
366	.10	.35	.17	.20	215	292	135	195	58	66	49	67	

LIFE GOALS

VAR.	INTRACLASS R				PAIRS				MEAN OR PERCENT				SD
NO.	IM	IF	FM	FF	IM	IF	FM	FF	IM	IF	FM	FF	NG
367	.26	.37	.05	.29	212	293	134	194	1.26	1.21	1.28	1.24	.50
368	.22	.30	.06	.13	213	289	133	194	2.17	2.46	2.23	2.47	.70
369	.31	.23	.18	.00	208	285	130	186	3.39	3.69	3.42	3.55	.68
370	.40	.33	.15	.17	205	288	130	189	2.27	1.97	2.18	1.96	.83
371	.23	.44	.05	.22	211	285	130	189	3.48	3.30	3.46	3.38	.83
372	.33	.27	.03	.22	214	289	134	195	1.72	1.61	1.79	1.56	.84
373	.34	.23	-.09	.12	211	291	133	191	2.04	2.41	1.98	2.49	.94
374	.36	.32	.15	.14	213	287	133	193	1.92	1.72	1.83	1.80	.79
375	.43	.36	.25	.14	212	289	134	193	3.20	3.65	3.21	3.63	.79
376	.38	.36	.07	.15	212	290	132	195	2.28	2.03	2.15	1.97	.82
377	.41	.36	.23	.27	213	288	133	193	2.88	3.11	2.82	3.02	.85
378	.39	.36	.19	.26	211	290	132	194	3.00	3.33	2.98	3.36	.79
379	.14	.00	.13	.18	214	292	134	195	1.20	1.12	1.18	1.08	.42
380	.51	.54	.45	.49	211	286	134	191	2.02	2.01	1.95	1.90	1.05
381	.28	.15	.15	.07	212	287	134	195	1.87	1.86	1.84	1.87	.92
382	.33	.30	.18	.07	212	286	132	192	3.16	3.53	3.14	3.51	.80
383	.36	.27	.15	.08	210	286	132	191	3.13	3.55	3.19	3.55	.79
384	.31	.39	.09	.01	209	286	131	193	3.60	3.48	3.60	3.52	.74
385	.26	.32	.14	.33	207	290	132	194	2.23	2.05	2.22	1.98	.85
386	.26	.32	.14	.13	210	286	132	194	2.87	3.02	2.86	3.06	.85

TWIN DATA (CONT.)

VAR.	INTRACLASS R				PAIRS				MEAN OR PERCENT				SD
NO.	IM	IF	FM	FF	IM	IF	FM	FF	IM	IF	FM	FF	NG
387	.26	.21	.15	.22	210	288	131	190	2.80	2.81	2.74	2.72	.93
388	.25	.18	.04	.21	214	288	132	189	1.75	1.58	1.56	1.58	.71
389	.29	.42	.04	.15	214	285	133	192	3.54	3.33	3.58	3.30	.97
390	.33	.60	.32	.40	212	289	131	188	3.63	3.54	3.56	3.61	.75
391	.37	.22	.07	.12	212	284	131	194	3.26	3.68	3.40	3.65	.73
392	.38	.40	.19	.25	213	291	134	193	2.28	2.27	2.18	2.22	.83
393	.19	.25	.10	.17	213	287	132	193	1.82	1.66	1.82	1.56	.72
394	.18	.25	.14	.56	213	288	134	194	1.17	1.11	1.24	1.09	.45
395	.11	.17	.22	.43	214	286	133	194	1.14	1.10	1.22	1.07	.44
396	.18	.05	.13	.11	213	288	134	193	1.18	1.14	1.24	1.12	.45
397	.61	.60	.54	.62	211	291	134	194	2.21	2.07	2.10	1.99	.98
398	.22	.24	.14	.24	213	287	130	192	2.56	2.98	2.52	2.88	.85
399	.17	.09	.04	-.08	208	291	128	189	3.74	3.81	3.81	3.85	.55
400	.21	.29	.03	.14	214	288	133	191	2.25	2.30	2.19	2.29	.84
401	.31	.23	.13	.24	212	289	133	193	2.42	3.01	2.53	2.83	1.03

ATTITUDES

VAR.	INTRACLASS R				PAIRS				MEAN OR PERCENT				SD
402	.65	.47	.63	.68	191	270	128	182	1.34	1.19	1.42	1.22	.71
403	.44	.30	.31	.46	198	281	124	185	2.14	2.09	2.10	2.12	.55
404	.24	.29	.29	.01	184	226	110	143	1.92	1.95	1.94	1.96	.67

DATING

VAR.	INTRACLASS R				PAIRS				MEAN OR PERCENT				SD
405	.46	.58	.33	.37	212	289	133	192	5.62	5.48	5.57	5.45	1.03
406	.13	.38	.19	.21	189	271	126	186	3.31	3.76	3.03	4.16	5.73
407	.26	.50	.25	.24	200	277	131	186	4.39	4.85	3.95	5.24	5.89
408	.26	.41	.10	.44	194	274	125	179	1.04	.79	.90	.78	1.71

DONE DURING PAST YEAR

VAR.	INTRACLASS R				PAIRS				MEAN OR PERCENT			
409	.14	.33	.23	.13	214	290	134	194	37	16	37	14
410	.24	.32	.04	.20	214	290	134	194	15	22	18	26
411	.34	.20	-.07	.49	214	290	134	194	9	3	6	1
412	.17	.39	.25	.23	214	289	134	193	57	55	68	56
413	.32	.63	.25	.29	215	291	134	193	9	48	11	55
414	.29	.37	.01	.08	215	289	134	193	14	9	12	9
415	.38	.26	.09	.24	215	288	134	188	45	9	39	9
416	.24	.31	.27	.24	207	291	126	193	4	42	5	47
417	.29	.35	.17	.17	210	289	133	191	63	69	67	68
418	.41	.40	.10	.30	215	291	134	193	20	21	19	15

TWIN DATA (CONT.)

VAR. NO.	INTRACLASS R				PAIRS				MEAN OR PERCENT				SD NG
	IM	IF	FM	FF	IM	IF	FM	FF	IM	IF	FM	FF	
419	.15	.20	.27	-.02	214	290	134	191	5	3	5	2	
420	-.02	-.01	-.04	-.01	214	290	134	192	2	1	4	1	
421	.27	.39	-.02	.29	214	290	134	192	2	19	2	23	
422	.15	.36	.27	.02	213	287	134	192	17	8	20	6	
423	.13	-.00	-.02	-.01	215	291	134	192	3	1	2	1	
424	.14	.39	-.09	.27	211	289	132	191	5	2	8	2	
425	.32	.39	.32	.42	215	291	133	191	54	57	52	54	
426	.45	-.01	.10	-.01	207	285	134	190	10	1	9	1	
427	.16	.36	.19	.22	215	291	134	193	74	79	74	83	
428	.31	.58	.39	.47	215	291	134	193	45	29	50	26	
429	-.00	0.00	0.00	-.00	215	291	133	193	0	0	0	0	
430	.32	.24	-.02	.32	211	290	131	192	1	1	2	2	
431	.28	.35	.01	.22	215	288	134	193	43	51	49	49	
432	.32	.39	.35	.26	215	290	133	193	79	84	85	85	
433	-.01	.33	-.02	-.00	214	290	134	192	1	1	2	1	
434	.16	.54	.25	.26	215	289	134	192	5	11	5	12	
435	.32	0.00	.23	0.00	214	291	134	192	13	0	17	0	
436	.54	.63	.27	.44	215	291	134	191	4	15	3	18	
437	.39	.19	-.01	.31	214	289	134	191	4	4	1	7	
438	.43	.34	.26	.13	214	289	134	192	26	27	25	30	
439	.19	.38	.20	.17	214	289	134	192	10	10	12	13	
440	.17	.22	.05	.12	214	287	134	191	25	22	27	19	
441	.26	.47	.08	.31	213	286	133	191	44	48	43	47	
442	.14	.19	.00	.12	211	286	134	190	22	21	23	18	
443	.35	.57	.55	.66	212	287	134	191	9	8	13	8	
444	.27	.26	.15	.45	214	289	132	191	17	13	16	14	
445	-.02	.29	.03	.05	214	285	133	190	16	8	18	5	
446	.26	.47	.28	.28	215	287	134	191	64	76	66	78	
447	.38	.50	.32	.47	214	288	134	191	30	33	41	36	
448	.16	.21	-.03	-.01	215	289	134	192	3	2	3	1	
449	.70	-.00	-.01	0.00	215	287	134	191	3	1	1	0	
450	.13	.26	.33	-.02	213	287	134	192	7	5	7	2	
451	.20	.31	.22	.40	214	288	132	192	83	86	81	83	
452	.36	.33	.23	.59	213	288	134	191	21	18	17	17	
453	.50	.58	.40	.43	214	288	134	192	80	84	84	87	
454	.11	.13	.11	.13	213	284	133	188	67	76	70	74	
455	.17	.20	.19	.26	213	289	134	192	4	6	3	4	
456	.29	.36	.09	.02	212	289	134	190	29	89	28	91	
457	-.02	-.02	-.01	-.02	213	288	133	192	2	2	2	2	
458	.32	.13	-.00	-.03	214	289	134	191	1	4	0	3	
459	.06	.30	.11	.13	214	287	134	191	5	7	5	8	
460	.22	.28	.23	.25	214	286	134	191	20	26	27	31	

TWIN DATA (CONT.)

| VAR. | INTRACLASS R | | | | PAIRS | | | | MEAN OR PERCENT | | | | SD |
| NO. | IM | IF | FM | FF | IM | IF | FM | FF | IM | IF | FM | FF | WG |

SELF-RATINGS

461	.63	.65	.50	.59	206	284	130	188	2.34	2.06	2.28	2.18	1.21
462	.40	.46	.13	.30	205	281	130	190	2.36	2.35	2.57	2.45	.84
463	.41	.34	.12	.27	204	282	130	190	1.89	1.72	1.97	1.88	.95
464	.24	.41	-.00	.37	204	281	132	189	2.50	2.49	2.61	2.66	1.29
465	.29	.29	.19	.13	203	283	131	191	2.07	1.89	2.12	2.05	.87
466	.28	.48	.15	.13	205	285	132	190	2.04	1.82	2.13	1.98	.89
467	.22	.21	.33	.08	205	286	131	191	1.64	1.60	1.74	1.56	.77
468	.33	.26	.15	.18	204	283	132	191	1.81	1.84	1.89	1.90	.91
469	.18	.23	.10	.22	204	280	131	189	2.34	2.32	2.50	2.46	1.19
470	.20	.37	.00	-.01	203	282	131	190	4.56	4.35	4.44	4.19	1.84
471	.37	.22	.22	.16	205	285	132	191	1.73	1.64	1.83	1.69	.75
472	.23	.26	.08	.12	202	283	132	188	4.92	4.77	4.72	4.79	1.63
473	.12	.16	-.05	.05	202	278	132	191	3.27	3.32	3.24	3.25	1.47
474	.33	.29	-.11	.04	195	270	123	179	3.60	3.47	3.48	3.36	1.47
475	.20	.31	.05	.16	199	277	129	188	3.43	3.51	3.35	3.27	1.40
476	.34	.33	.03	-.01	205	286	132	192	3.33	3.00	3.29	3.11	1.70
477	.42	.30	.10	.19	205	285	132	192	2.36	2.36	2.42	2.37	1.21
478	.23	.36	-.05	.08	203	284	132	190	5.08	5.31	5.02	5.26	1.54
479	.16	.29	.05	-.07	200	281	131	188	4.91	4.94	4.75	4.76	1.74
480	.12	.18	-.02	-.04	198	276	125	187	4.04	3.80	3.96	3.72	1.59
481	.48	.48	.21	.27	206	285	132	191	2.26	1.99	2.21	2.12	1.35
482	.38	.35	.21	.25	204	281	131	184	3.40	3.28	3.50	3.47	1.49
483	.21	.32	.12	-.04	204	285	131	188	4.23	3.87	4.29	3.91	1.35
484	.36	.40	.42	.29	200	275	130	186	3.68	3.57	3.67	3.59	1.48
485	.11	.27	.09	-.03	194	279	129	186	5.34	5.53	5.24	5.28	1.38
486	.25	.21	.08	.16	202	285	132	191	2.56	3.11	2.73	3.02	1.48
487	.16	.13	-.10	.01	203	285	132	190	2.89	2.69	2.95	2.95	1.50
488	.28	.28	-.04	.09	201	283	130	189	2.38	2.34	2.36	2.41	.90
489	.37	.28	.11	.05	201	282	132	192	2.22	2.38	2.30	2.50	1.15
490	.21	.32	.15	.06	204	283	132	192	1.76	1.54	1.78	1.76	.78
491	.28	.29	.01	.10	204	286	131	191	2.52	2.71	2.65	2.80	1.20
492	.23	.37	.12	.09	205	284	132	191	2.46	2.66	2.61	2.77	1.15
493	.56	.56	.19	.28	205	285	132	192	2.36	2.30	2.41	2.38	1.01
494	.34	.20	-.00	.03	206	286	131	192	1.96	1.81	2.03	1.96	.74
495	.37	.43	-.03	.03	205	286	132	191	1.83	1.95	2.02	2.15	1.01
496	.39	.47	.08	.20	204	284	132	192	2.32	3.63	2.44	3.54	1.35
497	.27	.28	.12	.10	205	284	132	192	3.95	4.52	3.77	4.15	2.00
498	.43	.43	-.04	.21	204	286	131	190	3.03	3.54	3.04	3.36	1.58
499	.26	.32	.01	.11	206	284	132	190	1.86	1.86	1.90	1.92	.84
500	.25	.24	.12	.12	202	282	132	191	4.29	3.78	4.24	3.84	1.58
501	.23	.15	-.05	.01	204	285	131	192	4.08	3.81	4.06	4.24	1.99
502	.25	.38	.24	.15	204	283	132	190	1.78	5.16	1.75	6.03	.91
503	.26	.32	.00	.12	204	281	130	190	2.29	2.98	2.32	2.93	1.32
504	.16	.14	.04	.00	204	283	129	190	2.27	2.38	2.21	2.41	1.19

TWIN DATA (CONT.)

VAR.	INTRACLASS R				PAIRS				MEAN OR PERCENT				SD
NO.	IM	IF	FM	FF	IM	IF	FM	FF	IM	IF	FM	FF	NG
505	.32	.46	.14	-.01	203	284	129	188	4.17	4.27	4.11	4.30	1.59
506	.30	.42	.10	.23	204	285	132	192	3.59	3.97	3.56	3.89	1.48
507	.15	.37	.05	.09	205	285	132	191	4.08	4.22	4.04	4.29	1.85

IDEAL SELF

508	.55	.57	.29	.60	207	285	132	193	1.88	1.67	1.88	1.70	1.12
509	.30	.44	.05	.21	206	286	131	193	1.51	1.48	1.52	1.44	.53
510	.06	.44	-.10	.07	206	284	130	193	1.14	1.11	1.14	1.10	.40
511	.26	.42	-.05	.11	204	285	130	191	1.31	1.34	1.44	1.45	.76
512	.29	.19	.05	.18	205	286	130	189	1.30	1.11	1.24	1.14	.45
513	.23	.26	.05	.21	208	286	131	192	1.20	1.15	1.20	1.17	.50
514	.21	.15	.05	.04	208	286	132	191	1.13	1.13	1.14	1.15	.48
515	.35	.32	.20	.20	207	287	132	191	1.35	1.50	1.35	1.42	.73
516	.22	.34	.10	.29	203	281	130	187	1.90	1.83	2.11	1.83	1.08
517	.15	.20	.14	.16	205	285	131	190	5.73	5.04	5.78	5.94	1.45
518	.05	.24	-.01	.16	208	284	132	191	1.21	1.21	1.18	1.18	.55
519	.13	.24	.08	.02	205	285	131	192	6.31	6.37	6.38	6.34	1.05
520	.15	.22	.04	.09	205	283	129	190	3.31	3.67	3.36	3.67	1.13
521	.23	.21	.17	.04	196	266	124	179	3.03	2.87	3.04	2.73	1.32
522	.25	.23	-.00	.17	204	279	130	183	4.44	5.09	4.48	5.08	1.57
523	.26	.27	.05	.14	208	285	132	192	3.00	2.91	3.02	2.98	1.35
524	.15	.19	.13	.15	206	284	131	190	1.70	1.72	1.65	1.68	.92
525	.18	.29	.02	.08	206	287	131	192	6.38	5.61	6.40	6.63	.93
526	.08	.32	.13	.15	206	285	130	192	6.18	5.59	6.23	6.58	1.09
527	.07	.27	-.04	.05	202	280	127	188	5.18	5.64	5.19	5.43	1.37
528	.24	.34	.10	.16	207	288	130	190	1.49	1.39	1.46	1.44	.92
529	.38	.48	.25	.40	205	284	130	184	3.81	3.76	3.82	3.94	1.76
530	.22	.37	.14	.07	204	287	128	187	5.41	4.80	5.32	4.87	1.22
531	.29	.20	.43	.21	205	278	127	177	3.79	3.52	3.59	3.47	1.62
532	.14	.27	.11	.10	199	284	126	183	6.22	5.33	6.21	6.35	1.05
533	.05	.16	.09	-.07	207	287	131	190	1.36	1.36	1.37	1.40	.64
534	.11	.19	.25	.16	206	288	131	190	1.46	1.23	1.37	1.24	.63
535	.05	.24	.07	.08	206	287	131	191	1.20	1.32	1.24	1.32	.55
536	.03	.15	.00	.02	205	286	130	191	1.70	2.05	1.70	2.09	1.02
537	.32	.33	-.05	.10	206	288	130	190	1.17	1.10	1.17	1.15	.44
538	.09	.44	-.02	.29	206	288	131	190	1.50	1.47	1.45	1.54	.79
539	.20	.16	.17	.17	208	288	131	191	1.45	1.99	1.44	1.99	.90
540	.28	.39	.09	.14	208	287	131	192	1.42	1.43	1.39	1.49	.59
541	.19	.17	.19	.12	208	288	131	191	1.30	1.11	1.26	1.13	.51
542	.19	.10	.01	.03	207	288	130	192	1.31	1.37	1.27	1.36	.73
543	.21	.37	-.04	.23	206	287	131	191	1.66	3.92	1.57	3.90	1.53
544	.25	.23	.09	.13	205	287	131	192	4.39	4.87	4.28	4.67	1.88
545	.22	.23	.03	.12	204	281	130	188	1.90	2.13	1.81	2.19	1.23
546	.23	.26	-.04	.08	207	286	131	192	1.36	1.20	1.24	1.22	.53

TWIN DATA (CONT.)

VAR.	INTRACLASS R				PAIRS				MEAN OR PERCENT				SD
NO.	IM	IF	FM	FF	IM	IF	FM	FF	IM	IF	FM	FF	M3
547	.15	.19	.09	.10	206	286	130	191	6.22	5.20	6.34	6.18	1.21
548	-.01	.22	.23	.10	206	288	131	191	6.22	5.26	6.34	6.39	1.35
549	.13	.35	.08	.38	208	288	131	190	1.37	5.50	1.28	6.46	.81
550	.20	.26	.03	.02	208	287	130	189	1.30	1.45	1.29	1.48	.81
551	.16	.25	.17	.12	205	288	130	190	1.61	1.62	1.50	1.51	1.00
552	.09	.33	.05	.19	207	286	131	192	5.42	5.51	5.44	5.55	1.35
553	.36	.36	.13	.28	205	286	127	192	3.06	2.91	3.05	2.85	1.63
554	.08	.21	.07	-.05	205	286	129	191	4.10	4.64	4.13	4.63	1.71

PROBLEMS OF YOUNG PEOPLE

VAR.	IM	IF	FM	FF	IM	IF	FM	FF	IM	IF	FM	FF	SD
555	.23	.19	.18	.04	215	292	131	193	1.40	1.41	1.34	1.45	.59
556	.30	.31	.13	.18	214	290	132	195	2.25	2.04	2.24	2.03	.57
557	.14	.13	.13	.06	214	288	131	192	1.78	1.76	1.77	1.71	.55
558	.32	.11	.00	.04	215	291	131	194	1.52	1.52	1.57	1.46	.65
559	.32	.25	.18	.15	215	291	130	193	2.34	2.22	2.36	2.16	.57
560	.19	.12	-.02	.02	215	291	130	195	2.01	1.91	1.98	1.86	.55
561	.13	.18	.13	.05	212	286	129	192	2.09	2.00	2.07	1.98	.58
562	.22	.15	.18	.00	214	289	130	194	1.63	1.60	1.60	1.62	.67
563	.27	.18	.05	.18	215	291	130	195	2.36	2.14	2.27	2.17	.70
564	.15	.16	.05	.22	215	291	130	194	2.12	2.28	2.15	2.32	.65
565	.22	.25	.10	.23	215	291	130	195	1.51	1.44	1.50	1.43	.60
566	.27	.23	.29	.18	214	291	130	195	1.83	1.93	1.83	1.95	.75
567	.18	.27	.10	-.04	214	292	129	194	2.08	2.00	2.04	2.02	.65
568	.11	.31	.09	.16	215	292	130	195	1.55	1.49	1.49	1.52	.63
569	.24	.29	.13	.22	215	291	129	195	2.46	2.22	2.44	2.20	.70
570	.22	.24	.11	.04	215	292	129	195	2.11	2.13	2.12	2.15	.69
571	.18	.23	.03	.01	214	292	129	193	2.23	2.22	2.24	2.21	.72
572	.12	.28	.11	.05	215	291	129	195	2.48	2.43	2.49	2.46	.68
573	.14	.19	-.05	.10	215	288	128	193	2.26	2.10	2.16	2.16	.70
574	.15	.35	.23	.06	214	290	129	195	1.94	1.89	2.00	1.85	.69

ITEMS IN THE HOME

VAR.	IM	IF	FM	FF	IM	IF	FM	FF	IM	IF	FM	FF	
575	.43	.39	-.03	.14	215	292	132	194	94	94	97	95	
576	.75	.68	.71	.56	215	290	132	193	61	60	66	69	
577	.64	.74	.62	.71	214	288	132	192	41	39	48	43	
578	.75	.75	.73	.82	215	291	132	193	62	70	67	72	
579	.41	.54	.32	.36	214	289	132	192	57	65	57	71	
580	.26	.54	-.03	.42	215	292	132	193	97	92	97	92	
581	.90	.86	.91	.94	215	291	132	194	84	92	90	96	
582	.26	.43	.31	.21	215	291	132	193	87	90	88	94	
583	.65	.74	.68	.95	213	288	129	194	4	4	11	6	

TWIN DATA (CONT.)

VAR. NO.	INTRACLASS R				PAIRS				MEAN OR PERCENT				SD NG
	IM	IF	FM	FF	IM	IF	FM	FF	IM	IF	FM	FF	
584	.83	.75	.62	.83	215	292	130	194	82	71	83	68	
585	.63	.68	.47	.70	213	291	132	194	50	55	57	47	
586	.74	.75	.73	.79	214	291	132	194	73	72	76	65	
587	.41	.65	.58	.49	215	292	132	192	24	25	29	25	
588	.33	.36	.34	.42	215	291	132	193	41	41	44	41	
589	.42	.65	.51	.63	214	290	131	192	19	29	23	28	
590	.84	.86	.75	.91	215	292	132	193	11	14	11	9	
591	.82	.49	.79	.66	215	292	132	193	4	5	4	2	
592	.44	.69	.55	.64	215	292	132	194	74	80	77	84	
593	.95	.98	.95	.97	214	291	132	194	59	64	56	51	
594	.65	.83	.72	.86	211	284	130	190	24	31	29	31	
595	.68	.78	.67	.80	215	292	131	194	21	12	23	13	
596	.67	.77	.59	.86	215	291	131	192	21	21	21	21	
597	.52	.59	.49	.52	215	291	131	192	23	12	25	12	
598	.53	.62	.77	.59	214	292	130	194	13	6	18	3	
599	.50	.57	.27	.42	214	291	131	194	9	7	9	5	
600	.93	.93	.93	.93	214	292	131	194	32	23	33	20	
601	.94	.90	.88	.89	214	292	131	194	44	40	49	42	
602	.66	.58	.39	.65	213	290	131	193	11	9	13	9	
603	.82	.80	.65	.70	214	292	131	194	88	92	95	96	
604	.74	.81	.85	.75	214	292	131	194	87	87	89	82	
605	.47	.46	.43	.47	214	289	131	193	40	36	48	38	
606	.43	.43	.34	.37	214	291	131	190	76	78	81	84	
607	.58	.66	.52	.76	214	290	131	194	48	52	56	59	
608	.58	.58	.61	.71	213	288	131	193	64	66	71	64	
609	.41	.67	.45	.67	214	291	131	191	50	55	62	58	
610	.68	.61	.88	.64	214	290	131	194	15	13	19	11	
611	.85	.77	.84	.87	212	292	131	194	62	51	70	49	
612	.69	.68	.71	.76	213	290	131	193	32	33	30	32	
613	.59	.61	.58	.67	214	287	131	191	59	61	58	58	
614	.86	.85	.95	.93	214	292	131	194	68	63	69	61	
615	1.00	.91	.92	.92	215	292	131	194	99	98	95	97	

ADJECTIVE CHECKLIST

VAR. NO.	INTRACLASS R				PAIRS				MEAN OR PERCENT				SD NG
616	.18	.10	.04	.02	216	293	135	195	13	18	16	17	
617	.19	.26	-.03	.29	216	293	135	195	66	71	69	70	
618	.20	.24	-.05	.06	216	293	135	195	41	21	42	25	
619	.02	.32	.19	.10	216	293	135	195	72	68	73	68	
620	.39	.29	.06	-.04	216	293	135	195	6	7	6	9	
621	.25	.23	-.02	.18	216	293	135	195	67	67	67	64	
622	.21	.23	.04	.22	216	293	135	195	39	47	41	45	
623	.22	.07	.20	.28	216	293	135	195	5	6	6	5	
624	.19	.28	.11	.07	216	293	135	195	34	28	41	34	
625	.42	.39	.03	-.02	216	293	135	195	23	30	21	31	

TWIN DATA (CONT.)

| VAR. | INTRACLASS R | | | | PAIRS | | | | MEAN OR PERCENT | | | | SD |
NO.	IM	IF	FM	FF	IM	IF	FM	FF	IM	IF	FM	FF	WG
626	.07	.27	.12	.15	216	293	135	195	15	13	20	12	
627	.24	.40	.17	.37	216	293	135	195	34	51	32	50	
628	.10	.05	.09	.07	216	293	135	195	13	6	18	7	
629	.12	.30	.12	.22	216	293	135	195	31	24	33	26	
630	.04	.24	-.12	.10	216	293	135	195	62	53	60	50	
631	.20	.26	.05	.01	216	293	135	195	74	79	76	79	
632	.24	.16	.06	.04	216	293	135	195	35	31	33	37	
633	-.01	.10	.05	-.03	216	293	135	195	7	8	7	8	
634	.10	.24	-.06	.03	216	293	135	195	58	60	61	57	
635	.14	.35	.17	.03	216	293	135	195	65	77	69	76	
636	.12	.20	.04	.09	216	293	135	195	68	54	67	54	
637	.22	.24	.03	.10	216	293	135	195	37	26	36	23	
638	.16	.22	.12	.28	216	293	135	195	14	19	17	21	
639	.08	.14	-.05	.19	216	293	135	195	53	39	49	40	
640	.19	.27	.09	.09	216	293	135	195	22	23	21	24	
641	.15	.28	-.05	.13	216	293	135	195	10	22	11	20	
642	.25	.33	.29	.11	216	293	135	195	57	62	63	68	
643	.12	.27	-.07	.22	216	293	135	195	16	17	20	21	
644	.06	.20	-.04	.10	216	293	135	195	73	76	71	76	
645	.19	.36	.23	.28	216	293	135	195	28	32	31	37	
646	.25	.22	.15	.19	216	293	135	195	57	67	65	70	
647	.17	.18	.04	.01	216	293	135	195	8	8	13	9	
648	.19	.19	-.09	.04	216	293	135	195	25	29	30	28	
649	.17	.23	.13	.22	216	293	135	195	16	14	24	13	
650	.29	.21	.13	.18	216	293	135	195	81	84	79	84	
651	.13	.13	.05	-.01	216	293	135	195	17	24	15	21	
652	.15	.28	.04	.09	216	293	135	195	68	73	74	68	
653	.32	.12	-.01	-.04	216	293	135	195	7	10	9	9	
654	.07	.23	.11	.05	216	293	135	195	17	23	25	19	
655	.10	.18	-.01	.04	216	293	135	195	8	7	9	5	
656	.01	.13	.01	.13	216	293	135	195	13	12	21	15	
657	.13	.03	-.04	.06	216	293	135	195	5	5	4	5	
658	.15	.26	-.08	.07	216	293	135	195	53	47	53	49	
659	.08	.20	.05	.27	216	293	135	195	52	56	53	55	
660	.15	.27	-.04	.13	216	293	135	195	10	5	11	6	
661	.16	.27	.02	.11	216	293	135	195	30	47	28	48	
662	.21	.39	-.01	.01	216	293	135	195	59	57	64	57	
663	.20	.17	.02	.12	216	293	135	195	48	65	53	64	
664	.23	.16	.14	.11	216	293	135	195	27	45	31	46	
665	.12	.28	-.07	.05	216	293	135	195	7	19	6	14	
666	-.02	.41	-.01	.24	216	293	135	195	2	64	1	61	
667	.13	.03	.05	-.07	216	293	135	195	27	11	26	14	
668	.09	.23	.05	.15	216	293	135	195	22	28	26	24	
669	.20	.27	-.04	.26	216	293	135	195	53	45	51	52	
670	.19	.22	.13	-.02	216	293	135	195	82	88	86	89	
671	.30	.25	.07	.03	216	293	135	195	51	56	49	53	
672	.25	.38	.02	.26	216	293	135	195	45	42	40	41	

TWIN DATA (CONT.)

VAR. NO.	INTRACLASS R				PAIRS				MEAN OR PERCENT				SD NG
	IM	IF	FM	FF	IM	IF	FM	FF	IM	IF	FM	FF	
673	.13	.17	.03	.12	216	293	135	195	68	71	73	67	
674	.06	.25	.13	.17	216	293	135	195	61	72	68	71	
675	.02	.26	-.01	.01	216	293	135	195	6	16	15	16	
676	.09	.23	.31	-.00	216	293	135	195	81	85	84	87	
677	-.03	.08	-.03	.11	216	293	135	195	3	3	3	4	
678	.19	.19	.09	.14	216	293	135	195	63	57	65	58	
679	.16	.24	.01	.38	216	293	135	195	29	29	31	30	
680	.24	.37	.22	.27	216	293	135	195	45	45	44	46	
681	.04	.42	.00	.31	216	293	135	195	5	14	9	11	
682	.02	.18	.11	.11	216	293	135	195	19	26	27	30	
683	.07	.26	.08	.04	216	293	135	195	12	24	21	22	
684	.08	.21	.02	.02	216	293	135	195	44	41	50	46	
685	.16	.36	-.05	.22	216	293	135	195	43	36	49	38	
686	.25	.34	.16	.20	216	293	135	195	20	9	24	11	
687	.37	.35	.27	.16	216	293	135	195	10	11	11	12	
688	.23	.30	-.05	.15	216	293	135	195	9	5	12	11	
689	.24	.46	-.05	.27	216	293	135	195	76	69	73	68	
690	-.04	-.03	-.04	-.03	216	293	135	195	3	3	4	3	
691	-.03	.18	.08	.10	216	293	135	195	8	13	14	14	
692	.14	.36	.15	.20	216	293	135	195	26	32	31	32	
693	.24	.15	.13	.05	216	293	135	195	73	80	73	78	
694	.16	.24	-.12	.14	216	293	135	195	9	14	11	13	
695	.08	.19	.07	-.02	216	293	135	195	28	32	31	34	
696	.23	.27	.19	.24	216	293	135	195	63	53	66	57	
697	.13	.23	-.03	.03	216	293	135	195	59	66	66	69	
698	.27	-.02	-.03	-.02	216	293	135	195	2	2	3	2	
699	.25	.29	.09	.15	216	293	135	195	53	64	58	65	
700	.08	-.01	.07	-.03	216	293	135	195	60	1	64	3	
701	.10	.30	.06	.25	216	293	135	195	57	49	61	51	
702	.12	.19	.04	-.11	216	293	135	195	6	10	7	10	
703	.09	.14	-.04	.11	216	293	135	195	6	8	10	8	
704	.17	.17	.01	.19	216	293	135	195	18	13	21	19	
705	.09	.12	.07	.14	216	293	135	195	32	32	33	31	
706	.07	.28	.04	.10	216	293	135	195	19	26	21	26	
707	.14	.25	.07	.12	216	293	135	195	46	58	45	55	
708	.20	.18	-.03	.00	216	293	135	195	25	34	30	36	
709	-.04	.15	-.08	.25	216	293	135	195	4	18	7	17	
710	.03	.38	-.05	.15	216	293	135	195	17	37	21	34	
711	.17	.24	.14	.17	216	293	135	195	24	27	31	25	
712	.20	.35	.05	.17	216	293	135	195	20	21	19	24	
713	.27	.25	.02	.05	216	293	135	195	36	29	36	32	
714	.28	.27	-.01	.07	216	293	135	195	30	34	28	37	
715	.27	.14	.19	.03	216	293	135	195	18	14	22	15	
716	-.01	.24	.02	.00	216	293	135	195	49	54	50	51	
717	.14	.31	.11	.03	216	293	135	195	42	40	50	40	
718	.17	.22	.10	.18	216	293	135	195	60	69	58	68	
719	.20	.32	-.03	.11	216	293	135	195	9	10	13	8	

TWIN DATA (CONT.)

VAR. NO.	INTRACLASS R IM	IF	FM	FF	PAIRS IM	IF	FM	FF	MEAN OR PERCENT IM	IF	FM	FF	SD WG
720	.14	.32	-.09	.14	216	293	135	195	53	60	61	57	
721	.10	.25	-.01	-.03	216	293	135	195	10	13	15	12	
722	.05	.24	.15	.12	216	293	135	195	15	15	17	14	
723	.13	.23	-.03	-.05	216	293	135	195	34	39	37	37	
724	.18	.26	.07	.18	216	293	135	195	49	48	50	44	
725	.11	.20	.01	-.01	216	293	135	195	63	69	65	63	
726	.13	.31	-.02	.10	216	293	135	195	12	13	18	14	
727	-.03	-.03	.11	-.04	216	293	135	195	3	3	5	4	
728	.16	.06	.03	.01	216	293	135	195	32	30	37	34	
729	.14	.27	.15	.09	216	293	135	195	68	69	69	73	
730	.05	.29	-.08	.07	216	293	135	195	5	10	8	7	
731	.20	.24	.03	-.03	216	293	135	195	34	38	37	36	
732	.16	.36	.09	.23	216	293	135	195	34	26	41	26	
733	.20	.21	.20	.17	216	293	135	195	60	67	69	70	
734	.13	.16	.13	.02	216	293	135	195	18	21	24	21	
735	-.03	.23	-.02	.20	216	293	135	195	3	3	2	2	
736	.22	.45	.01	.20	216	293	135	195	17	21	27	21	
737	.13	.19	-.11	.08	216	293	135	195	9	7	10	9	
738	.22	.20	-.04	.15	216	293	135	195	36	29	40	28	
739	.26	.29	-.03	-.01	216	293	135	195	36	60	37	57	
740	.10	.14	-.11	-.00	216	293	135	195	64	60	62	61	
741	.19	.08	.04	-.03	216	293	135	195	11	5	13	3	
742	.26	.31	.13	-.01	216	293	135	195	24	33	27	32	
743	.19	.22	-.00	.12	216	293	135	195	62	76	64	77	
744	.13	.10	-.08	-.04	216	293	135	195	5	8	7	9	
745	-.02	.33	.23	.20	215	293	135	195	2	6	3	2	
746	.30	.34	.10	.12	216	293	135	195	49	59	51	61	
747	.24	.21	-.12	-.01	216	293	135	195	10	10	10	11	
748	.32	.29	.04	.11	216	293	135	195	42	42	49	40	
749	.12	.19	-.00	.12	216	293	135	195	30	36	34	38	
750	.15	.20	-.07	.05	216	293	135	195	7	9	7	8	
751	.08	.27	.01	.30	215	293	135	195	21	23	27	17	
752	.09	.30	.08	-.08	216	293	135	195	10	14	18	11	
753	.15	.21	.15	.17	216	293	135	195	36	38	39	37	
754	.26	.29	-.02	-.01	216	293	135	195	36	48	36	48	
755	.10	.16	-.07	.07	216	293	135	195	18	23	18	28	
756	-.01	.22	.03	-.05	216	293	135	195	10	19	14	17	
757	.20	.25	.01	.19	216	293	135	195	31	31	37	31	
758	.22	.16	.09	.10	216	293	135	195	70	75	69	74	
759	.24	.25	-.09	.10	216	293	135	195	11	18	13	14	
760	-.03	.22	.25	-.03	216	293	135	195	3	5	5	3	
761	.15	.12	.06	.15	216	293	135	195	5	9	10	7	
762	.23	.38	-.04	.20	216	293	135	195	8	6	14	6	
763	-.01	-.02	-.01	-.01	216	293	135	195	1	2	1	1	
764	.01	.07	.03	.02	216	293	135	195	9	7	16	6	
765	.31	.27	.05	-.09	215	293	135	195	6	6	10	8	
766	.28	.30	.22	.29	216	293	135	195	47	42	55	39	

TWIN DATA (CONT.)

VAR. NO.	INTRACLASS R				PAIRS				MEAN OR PERCENT				SD
	IM	IF	FM	FF	IM	IF	FM	FF	IM	IF	FM	FF	NG
767	.26	.30	.15	.16	216	293	135	195	44	57	43	55	
768	.17	.30	.15	.23	216	293	135	195	57	56	59	59	
769	.24	.19	.23	.17	216	293	135	195	60	64	66	66	
770	-.01	.14	-.03	-.04	216	293	135	195	1	4	3	4	
771	.23	.28	.13	.30	216	293	135	195	35	47	34	47	
772	.13	.27	-.08	.08	216	293	135	195	9	7	13	9	
773	.23	.38	.01	-.08	216	293	135	195	35	30	39	33	
774	.19	.30	-.10	.11	216	293	135	195	16	32	27	33	

HEALTH

VAR. NO.	INTRACLASS R				PAIRS				MEAN OR PERCENT				SD
775	.48	.32	.23	.20	210	289	132	190	2.32	2.18	2.22	2.17	1.11
776	-.00	.11	-.04	.18	213	289	131	194	1.10	1.12	1.17	1.09	.44
777	.24	.25	.27	.35	212	290	133	191	2.00	2.19	2.03	2.25	.85
778	.33	.22	.12	.12	212	291	133	194	1.97	1.95	2.01	1.92	.38
779	.16	.39	.24	.09	190	281	125	182	2.73	2.56	2.73	2.55	.50
780	.32	.48	-.03	.22	196	283	127	183	2.72	2.71	2.75	2.72	.57
781	.26	.36	.19	.17	192	281	126	185	2.84	2.90	2.79	2.97	.35
782	.17	.22	-.04	.09	200	280	125	184	2.73	2.91	2.73	2.89	.38
783	0.00	-.00	0.00	-.00	195	281	126	184	3.00	3.00	3.00	3.00	.05
784	-.03	-.02	-.03	.11	196	279	126	183	2.97	2.98	2.97	2.97	.17
785	.18	.33	.04	.06	196	284	127	184	2.78	2.54	2.69	2.53	.55
786	.30	.25	.04	-.00	207	286	130	192	2.20	1.99	2.19	1.99	.51
787	.21	.17	-.05	.21	195	278	127	185	2.85	2.74	2.81	2.76	.45
788	.35	.09	-.03	.15	197	280	125	183	2.93	2.97	2.96	2.96	.24
789	-.01	.10	-.03	-.02	197	280	125	184	2.99	2.97	2.97	2.96	.18
790	.29	.21	.14	.17	199	283	128	186	2.51	2.32	2.47	2.28	.59
791	.16	.28	.09	.18	191	275	119	179	2.77	2.76	2.80	2.75	.45
792	.17	.40	.09	.26	203	281	129	186	2.47	2.41	2.39	2.41	.51
793	.47	.59	.22	.25	196	284	125	184	2.77	2.79	2.82	2.80	.51
794	0.00	-.02	-.02	-.02	195	283	126	184	3.00	2.98	2.97	2.98	.14
795	-.03	.45	.17	-.03	196	281	126	184	2.97	2.94	2.94	2.96	.24
796	.35	.18	.38	.12	198	283	126	184	2.87	2.81	2.88	2.85	.38
797	.19	.40	.21	.35	199	280	129	185	2.73	2.62	2.74	2.57	.51
798	.26	.37	.26	.27	199	284	126	185	2.70	2.67	2.69	2.69	.48
799	.28	.32	.35	.16	199	282	126	187	2.60	2.38	2.58	2.43	.55
800	.22	.28	.09	.13	199	281	126	185	2.70	2.60	2.69	2.56	.51
801	.12	.18	-.04	.09	197	281	125	184	2.79	2.80	2.80	2.72	.45
802	.18	.21	.26	.22	201	279	128	183	2.60	2.65	2.59	2.53	.52
803	.19	.24	.17	.16	196	280	127	184	2.63	2.58	2.64	2.56	.54
804	-.01	.29	-.00	.19	185	279	117	181	2.99	2.63	3.00	2.72	.45
805	.21	.29	.03	.16	201	277	124	183	2.56	2.60	2.58	2.61	.52
806	.52	.56	.15	.30	201	280	131	182	2.30	2.56	2.31	2.53	.53
807	.06	.25	.02	.19	200	281	128	181	2.54	2.58	2.55	2.59	.54
808	.22	.17	.01	.24	207	287	128	189	2.22	2.05	2.21	2.08	.43

TWIN DATA (CONT.)

VAR.	INTRACLASS R				PAIRS				MEAN OR PERCENT				SD
NO.	IM	IF	FM	FF	IM	IF	FM	FF	IM	IF	FM	FF	MG
809	.35	.27	.14	.21	207	275	127	187	1.88	1.89	1.83	1.91	.33

ITEMS IN ROOM

810	.11	.08	.42	.38	216	293	135	195	3	3	3	3	
811	.35	.54	.40	.28	216	293	135	195	14	15	16	15	
812	.67	.68	.49	.64	216	293	135	195	35	40	34	34	
813	.51	.41	.20	.51	216	293	135	195	6	11	6	12	
814	.55	.51	.62	.42	216	293	135	195	20	5	16	6	
815	.31	.55	.23	.32	216	293	135	195	3	4	3	2	
816	.50	.59	.25	.44	216	293	135	195	20	17	19	17	
817	.31	.33	.08	.32	216	293	135	195	8	1	9	2	
818	.58	.65	.33	.64	216	293	135	195	40	40	33	40	
819	.47	.41	.25	.49	216	293	135	195	26	27	21	20	
820	.43	.51	.20	.24	216	293	135	195	17	16	16	14	
821	.52	.50	.34	.43	216	293	135	195	59	55	53	52	
822	.60	.49	.35	.43	216	293	135	195	9	8	6	11	
823	.50	.52	.35	.51	216	293	135	195	35	50	37	48	
824	.52	.45	.20	.51	216	293	135	195	34	56	33	55	
825	.41	.47	.25	.24	216	293	135	195	6	8	5	8	
826	.63	.24	.21	.38	216	293	135	195	12	8	12	7	
827	.44	.41	.39	.40	216	293	135	195	26	17	24	15	
828	.39	.66	.65	-.00	216	293	135	195	1	1	1	0	
829	.42	.42	.45	.53	216	293	135	195	11	7	7	6	
830	.45	.53	.47	.47	216	293	135	195	31	11	29	12	
831	.51	.27	.12	.23	216	293	135	195	23	9	23	7	
832	.29	.34	.08	.17	216	293	135	195	17	24	20	23	

INTERPERSONAL RELATIONS

833	.29	.37	.30	.31	213	292	133	194	1.42	1.66	1.44	1.71	.63
834	.46	.44	.23	.26	211	290	133	194	1.62	1.41	1.79	1.47	.55
835	.54	.45	.12	.39	212	284	132	192	1.58	1.57	1.63	1.66	.73
836	.48	.52	.07	.33	199	277	126	181	1.59	1.67	1.62	1.70	.75
837	.27	.43	.12	.31	209	286	132	194	1.54	1.45	1.63	1.53	.60
838	.20	.45	.20	.17	206	284	130	188	1.55	1.45	1.60	1.52	.55

VOCATIONAL PREFERENCE INVENTORY

839	.21	.41	-.02	.30	212	293	132	194	66	39	70	39	
840	.36	.35	.22	.27	210	293	131	193	51	44	52	51	

TWIN DATA (CONT.)

VAR. NO.	INTRACLASS R				PAIRS				MEAN OR PERCENT				SD NG
	IM	IF	FM	FF	TM	IF	FM	FF	IM	IF	FM	FF	
841	.26	.31	.35	.11	209	291	131	193	5	27	6	26	
842	.41	.35	.11	.30	213	293	131	193	52	45	53	54	
843	.43	.39	.15	.20	210	293	131	193	11	15	10	12	
844	.16	.02	.07	-.04	210	292	132	193	8	5	6	4	
845	.47	.14	.07	.15	210	292	130	193	49	17	47	20	
846	.36	.33	-.09	.09	213	292	132	194	45	50	49	48	
847	.29	.22	.04	.27	211	292	131	194	48	60	48	59	
848	.35	.41	.21	.28	211	292	127	194	54	34	48	31	
849	.26	.14	-.03	.05	211	293	132	193	35	9	34	8	
850	.23	.14	.17	.24	208	291	131	193	32	26	35	24	
851	.20	.31	.23	.20	211	293	132	194	29	58	33	57	
852	.25	.34	.17	.23	212	292	131	193	17	26	15	25	
853	.05	.33	.09	.07	210	291	131	193	24	14	23	13	
854	.28	.35	.00	.18	213	292	131	193	21	38	21	37	
855	.31	.41	.04	.29	212	292	130	194	58	47	58	45	
856	.19	.31	.15	.27	210	292	131	193	31	39	30	35	
857	-.04	.38	-.03	.22	213	292	130	193	4	56	3	53	
858	.27	.33	.04	.11	210	291	131	191	58	49	60	51	
859	.35	.34	.30	.09	210	291	131	194	46	25	50	24	
860	.44	.26	.18	.24	211	292	131	191	45	44	39	41	
861	.37	.29	.10	.23	213	291	131	194	59	62	49	62	
862	.13	.25	.05	.04	209	290	129	191	19	9	23	8	
863	.34	.31	.17	.22	209	291	131	194	29	38	28	40	
864	.29	.36	.29	.17	211	292	131	193	19	24	20	23	
865	.17	.09	-.04	-.06	211	292	131	193	16	5	23	5	
866	.23	.20	.11	.08	211	290	131	192	26	30	28	28	
867	.19	.28	.14	.25	211	291	131	193	18	62	15	60	
868	.26	.18	.14	.12	211	291	131	193	35	34	29	35	
869	.21	-.05	-.06	.18	208	291	131	193	14	4	15	3	
870	.28	.31	.27	.14	210	289	131	193	45	35	41	35	
871	.34	.22	.09	.00	211	292	132	192	38	64	37	63	
872	.14	.21	.07	.02	209	291	131	193	12	7	12	6	
873	.19	.26	.18	-.05	209	291	131	193	17	6	18	5	
874	.44	.36	.28	.16	211	291	129	193	32	44	36	46	
875	.23	.09	-.09	-.02	211	291	131	193	14	5	13	2	
876	.22	.31	.05	.38	209	291	130	193	48	45	50	44	
877	.23	.31	.13	.21	209	289	131	192	54	28	53	28	
878	.15	.16	-.10	-.03	210	291	131	193	16	4	17	3	
879	.15	.06	.16	.18	209	291	131	193	9	4	7	3	
880	.25	.19	.13	.16	208	289	131	193	51	24	56	19	
881	.22	.29	.07	.16	209	290	131	193	14	53	10	54	
882	.30	-.12	-.09	.10	209	290	131	192	12	7	14	4	
883	.07	.15	.15	.23	210	291	130	193	25	18	24	13	
884	.32	.40	.19	.14	210	291	130	194	40	56	33	54	
885	.30	.23	.16	.07	209	291	131	194	22	14	19	10	
886	.34	.18	.19	.06	210	290	131	193	47	19	38	12	
887	.31	.39	.04	.11	210	292	131	194	28	75	22	76	

TWIN DATA (CONT.)

VAR. NO.	INTRACLASS R				PAIRS				MEAN OR PERCENT				SD
	IM	IF	FM	FF	IM	IF	FM	FF	IM	IF	FM	FF	MS
888	.41	.45	.20	.21	210	292	131	194	36	53	31	51	
889	.32	.12	.04	-.02	210	293	131	194	15	2	16	2	
890	.22	.33	.12	.17	208	292	131	191	36	32	33	31	
891	.09	.35	.15	.16	209	293	131	194	18	53	21	56	
892	.16	.18	.09	.08	210	292	131	193	23	16	26	21	
893	.33	.26	.25	.05	212	293	131	194	36	32	28	30	
894	.23	.32	.07	.14	211	293	131	194	26	45	26	44	
895	.28	.31	.09	.15	208	293	131	195	21	20	18	23	
896	.33	.32	.10	.23	209	293	130	193	43	45	43	47	
897	.25	.37	.01	.30	209	293	131	194	20	37	15	38	
898	.26	.24	.10	.22	210	293	131	193	36	7	34	10	
899	.31	.25	.15	.07	210	293	131	195	35	13	35	10	
900	.27	.38	.17	.26	210	293	130	194	32	30	30	30	
901	.47	.43	.25	.32	211	292	131	194	40	50	34	48	
902	.25	.27	-.04	.09	210	293	131	194	6	34	3	31	
903	.33	.31	.05	.21	210	293	131	194	28	27	24	23	
904	.30	.40	.09	.19	210	291	131	194	33	38	27	37	
905	.24	.26	.17	.12	212	293	131	195	32	23	29	19	
906	.22	.35	.09	.27	210	293	131	194	49	44	52	42	
907	.34	.37	.15	.16	211	292	132	194	56	32	53	31	
908	.26	.18	.12	.17	210	292	131	193	22	8	25	7	
909	.20	.16	.04	.14	209	293	131	193	19	6	22	3	
910	.36	.32	.10	.21	209	293	131	195	56	39	51	38	
911	.28	.35	.05	.28	210	293	131	195	18	45	13	42	
912	.21	.17	.15	.22	210	293	131	194	19	24	16	23	
913	.27	.31	.15	.16	209	293	130	194	54	32	46	27	
914	.35	.28	.47	.33	209	293	131	194	16	30	18	27	
915	.23	.37	.19	.25	211	293	131	195	16	18	13	18	
916	.17	.29	.13	.11	210	293	131	194	14	22	13	20	
917	.36	.15	.20	.08	210	293	131	194	45	19	37	11	
918	.30	.27	.33	.01	209	293	131	194	35	20	30	19	
919	.30	.26	.15	.01	209	293	131	194	30	17	33	15	
920	.41	.37	.11	.20	207	292	131	193	50	39	48	33	
921	.24	.38	.29	.36	209	293	131	193	30	47	30	47	
922	.14	.03	-.07	-.05	209	293	131	193	17	7	18	5	
923	.16	.29	.22	.18	209	293	131	194	8	18	8	16	
924	.05	.25	.10	.21	210	293	131	194	15	34	14	34	
925	.32	.16	.01	.16	209	292	131	194	24	10	26	15	
926	.28	.29	.01	.09	209	293	131	194	23	20	23	19	
927	.37	.18	.05	.25	209	293	131	194	34	11	31	13	
928	.26	.21	.03	.06	210	292	131	194	6	8	7	5	
929	.37	.15	.14	.16	209	289	129	193	15	5	10	3	
930	.31	.15	.13	.09	209	293	131	195	32	16	24	16	
931	.17	.26	.02	.11	209	293	131	193	29	37	24	32	
932	.09	.04	.10	.03	209	292	131	194	13	7	14	6	
933	.31	.25	-.15	.20	210	293	132	194	29	31	30	26	
934	.38	.28	.03	.25	209	293	131	193	15	33	15	31	

TWIN DATA (CONT.)

VAR. NO.	INTRACLASS R				PAIRS				MEAN OR PERCENT				SO NG
	IM	IF	FM	FF	IM	IF	FM	FF	IM	IF	FM	FF	
935	.22	.05	.05	.05	209	293	131	195	23	6	29	5	
936	.14	.29	-.07	.07	210	293	131	194	23	35	29	40	
937	.29	.30	.15	.27	211	293	131	195	27	48	25	44	
938	.29	.09	.14	-.05	211	293	131	194	21	12	20	10	
939	.19	.26	.13	.01	209	293	131	195	12	12	13	10	
940	.11	.22	.10	.03	206	293	131	194	20	15	16	11	
941	-.01	.28	.07	.20	209	293	129	195	12	37	15	34	
942	.31	.36	.14	.19	208	293	131	195	45	35	42	42	
943	.16	.11	.05	-.06	208	292	131	194	10	8	7	6	
944	.29	.40	.10	.29	207	292	131	194	14	30	11	30	
945	.39	.30	.19	.32	210	292	131	195	60	47	60	53	
946	.21	.28	.01	.11	208	291	131	194	41	35	44	32	
947	.18	.26	.27	.12	206	292	131	193	18	4	19	3	
948	.30	.33	.15	.25	211	292	131	195	59	50	51	48	
949	.22	.07	.15	.10	208	292	131	194	19	5	21	4	
950	.29	.29	.19	.27	209	292	130	195	33	29	30	26	
951	.17	.15	.09	.24	209	292	131	194	19	19	14	16	
952	.17	.06	.09	-.09	208	292	131	194	20	8	20	8	
953	.31	.19	.06	.24	210	292	131	194	15	8	13	4	
954	.32	.29	.27	.35	209	292	131	192	22	34	20	34	
955	.37	.43	.05	.18	210	293	131	195	43	42	47	38	
956	.28	.24	.24	.07	209	293	131	194	33	22	32	19	
957	.24	.33	-.00	.18	209	292	131	194	18	43	15	42	
958	.28	.03	.04	.17	209	293	130	194	21	4	26	5	
959	.19	.19	-.04	.31	209	293	130	193	17	7	21	7	
960	.28	.29	.10	.20	209	293	128	192	28	31	27	29	
961	.28	.29	.19	.15	211	293	129	194	26	58	23	54	
962	.17	.16	.15	-.07	209	293	130	194	15	8	16	6	
963	.19	.18	.07	.08	210	292	129	192	17	13	21	11	
964	.28	.27	.21	.14	210	293	129	193	18	35	18	33	
965	.30	.40	.10	.14	209	293	131	193	54	46	58	43	
966	.44	.30	.11	.20	209	293	130	194	41	30	41	29	
967	.34	.23	.20	.09	209	291	130	193	27	11	36	11	
968	.32	.24	.23	.16	210	292	130	194	39	29	38	29	
969	-.00	.11	.01	.07	210	290	130	191	12	14	12	12	
970	.42	.30	.10	.19	210	293	130	194	54	40	46	36	
971	.25	.28	.09	.12	210	293	130	194	27	58	25	60	
972	.10	.36	.03	.24	210	292	130	194	10	13	7	13	
973	.36	.33	.15	.31	210	292	130	193	34	14	28	15	
974	.38	.24	.04	.32	209	293	130	194	26	36	20	35	
975	.27	.27	.15	.28	210	293	131	194	56	31	56	27	
976	.30	.38	.14	.24	209	291	130	195	47	41	49	42	
977	-.03	.36	-.03	.21	210	293	130	194	3	50	3	48	
978	.39	.26	.15	.35	208	293	130	194	22	4	24	4	
979	.30	.02	.07	.15	209	293	130	195	36	9	36	9	
980	.42	.28	.30	.14	208	292	130	194	46	31	46	33	
981	.30	.22	.12	.10	210	293	130	194	18	44	15	40	

TWIN DATA (CONT.)

VAR.	INTRACLASS R				PAIRS				MEAN OR PERCENT				SD
NO.	IM	IF	FM	FF	IM	IF	FM	FF	IM	IF	FM	FF	NO
982	.17	.16	.24	.04	207	293	130	192	22	8	20	6	
983	.33	.27	.12	.26	208	293	129	194	17	15	17	11	
984	.20	.30	-.14	.16	208	291	130	194	29	41	29	34	
985	.24	.33	.09	.20	210	293	131	195	40	14	42	19	
986	.12	.21	-.06	.05	208	293	131	195	15	20	15	19	
987	.28	.31	.15	.11	209	293	131	194	21	65	21	61	
988	.21	.05	-.00	.28	208	293	130	194	10	4	9	3	
989	.40	.21	-.07	.05	204	292	130	193	6	5	6	5	
990	.31	.27	.14	.20	211	292	131	192	52	31	49	27	
991	.31	.24	.12	.25	209	293	130	193	46	41	49	38	
992	.11	.29	-.00	.08	208	293	130	193	10	7	9	7	
993	.11	.41	.16	.21	208	293	131	194	37	49	41	47	
994	.09	.04	.28	.16	209	292	130	193	9	7	7	7	
995	.34	.22	.13	.02	208	293	130	194	8	6	8	6	
996	.23	-.02	-.03	-.01	209	293	130	193	2	2	3	1	
997	.17	.15	-.05	-.01	209	293	130	194	5	14	5	11	
998	-.04	.17	-.03	.26	209	290	128	189	4	8	3	5	

HONORS

VAR.	INTRACLASS R				PAIRS				MEAN OR PERCENT				SD
NO.	IM	IF	FM	FF	IM	IF	FM	FF	IM	IF	FM	FF	NO
999	.32	.22	.12	.18	216	293	135	195	9	4	8	3	
1000	.34	.27	.42	.15	216	293	135	195	25	13	25	12	
1001	.37	.46	.04	.20	216	293	135	195	10	4	7	2	
1002	-.00	-.00	0.00	-.00	216	293	135	195	0	0	0	0	
1003	-.01	-.00	-.00	0.00	215	293	135	195	1	0	0	0	
1004	.21	.17	.19	-.02	216	293	135	195	12	2	18	2	
1005	.49	.43	.22	.30	216	293	135	195	24	16	24	14	
1006	.56	.39	-.02	0.00	215	293	135	195	3	1	2	0	
1007	-.01	0.00	0.00	-.00	216	293	135	195	1	0	0	0	
1008	.16	-.01	-.03	.49	216	293	135	195	3	1	3	2	
1009	.38	.44	.42	.80	216	293	135	195	3	2	3	1	
1010	.39	.39	.14	.12	216	293	135	195	6	4	7	3	
1011	.33	.25	.29	.18	216	293	135	195	8	3	9	5	
1012	-.00	-.00	-.00	0.00	216	293	135	195	0	1	0	0	
1013	.27	.19	.72	.48	216	293	135	195	2	2	4	3	
1014	.16	.24	-.03	.22	216	293	135	195	3	1	3	4	
1015	.41	.47	.11	.10	216	293	135	195	6	5	8	6	
1016	.41	.39	.38	.08	216	293	135	195	12	11	18	11	
1017	.35	.43	.48	.26	216	293	135	195	21	29	27	33	
1018	.49	.31	.23	.48	216	293	135	195	3	7	3	3	
1019	.79	.36	-.02	.26	216	293	135	195	2	4	2	5	
1020	.41	.51	.14	.56	216	293	135	195	10	9	7	6	
1021	.44	.48	.30	.33	216	293	135	195	22	35	28	37	
1022	.10	.48	-.05	.48	216	293	135	195	3	4	4	3	
1023	.33	.42	.14	.19	216	293	135	195	9	7	14	6	

TWIN DATA (CONT.)

VAR.	INTRACLASS R				PAIRS				MEAN OR PERCENT				SD
NO.	IM	IF	FM	FF	IM	IF	FM	FF	IM	IF	FM	FF	N3
1024	.39	.57	.32	-.01	216	293	135	195	2	1	2	1	
1025	.17	.27	.10	.29	216	293	135	195	4	2	5	6	
1026	-.01	.24	.39	0.00	216	293	135	195	1	1	2	0	
1027	.32	.44	.23	-.01	216	293	135	195	1	2	3	1	
1028	.71	.65	.57	.50	216	293	135	195	23	23	28	26	
1029	.57	.65	.50	.64	216	293	135	195	28	31	36	35	
1030	.47	.33	.31	-.01	216	293	135	195	6	1	6	1	
1031	.38	-.00	.25	-.00	216	293	135	195	3	0	5	0	
1032	.39	.50	.27	-.01	216	293	135	195	1	1	3	1	
1033	.55	.56	.47	.48	216	293	135	195	7	9	16	12	
1034	.41	.14	.22	.32	216	293	135	195	3	4	8	8	
1035	.52	.62	.07	.50	216	293	135	195	3	5	6	5	
1036	.45	.53	.30	.28	216	293	135	195	5	6	4	5	
1037	.35	-.01	.27	.49	216	293	135	195	3	1	5	1	
1038	-.01	-.01	0.00	.32	216	293	135	195	1	1	0	2	
1039	-.01	.33	-.01	.16	216	293	135	195	1	3	1	3	
1040	-.03	.46	-.05	.21	216	293	135	195	3	5	4	6	
1041	.23	.32	.05	.23	216	293	135	195	5	10	7	11	
1042	-.00	.33	-.00	-.00	216	293	135	195	0	1	0	0	
1043	-.00	-.01	-.01	-.02	216	293	135	195	0	1	1	2	
1044	-.02	.54	-.01	.12	216	293	135	195	2	2	1	3	
1045	-.02	.27	-.02	-.03	216	293	135	195	2	3	2	3	
1046	-.02	.25	.23	.32	216	293	135	195	2	3	3	2	
1047	.19	.34	.08	.27	216	293	135	195	4	9	6	9	
1048	.17	.17	.10	.37	216	293	135	195	4	5	5	5	
1049	.43	.47	.15	.40	216	293	135	195	20	25	19	27	
1050	.32	.33	.14	.40	216	293	135	195	16	23	21	21	
1051	.39	.39	-.01	.27	216	293	135	195	1	2	1	2	
1052	.26	.22	.17	.12	216	293	135	195	6	5	7	6	

THE TWINSHIP

VAR.	INTRACLASS R				PAIRS				MEAN OR PERCENT				SD
1053	.21	.39	.36	.43	214	288	133	192	1.99	2.03	2.02	2.01	.48
1054	.74	.83	.82	.87	212	291	131	192	1.95	1.96	1.94	1.95	.81
1055	.33	.57	.49	.58	213	290	132	193	1.96	2.04	1.98	1.99	.82
1056	.41	.49	.59	.63	212	287	133	188	2.02	2.04	1.98	2.00	.70
1057	.39	.53	.58	.68	211	290	132	192	2.05	1.90	1.96	2.05	.74
1058	.57	.57	.65	.73	214	288	132	192	1.96	1.95	1.96	1.98	.71
1059	.40	.65	.55	.57	214	291	132	193	2.02	1.99	2.11	2.05	.87
1060	.29	.38	.35	.57	212	290	132	190	2.02	2.03	2.14	2.04	.82
1061	.68	.75	.69	.78	210	285	133	191	2.02	2.01	1.89	2.08	.71
1062	.65	.59	.65	.74	214	288	130	191	1.98	1.98	1.95	1.99	.53
1063	.54	.44	.57	.55	213	291	133	192	1.98	1.97	1.99	1.94	.74
1064	.54	.64	.58	.68	213	291	133	192	2.00	2.01	2.00	2.01	.59
1065	.48	.38	.51	.53	211	290	132	193	2.00	1.99	1.97	1.92	.68

TWIN DATA (CONT.)

VAR. NO.	INTRACLASS R				PAIRS				MEAN OR PERCENT				SD WG
	IM	IF	FM	FF	IM	IF	FM	FF	IM	IF	FM	FF	
1066	.29	.54	.60	.57	211	290	132	192	1.99	1.99	2.10	1.99	.71
1067	.59	.48	.38	.36	212	289	132	191	2.03	2.00	2.07	1.96	.52
1068	.55	.55	.74	.68	214	290	132	193	1.95	1.95	2.04	2.00	.75
1069	.21	.51	.31	.36	214	290	130	189	2.01	2.01	2.07	1.97	.41
1070	.26	.39	.29	.34	205	282	126	181	2.02	2.01	2.04	2.03	.41
1071	.15	.36	.31	.30	214	287	133	188	1.99	2.02	2.05	2.03	.56
1072	.11	.33	.26	.41	214	287	132	188	2.00	2.00	2.04	2.03	.55
1073	.06	.23	.10	.34	212	290	133	191	1.98	1.98	1.97	2.00	.52
1074	.47	.28	.45	.52	213	290	133	192	1.99	2.04	1.96	1.98	.57
1075	.21	.46	.45	.45	212	290	133	193	2.06	1.96	1.94	1.99	.84
1076	.60	.64	.63	.68	213	290	133	189	1.99	2.04	1.94	1.96	.79
1077	.25	.48	.42	.63	213	291	133	193	2.01	2.00	1.97	2.03	.62
1078	.60	.62	.38	.70	212	290	132	193	1.54	1.37	1.83	1.55	.68
1079	.52	.59	.44	.59	213	291	132	191	2.08	1.96	2.36	2.16	.84
1080	.62	.64	.47	.61	211	288	131	185	1.95	1.83	2.26	2.01	.79
1081	.59	.60	.52	.45	209	284	132	189	2.33	2.35	2.51	2.57	.68
1082	.44	.45	.26	.40	212	285	128	192	2.23	2.16	2.47	2.40	.65
1083	.14	.41	.18	.32	212	290	132	191	2.59	2.44	2.70	2.63	.59
1084	.53	.61	.49	.55	212	291	133	192	2.22	2.30	2.23	2.20	.58
1085	.81	.89	.72	.89	215	293	133	194	3.29	2.98	3.74	3.43	.92
1086	.51	.64	.37	.62	215	292	131	195	1.83	1.73	2.21	2.06	.68
1087	.97	1.00	.98	1.00	215	293	133	195	1.90	1.91	2.09	1.95	1.00
1088	.82	.87	.82	.91	211	290	132	195	3.48	3.11	3.97	3.49	1.51
1089	.74	.64	.64	.74	214	292	131	194	2.40	1.88	2.95	2.34	1.08
1090	.51	.63	.33	.42	214	290	133	193	2.23	1.92	2.23	1.95	1.15
1091	.57	.61	.39	.60	214	292	133	194	2.30	2.24	2.67	2.61	.83

TIME TO DO BOOKLET

VAR. NO.	INTRACLASS R				PAIRS				MEAN OR PERCENT				SD WG
1092	.64	.70	.45	.62	204	267	128	187	103.97	109.37	109.32	108.83	46.55

CALIFORNIA PSYCHOLOGICAL INVENTORY

VAR. NO.	INTRACLASS R				PAIRS				MEAN OR PERCENT				SD WG
1093	.24	.36	.07	.29	201	288	124	193	78	85	74	85	
1094	-.02	.21	-.01	-.02	202	288	124	193	2	2	1	2	
1095	.51	.59	.32	.45	198	285	124	192	52	55	48	63	
1096	.32	.35	.05	.13	202	286	124	192	59	53	61	59	
1097	.08	.23	.01	.16	202	287	124	193	23	26	25	28	
1098	.04	.29	.19	.19	202	287	124	192	92	76	91	74	
1099	.18	.26	.14	.22	202	288	124	193	25	33	23	32	
1100	.30	.35	-.00	.20	200	286	122	190	51	73	48	73	
1101	.18	.09	.79	.20	202	288	124	193	6	7	6	8	
1102	.06	.03	-.05	-.05	202	287	124	193	93	93	95	95	

TWIN DATA (CONT.)

VAR. NO.	INTRACLASS R				PAIRS				MEAN OR PERCENT				SD NS
	IM	IF	FM	FF	IM	IF	FM	FF	IM	IF	FM	FF	
1103	.11	.17	.04	.13	202	287	124	192	15	25	21	19	
1104	.02	.28	.05	.15	197	283	123	190	9	10	10	12	
1105	-.00	.28	.05	.24	202	287	124	192	26	29	28	28	
1106	.07	.42	.03	.14	202	288	124	192	26	26	24	19	
1107	.36	.33	.03	.14	202	288	124	193	8	11	11	11	
1108	.20	.38	-.03	.14	202	288	124	193	6	3	3	3	
1109	.22	.25	.18	.16	201	288	124	193	16	19	14	19	
1110	.18	.18	.15	.24	202	287	124	193	69	69	70	70	
1111	.23	.15	.24	.03	202	288	124	193	31	5	35	9	
1112	.31	.29	.23	.11	202	288	124	192	26	25	27	22	
1113	.25	.22	.32	.33	201	288	124	193	72	73	72	77	
1114	.17	.18	-.00	.16	201	288	124	191	86	86	82	87	
1115	.39	.37	.08	.20	202	285	124	193	38	49	33	48	
1116	.15	.18	-.03	.09	202	288	124	192	76	78	73	78	
1117	.17	.25	.01	.18	202	284	124	193	48	50	53	53	
1118	.46	.31	.15	.12	199	288	124	191	27	20	28	16	
1119	.34	.19	.07	.01	201	288	124	192	17	16	17	14	
1120	.03	.40	.19	.17	202	288	124	193	6	49	4	49	
1121	.13	.11	.13	.05	200	288	124	192	20	14	19	20	
1122	.16	.26	.13	.15	202	288	124	193	66	91	68	91	
1123	.32	.33	-.04	.16	201	285	124	192	24	36	24	35	
1124	.19	.28	.23	.21	201	288	123	193	41	42	35	42	
1125	.33	.30	.08	.17	202	287	124	191	12	33	12	30	
1126	.10	.21	-.04	.12	201	287	123	193	90	89	89	85	
1127	.29	.24	.39	.16	202	287	124	193	35	62	35	66	
1128	.32	.39	-.04	.23	202	289	124	193	1	1	4	2	
1129	.28	.29	.14	.05	201	285	124	192	42	43	42	40	
1130	.23	.38	.05	.09	202	288	124	192	41	41	42	39	
1131	.29	.32	.17	.26	202	287	124	193	52	38	55	41	
1132	.22	.28	.14	.05	202	287	123	193	43	60	45	62	
1133	.21	.20	-.00	.18	202	288	124	192	47	46	53	41	
1134	.15	.23	-.05	.02	202	288	124	193	70	68	74	68	
1135	.36	.22	.17	.18	202	287	124	193	19	17	18	13	
1136	.26	.26	.17	.26	202	287	124	193	46	44	55	48	
1137	.20	.37	.23	.23	202	287	124	193	72	71	67	68	
1138	.33	.35	-.02	.20	202	288	124	193	54	64	49	62	
1139	.27	.32	.45	.48	202	288	124	193	23	27	21	27	
1140	.28	.27	.15	.29	201	287	124	193	57	54	55	49	
1141	.26	.26	.14	.12	201	287	124	192	29	14	22	13	
1142	.37	.08	.28	.13	202	288	123	193	95	90	91	87	
1143	.18	.29	.23	-.04	202	287	124	192	85	85	82	91	
1144	.27	.41	.29	.30	202	287	124	193	45	49	48	52	
1145	.22	.32	.11	.21	202	287	124	193	70	53	70	53	
1146	.20	.23	.15	.03	202	287	124	192	12	12	20	15	
1147	.37	.38	.21	.37	202	288	124	193	61	72	64	72	
1148	.11	.20	-.12	.05	202	288	124	193	68	67	67	72	
1149	.23	.26	.11	.16	202	286	124	193	44	47	50	52	

TWIN DATA (CONT.)

VAR.	INTRACLASS R				PAIRS				MEAN OR PERCENT				SD
NO.	IM	IF	FM	FF	IM	IF	FM	FF	IM	IF	FM	FF	NG
1150	.24	.24	.04	.22	202	287	123	192	50	65	57	68	
1151	.16	.20	.13	.09	202	287	124	193	65	62	62	68	
1152	.30	.31	.08	.21	201	288	124	193	43	33	44	29	
1153	.21	.20	.02	.07	202	288	123	193	90	93	92	90	
1154	.25	.30	.05	.16	198	284	123	192	60	68	61	62	
1155	.11	.31	-.01	.10	201	288	124	192	42	41	45	34	
1156	.08	.24	.17	.30	202	288	124	193	4	14	4	15	
1157	.15	.31	.08	.19	202	287	124	192	16	35	10	33	
1158	.40	.36	.04	.31	201	288	124	193	87	77	89	82	
1159	.58	.61	.53	.60	201	286	124	191	47	43	46	42	
1160	.33	.36	.15	.38	201	288	124	193	17	64	18	55	
1161	.27	.29	.37	.22	202	288	124	192	73	83	74	96	
1162	.35	.22	.11	.15	202	288	124	193	38	44	42	46	
1163	.17	.29	.05	.05	202	288	124	193	21	45	27	45	
1164	.50	.59	.30	.44	202	288	124	193	8	57	7	60	
1165	.33	.32	.12	.25	202	288	124	192	18	13	16	10	
1166	.26	.16	.03	.18	202	288	124	193	41	40	42	41	
1167	.12	.11	-.07	-.06	201	288	124	192	13	8	6	6	
1168	.17	.23	.23	.11	202	284	124	193	23	29	22	30	
1169	.26	.30	-.02	.11	202	288	124	193	55	60	67	63	
1170	.22	.32	-.02	.17	202	288	124	191	64	61	63	69	
1171	.48	.60	.48	.45	202	288	124	193	20	27	15	35	
1172	.27	.28	.13	.08	202	288	124	193	88	89	92	91	
1173	.13	.12	.21	.02	202	288	124	193	40	43	49	48	
1174	.47	.30	.15	.24	202	288	124	193	25	5	28	7	
1175	.36	.35	.28	.33	202	287	124	193	31	29	34	26	
1176	.23	.27	.15	.28	202	288	124	193	68	75	68	74	
1177	.15	.31	.19	.08	202	288	123	192	41	44	48	43	
1178	.21	.17	.03	.12	201	297	124	191	49	50	52	49	
1179	.34	.28	.10	.21	201	286	124	190	79	26	80	23	
1180	.16	.19	.20	.22	202	287	124	192	74	86	83	90	
1181	.18	.13	-.05	.17	202	287	124	192	6	6	5	7	
1182	.18	.07	-.02	-.03	202	288	124	192	2	3	2	3	
1183	.10	.29	.06	.16	202	288	124	193	61	54	66	52	
1184	.24	.15	.28	.14	202	288	124	193	28	34	31	33	
1185	.05	.23	.17	.05	202	287	124	193	5	6	4	5	
1186	.23	.19	.24	.22	202	288	124	193	8	8	8	8	
1187	.38	.21	.00	.07	202	288	124	193	72	64	69	63	
1188	.20	.25	-.00	.22	202	287	124	193	80	89	82	90	
1189	.28	.39	.07	.33	202	288	124	193	38	45	38	37	
1190	.18	.28	.02	.24	202	288	123	192	50	50	48	56	
1191	.22	.15	-.04	.08	202	288	124	193	20	18	22	18	
1192	.30	.45	.17	.37	201	288	124	193	71	37	77	43	
1193	.16	.26	.14	.16	202	288	124	192	39	36	42	37	
1194	.26	.39	.11	.26	200	288	124	191	35	41	44	40	
1195	.44	.47	.22	.32	202	288	124	193	31	38	35	40	
1196	.29	.40	.10	.23	202	288	124	193	70	66	67	68	

TWIN DATA (CONT.)

VAR.	INTRACLASS R				PAIRS				MEAN OR PERCENT				SD
NO.	IM	IF	FM	FF	TM	IF	FM	FF	IM	IF	FM	FF	NS
1197	.20	.31	.21	.18	202	287	124	193	29	30	34	37	
1198	.26	.30	.20	.06	201	287	124	192	52	50	54	51	
1199	.15	.11	.10	.06	201	287	124	192	74	75	75	75	
1200	.26	.25	.01	.13	202	288	124	193	67	54	65	51	
1201	.15	.25	.17	.04	202	288	124	193	70	78	73	80	
1202	.21	.25	.19	.18	202	287	124	193	55	78	56	76	
1203	.29	.32	.15	.11	202	287	124	193	37	36	41	35	
1204	.13	.18	.12	.31	202	288	123	193	72	81	76	82	
1205	.34	.37	.15	.43	202	288	124	192	20	16	16	14	
1206	.29	.19	.20	.06	202	288	124	192	41	17	46	19	
1207	.38	.19	.03	.19	201	288	124	193	40	52	33	50	
1208	.27	.04	.15	-.08	202	289	124	193	90	90	87	93	
1209	.37	.25	.17	.11	202	287	124	192	33	27	33	25	
1210	.29	.15	-.07	.05	202	286	123	192	92	92	93	95	
1211	.17	.28	.09	.28	202	288	124	193	22	25	22	24	
1212	.41	.40	.35	.38	201	287	124	192	68	67	73	72	
1213	.32	.30	-.10	.32	202	287	124	193	15	9	14	11	
1214	.48	.37	.32	.37	201	288	124	193	54	69	47	69	
1215	.09	.25	.19	.26	202	288	124	192	50	52	49	46	
1216	.23	.29	.14	-.03	202	287	124	193	40	36	46	35	
1217	.12	.07	.17	.12	201	288	124	193	86	81	81	77	
1218	.23	.39	.15	.22	202	288	124	193	80	57	80	60	
1219	.21	.15	.19	.12	202	288	124	193	72	80	70	74	
1220	.21	.27	.07	.09	199	288	124	192	44	37	44	41	
1221	.30	.26	.16	.12	202	288	124	193	49	17	53	22	
1222	.14	.29	.25	-.00	199	288	124	193	52	64	55	60	
1223	.35	.25	.13	.22	202	287	124	191	80	85	81	82	
1224	-.00	.07	.19	.01	202	288	123	192	17	17	15	17	
1225	.17	.24	.03	.16	202	288	121	191	75	70	71	70	
1226	.20	.25	.05	.11	201	287	123	193	44	52	46	54	
1227	.29	.31	.17	.20	202	288	124	193	49	54	46	59	
1228	.26	.31	-.05	.16	202	288	124	193	21	20	22	17	
1229	.38	.21	.19	.21	200	286	122	193	31	34	42	32	
1230	.09	.32	.09	.00	202	287	124	193	88	85	88	84	
1231	.27	.23	.18	.24	201	288	123	192	41	26	35	23	
1232	.21	.36	.11	.28	202	288	124	193	56	54	54	52	
1233	.30	.35	.00	.11	202	287	124	192	62	60	65	65	
1234	.18	.33	.23	.15	202	287	124	192	70	63	70	63	
1235	.27	.26	.00	.37	201	286	124	193	37	28	39	30	
1236	.19	.37	.23	.20	202	288	124	193	25	46	26	48	
1237	.10	.23	-.08	.04	200	287	124	192	19	24	19	28	
1238	.41	.31	.09	.15	202	288	124	193	61	78	68	78	
1239	.31	.27	.10	.13	202	288	124	193	52	65	56	57	
1240	.24	.17	.12	.24	199	282	122	190	57	30	61	24	
1241	.21	.26	.11	.10	201	287	124	192	51	49	50	47	
1242	.17	.16	.16	.15	201	287	124	193	62	76	66	77	
1243	.22	.17	.06	.20	201	287	123	193	31	30	33	33	

TWIN DATA (CONT.)

VAR.	INTRACLASS R				PAIRS				MEAN OR PERCENT				SD
NO.	IM	IF	FM	FF	IM	IF	FM	FF	IM	IF	FM	FF	NG
1244	.43	.52	.24	.36	202	288	124	193	69	81	74	75	
1245	.19	.18	-.11	.06	202	287	124	193	65	79	71	77	
1246	.41	.41	.22	.32	199	287	124	189	27	52	39	59	
1247	.20	.23	-.05	.26	202	286	124	192	39	34	42	34	
1248	.32	.26	.30	.09	202	288	124	193	21	13	20	11	
1249	.26	.24	.08	.07	201	287	124	192	15	10	19	8	
1250	.23	.23	.01	.09	200	288	124	193	12	16	15	19	
1251	.29	.28	.18	.15	202	287	124	193	46	49	44	52	
1252	.38	.42	.06	.30	201	288	124	193	36	50	33	52	
1253	.24	.17	.10	.17	202	288	124	193	46	62	51	69	
1254	.11	.06	.03	.04	202	286	124	192	90	91	89	95	
1255	.46	.43	.29	.20	202	289	123	193	82	87	76	88	
1256	.24	.29	.22	.28	202	288	124	193	13	12	15	15	
1257	.21	.26	-.04	.10	202	287	123	192	72	71	72	56	
1258	.33	.34	.08	.14	202	288	124	193	61	61	65	69	
1259	.29	.43	.19	.26	202	288	124	193	45	58	42	55	
1260	.41	.41	.23	.38	202	288	124	193	74	72	71	70	
1261	.52	.30	.11	.16	202	288	124	193	32	36	33	34	
1262	.15	.24	.13	.05	202	286	124	193	47	48	48	56	
1263	.42	.20	.28	.17	202	287	124	193	20	6	22	7	
1264	.45	.20	.21	.19	202	288	124	193	61	41	66	41	
1265	.12	.23	.11	.09	201	288	124	193	39	38	53	44	
1266	.12	.38	.05	.19	202	288	124	193	49	40	42	30	
1267	.23	.10	.21	.15	202	288	123	193	16	12	17	16	
1268	.22	.33	.18	.14	202	288	124	193	38	32	39	37	
1269	.27	.27	-.10	.15	202	287	124	192	24	33	22	34	
1270	.27	.17	-.00	.17	202	287	124	193	26	18	22	13	
1271	.37	.31	.11	.18	200	287	123	192	47	40	46	47	
1272	.23	.33	.16	.30	202	287	124	193	86	86	80	85	
1273	.50	.47	.19	.24	202	288	124	193	56	73	50	64	
1274	.20	.30	.09	.06	202	288	124	193	37	35	42	32	
1275	.08	.02	.18	.13	202	288	124	193	17	15	17	13	
1276	.29	.25	.11	.07	202	288	123	193	24	20	26	15	
1277	.22	.35	.10	.10	202	287	124	193	30	29	37	32	
1278	.12	.23	.05	.11	202	289	124	193	60	49	58	46	
1279	.23	.15	-.01	.00	202	287	124	193	39	53	42	55	
1280	.21	.31	.06	.13	201	287	123	192	42	34	41	35	
1281	.55	.21	.06	-.01	201	284	124	189	5	2	6	1	
1282	.38	.34	.14	.32	202	288	124	192	14	19	13	19	
1283	.20	.43	.14	.27	202	286	124	193	45	40	46	44	
1284	.24	.29	.03	.09	202	288	124	193	32	34	34	37	
1285	.30	.17	.15	.30	202	288	123	193	82	88	80	87	
1286	.27	.30	.05	.09	202	288	124	193	33	28	40	27	
1287	.24	.28	.18	.06	202	286	124	191	55	55	56	57	
1288	.43	.09	.09	.18	202	288	124	193	28	3	21	3	
1289	.23	.48	-.05	.29	202	287	124	193	93	82	95	89	
1290	.27	.24	.25	.04	202	288	124	191	68	66	73	66	

TWIN DATA (CONT.)

VAR.	INTRACLASS R				PAIRS				MEAN OR PERCENT				SD
NO.	IM	IF	FM	FF	IM	IF	FM	FF	IM	IF	FM	FF	NG
1291	.30	.26	.18	.15	202	288	123	193	41	12	34	9	
1292	.19	.14	.09	.08	202	288	124	193	78	73	81	72	
1293	.08	.44	.12	.28	202	288	124	193	19	16	16	20	
1294	.26	.36	.16	.19	202	283	123	189	67	49	68	48	
1295	.22	.21	.15	.13	201	288	124	192	67	69	65	75	
1296	.23	.34	.19	.00	201	288	124	193	38	44	35	38	
1297	.33	.41	.04	.04	202	288	124	193	25	15	19	15	
1298	.24	.20	.02	.20	202	288	123	192	28	20	17	18	
1299	.21	.22	.17	.30	198	284	124	189	28	29	27	28	
1300	.24	.42	.17	.22	202	287	124	193	53	50	54	52	
1301	.20	.31	.10	.12	202	287	124	193	40	34	38	34	
1302	.56	.38	.30	.34	202	288	124	193	48	13	46	15	
1303	.32	.28	.15	.13	202	285	124	193	57	48	58	47	
1304	.27	.29	.15	-.05	202	288	124	193	83	97	82	95	
1305	.22	.16	.18	.14	202	288	124	192	83	89	84	91	
1306	.54	.30	.12	.32	202	288	124	192	18	5	19	6	
1307	.21	.19	.31	.08	202	287	124	193	25	7	26	7	
1308	.19	.38	.10	.07	200	287	124	191	67	72	66	72	
1309	.16	.39	.01	.26	201	288	124	193	13	36	12	33	
1310	.46	.49	.48	.32	202	287	124	193	56	67	49	74	
1311	.24	.24	-.01	.16	202	288	123	193	36	26	34	34	
1312	.23	.39	.13	.10	202	288	124	193	16	6	15	12	
1313	.16	.15	.18	.24	201	285	124	192	88	89	88	95	
1314	.37	.42	.28	.32	202	288	124	192	46	51	45	53	
1315	.24	.39	.22	.32	201	287	124	192	44	52	45	49	
1316	.23	.12	-.05	.04	202	287	124	192	90	83	89	84	
1317	.17	.27	.15	.29	202	288	123	192	54	44	54	49	
1318	.20	.21	.02	.08	201	287	123	191	49	46	47	48	
1319	.31	.35	.10	.13	202	287	124	193	37	35	37	35	
1320	.30	.40	.24	.22	202	287	124	192	69	56	66	56	
1321	.30	.26	.11	.17	187	273	119	174	68	58	74	54	
1322	.36	.44	.30	.13	202	287	122	193	82	86	81	87	
1323	.29	.33	.15	.18	202	288	124	193	52	40	55	46	
1324	.27	.30	.19	.15	202	288	124	193	26	41	27	45	
1325	.09	.37	.09	.28	202	288	124	192	18	17	19	15	
1326	.35	.28	.11	.22	201	285	124	193	29	23	35	28	
1327	.20	.27	.10	.11	202	282	123	187	77	77	82	76	
1328	.24	.12	-.03	.06	202	288	124	193	19	20	17	22	
1329	.07	.27	.20	-.03	202	288	124	193	17	15	17	14	
1330	.23	.22	.08	.03	202	288	123	193	61	70	64	69	
1331	.31	.41	.08	.09	201	287	123	193	30	26	30	23	
1332	.10	.31	-.03	.07	202	288	124	193	6	39	3	41	
1333	.23	.35	.18	.24	202	288	123	193	54	56	53	58	
1334	.36	.38	.23	.13	200	286	122	193	59	64	60	63	
1335	.30	.16	.08	.12	202	288	124	193	35	38	37	40	
1336	.51	.33	.23	.24	202	288	124	193	20	43	18	42	
1337	.21	.38	.15	-.01	202	288	123	193	86	85	78	95	

TWIN DATA (CONT.)

VAR. NO.	INTRACLASS R				PAIRS				MEAN OR PERCENT				SD
	IM	IF	FM	FF	IM	IF	FM	FF	IM	IF	FM	FF	NS
1338	.23	.12	.25	.21	202	288	124	193	69	64	69	63	
1339	.23	.24	.15	.18	202	283	124	191	35	30	35	25	
1340	.23	.23	.01	.12	202	286	124	193	54	53	53	58	
1341	.42	.12	.15	-.06	202	288	123	193	42	6	46	5	
1342	.17	.26	.17	.14	202	286	124	193	35	29	37	34	
1343	.48	.35	.10	.20	202	288	124	193	41	35	38	38	
1344	.27	.21	.21	.19	202	288	124	193	37	43	40	51	
1345	.23	.31	-.05	.16	199	285	121	193	58	54	63	53	
1346	.16	.31	.17	.14	201	286	124	193	15	25	14	17	
1347	.34	.27	.28	.18	202	287	124	193	45	46	44	42	
1348	.15	.32	.15	.27	201	288	123	193	71	53	67	49	
1349	.31	.12	.04	.17	200	288	124	193	28	27	30	29	
1350	.15	.33	.23	.29	202	287	124	193	29	42	29	38	
1351	.07	.06	.22	.16	202	288	124	193	96	92	92	95	
1352	.12	.23	-.07	.30	202	288	122	192	82	84	79	81	
1353	.20	.11	-.01	.05	202	288	124	193	12	8	9	5	
1354	.12	.21	.29	.12	201	288	124	193	69	74	77	74	
1355	.30	.22	.19	.11	202	288	124	193	71	69	68	63	
1356	.30	-.00	.01	.02	202	288	124	193	76	85	85	87	
1357	.30	.40	.25	.31	202	288	124	193	33	57	35	57	
1358	.33	.17	.11	.37	201	288	124	193	44	28	38	28	
1359	.23	.23	-.11	.12	202	287	124	192	25	17	23	23	
1360	.40	.38	.05	.30	202	288	124	193	66	66	71	73	
1361	.43	.35	.17	.22	202	288	124	192	75	60	79	59	
1362	.25	.25	-.02	.06	202	288	124	193	20	24	19	27	
1363	.30	.43	.49	.27	202	288	124	191	20	21	24	20	
1364	.22	.36	.12	.13	199	288	124	193	35	55	35	60	
1365	.28	.15	.12	.03	202	287	124	193	22	28	24	28	
1366	.24	.14	-.00	.08	201	288	124	193	9	4	13	7	
1367	.27	.27	.18	.34	202	288	124	192	54	45	56	48	
1368	.28	.30	.11	.26	202	288	124	192	56	52	58	57	
1369	.49	.37	.33	.26	202	286	124	193	71	68	75	63	
1370	.42	.32	.25	.26	201	288	124	193	61	78	65	77	
1371	.19	.26	.19	.04	202	288	124	192	54	60	58	65	
1372	.13	.32	.20	.22	202	288	124	193	95	93	94	92	
1373	.19	-.01	.21	.15	201	288	124	193	13	9	13	7	
1374	.25	.20	.22	.14	201	286	122	193	65	66	68	69	
1375	.39	.40	.27	.19	202	288	124	193	67	50	67	47	
1376	.25	.22	-.02	.14	202	288	124	193	39	40	41	40	
1377	.17	.21	.06	.05	202	288	124	193	26	27	29	26	
1378	.29	.34	.20	.13	202	288	124	193	34	58	32	49	
1379	.38	.43	.23	.19	202	288	124	193	39	59	38	64	
1380	.26	-.01	.11	-.01	202	288	124	193	5	1	5	1	
1381	.17	.22	-.10	.08	202	287	124	193	71	84	72	83	
1382	.06	-.03	.12	.20	202	288	124	193	93	97	95	92	
1383	.33	.37	.13	.21	202	288	124	193	26	11	29	14	
1384	.29	.26	.10	.15	202	287	124	193	63	65	59	58	

TWIN DATA (CONT.)

VAR. NO.	INTRACLASS R				PAIRS				MEAN OR PERCENT				SD NS
	IM	IF	FM	FF	IM	IF	FM	FF	IM	IF	FM	FF	
1385	.23	.27	.27	.11	202	288	124	193	49	53	48	57	
1386	.29	.20	.16	.26	202	288	124	193	27	24	26	27	
1387	.15	.22	.14	.26	202	286	123	192	47	53	57	53	
1388	.38	.40	.15	-.02	202	288	124	193	35	34	31	33	
1389	.20	.21	.15	.11	202	288	124	192	20	21	27	26	
1390	.18	.27	.22	.04	202	288	124	193	31	37	35	40	
1391	.11	.03	.08	.05	202	288	124	193	6	7	6	5	
1392	.24	.28	.22	.15	202	287	123	193	28	28	25	28	
1393	.15	.38	.14	.18	202	288	124	193	9	32	10	32	
1394	.18	.23	.17	.32	202	288	123	193	25	18	27	24	
1395	.15	.22	.15	.10	201	286	124	191	43	42	43	46	
1396	.17	.20	.30	.39	202	286	124	192	84	83	86	88	
1397	.09	.24	.05	.02	202	288	124	193	83	86	87	89	
1398	.23	.09	-.05	.19	202	288	124	192	5	7	5	8	
1399	.26	.15	.15	.16	201	288	124	192	9	4	10	5	
1400	.17	.28	.17	.16	202	288	124	193	5	5	4	7	
1401	.20	.26	.09	.13	202	288	124	192	16	28	19	26	
1402	.25	.22	.04	.13	201	285	123	193	68	68	67	72	
1403	.16	.20	.17	.24	202	288	124	193	3	3	4	4	
1404	.11	.18	.30	-.03	202	287	124	193	94	97	93	97	
1405	.21	.08	-.01	-.06	202	287	124	193	80	83	81	80	
1406	.15	.13	.21	.17	202	287	124	193	63	65	60	63	
1407	.09	.24	.09	-.07	202	288	124	193	14	16	15	11	
1408	.09	.23	-.03	-.07	202	287	123	191	96	92	97	93	
1409	.03	.00	.15	.05	202	288	124	193	91	92	90	95	
1410	.14	.30	.05	.12	202	286	124	193	39	35	40	34	
1411	.35	.44	.24	.13	201	287	123	193	29	45	31	48	
1412	.31	.32	.11	.22	202	285	124	191	57	51	59	49	
1413	.05	.23	.05	.10	202	288	124	193	5	5	7	6	
1414	.16	.05	.08	-.03	202	288	124	193	95	96	94	97	
1415	.44	.47	.27	.12	201	287	124	193	87	94	85	90	
1416	.32	-.01	-.02	-.01	201	288	124	193	1	1	2	1	
1417	.12	.21	.04	.10	200	287	123	193	24	29	19	32	
1418	.11	.09	.10	-.02	201	288	124	193	90	90	86	92	
1419	.05	-.02	.02	-.06	201	288	124	193	12	7	12	6	
1420	.17	.22	.24	.31	200	284	123	193	65	61	60	63	
1421	.20	.22	.07	.05	202	287	124	192	58	56	59	60	
1422	.18	-.02	-.02	-.01	202	287	123	193	2	2	2	1	
1423	.23	.31	.19	.01	202	288	124	193	29	28	27	27	
1424	.12	.14	-.05	.12	201	288	124	193	6	4	6	3	
1425	.17	.01	.01	.09	202	288	124	192	92	95	92	96	
1426	.17	.22	.23	.17	201	288	124	192	52	67	57	70	
1427	.20	.20	.19	.18	202	288	124	192	53	64	58	66	
1428	.33	.36	.22	.39	202	288	124	193	55	53	60	59	
1429	.22	.25	-.04	-.01	201	288	124	193	4	5	4	8	
1430	.17	.18	.05	.05	202	288	124	193	10	5	10	5	
1431	.16	.15	.14	.20	202	288	124	193	5	4	4	4	

TWIN DATA (CONT.)

VAR. NO.	INTRACLASS R				PAIRS				MEAN OR PERCENT				SD
	IM	IF	FM	FF	IM	IF	FM	FF	IM	IF	FM	FF	NG
1432	.08	.17	.04	.07	202	287	124	193	29	28	27	30	
1433	.18	.32	.23	.19	200	287	124	193	20	19	18	22	
1434	.25	.05	.12	.09	202	288	124	193	93	92	92	93	
1435	.08	.29	.39	-.02	202	288	124	193	96	98	98	98	
1436	.24	.34	.15	.15	202	288	124	193	27	41	29	47	
1437	.08	.09	.10	-.08	202	288	123	193	11	5	9	8	
1438	.29	.27	-.01	.16	202	288	124	192	57	62	56	63	
1439	.11	.31	.14	.28	202	288	123	193	50	41	43	32	
1440	.19	.17	.12	.04	202	288	124	193	83	90	84	89	
1441	.14	-.01	-.05	-.03	202	288	124	193	3	1	4	3	
1442	.05	-.01	-.03	-.02	202	288	124	193	5	1	3	2	
1443	.22	.36	.12	.18	202	288	124	193	53	64	58	67	
1444	.26	.20	-.03	.04	202	288	124	193	6	7	7	6	
1445	.09	.19	.00	.01	202	288	123	193	12	10	13	12	
1446	.29	.30	.01	.07	201	287	124	193	60	61	63	62	
1447	.29	.39	.24	.12	202	288	124	193	37	26	35	21	
1448	.25	.34	.23	.05	202	288	124	193	50	59	55	54	
1449	.24	.28	.26	.24	202	288	124	192	49	45	52	40	
1450	.26	.18	.11	.27	202	287	124	193	41	39	41	40	
1451	.39	.42	-.01	.14	202	287	124	191	44	36	44	40	
1452	.14	.07	-.05	-.03	201	288	124	193	3	3	5	3	
1453	.14	.31	.05	.18	201	288	124	193	76	76	77	76	
1454	.30	.18	.08	.23	201	287	124	192	79	81	81	84	
1455	.13	.14	.29	-.03	200	287	124	192	32	41	37	44	
1456	.20	.28	.02	.18	201	287	123	193	27	18	28	23	
1457	.41	.12	-.01	-.03	202	288	124	193	3	2	1	3	
1458	.32	.16	-.05	.24	202	288	124	193	7	5	5	5	
1459	.40	.46	.18	.40	202	288	124	192	66	65	64	64	
1460	.25	.07	.13	-.04	201	287	124	191	88	93	89	91	
1461	.11	.17	.10	.16	202	288	121	192	23	17	20	17	
1462	.37	.45	.11	.15	202	286	124	192	27	31	23	34	
1463	.41	.31	.23	.21	202	288	123	193	82	86	79	87	
1464	.22	.16	.13	.07	202	288	124	193	9	15	15	18	
1465	.31	.39	.38	.02	201	288	124	192	82	72	79	78	
1466	.18	.15	-.05	-.02	202	288	124	193	6	2	5	2	
1467	.43	.27	.21	.15	202	285	123	190	56	42	56	44	
1468	.27	.08	.20	.07	202	288	123	192	52	54	47	59	
1469	.16	.19	.03	.21	201	287	124	191	49	49	53	48	
1470	.14	.12	.16	.22	202	288	124	193	9	10	7	8	
1471	.26	.22	.07	.09	202	287	124	193	36	50	38	42	
1472	.30	.37	.02	.15	201	284	123	192	76	77	74	73	
1473	.17	-.02	-.02	.09	202	288	124	193	5	2	2	4	
1474	.38	.29	.22	.21	202	288	124	193	74	70	76	72	
1475	.16	.30	.14	.14	202	288	124	193	26	36	25	36	
1476	.35	-.01	-.02	-.01	202	288	124	193	5	1	2	1	
1477	.12	.19	-.04	.26	202	288	123	192	13	21	11	18	
1478	.22	.26	.11	.18	202	288	124	193	49	52	53	54	

TWIN DATA (CONT.)

VAR.	INTRACLASS R				PAIRS				MEAN OR PERCENT				S)
NO.	IM	IF	FM	FF	IM	IF	FM	FF	IM	IF	FM	FF	NG
1479	.16	.22	.05	.05	202	288	124	193	64	70	67	69	
1480	.20	.15	.19	.10	200	285	123	192	53	51	59	58	
1481	.33	.16	.07	.24	202	285	124	193	61	60	55	52	
1482	.35	.16	.11	.03	202	288	123	193	10	5	9	6	
1483	.44	.40	.12	.07	202	288	124	192	37	51	35	49	
1484	.26	.25	.05	.09	202	287	123	193	56	48	51	49	
1485	.31	-.01	.06	.09	200	287	124	193	6	1	6	4	
1486	.28	.29	.17	.08	202	285	124	190	58	72	58	69	
1487	.27	.24	.25	.24	202	287	124	192	66	72	67	72	
1488	.26	.36	.23	.23	202	287	124	193	43	47	51	51	
1489	.23	.27	.08	-.02	202	288	124	193	47	43	51	53	
1490	.05	.34	.14	.31	202	288	124	193	5	4	4	3	
1491	.33	.35	.21	.25	202	287	124	191	43	34	51	31	
1492	.19	.27	.19	.21	202	287	124	193	56	59	52	52	
1493	.66	-.00	-.02	-.00	202	288	124	193	2	0	2	0	
1494	.19	-.02	.22	.07	202	288	123	193	4	2	3	5	
1495	.37	.36	.13	.03	202	286	122	191	32	26	38	27	
1496	.28	.21	.05	.15	202	286	124	193	41	39	41	42	
1497	.34	.33	.25	.19	200	286	123	190	19	17	17	21	
1498	.07	.10	.19	.05	202	287	124	192	9	8	15	10	
1499	.15	.10	-.05	.18	200	285	124	193	86	87	88	81	
1500	.25	.30	.15	.12	202	287	124	192	44	45	40	46	
1501	.20	.28	.16	.13	202	288	124	191	50	63	49	64	
1502	.22	.16	-.02	-.04	202	288	124	193	96	96	98	96	
1503	.02	.11	.08	.03	202	288	124	193	6	5	6	6	
1504	.31	.26	.05	.15	201	288	123	192	70	57	74	59	
1505	.04	.23	.05	.25	202	287	124	192	92	87	87	87	
1506	.22	-.03	-.04	-.03	202	288	124	193	96	97	96	97	
1507	.12	.18	.15	-.09	202	288	124	193	13	7	15	9	
1508	.24	.31	.14	.11	202	288	124	192	22	23	29	18	
1509	.29	.27	.04	.04	202	288	123	193	15	7	14	6	
1510	.24	.20	.19	.13	202	287	124	193	25	23	23	24	
1511	.14	.28	-.05	.11	201	288	124	192	16	18	18	17	
1512	.47	.36	.41	.40	202	288	124	193	32	16	36	16	
1513	.11	.22	-.03	.04	200	288	123	193	17	10	14	9	
1514	.27	.21	.31	.05	201	288	124	193	16	22	19	21	
1515	.09	.29	-.01	.43	201	287	124	191	4	3	1	2	
1516	.21	.18	.20	.10	201	285	123	191	46	76	42	72	
1517	.33	.19	.14	.11	201	288	124	192	28	30	25	34	
1518	.11	.15	-.08	.11	201	288	124	192	85	98	83	88	
1519	.24	.23	-.04	.05	201	287	124	193	91	88	89	86	
1520	.14	.39	.01	.31	201	287	124	192	17	20	17	16	
1521	.23	.39	.05	.18	201	288	124	192	30	48	34	50	
1522	.24	.37	.13	.30	201	288	124	193	12	17	17	18	
1523	.28	.25	.10	.10	201	288	124	193	10	3	12	4	
1524	.42	.13	.07	.17	199	288	124	193	83	84	85	86	
1525	.27	.11	.15	.14	199	288	124	193	76	86	82	85	

TWIN DATA (CONT.)

VAR. NO.	INTRACLASS R				PAIRS				MEAN OR PERCENT				SD
	IM	IF	FM	FF	IM	IF	FM	FF	IM	IF	FM	FF	
1526	.32	.13	.00	-.02	201	288	124	192	7	6	9	11	
1527	.43	.23	.15	.20	200	288	124	193	18	16	17	13	
1528	.45	.31	-.05	.12	201	288	124	193	6	6	11	8	
1529	.35	.27	-.01	.20	201	288	124	193	3	2	1	2	
1530	.21	.20	.20	.23	201	287	124	191	7	4	6	2	
1531	.37	.39	.20	.37	199	287	124	193	75	69	71	68	
1532	.19	.09	.17	.10	202	287	124	191	94	95	96	96	
1533	.29	.30	.15	.05	202	287	124	192	14	28	12	30	
1534	.20	.14	.15	-.02	202	285	124	192	68	66	67	73	
1535	.33	.27	.03	.04	201	285	123	191	67	87	65	91	
1536	.32	.27	.14	.20	201	287	124	192	14	15	17	15	
1537	.14	.06	-.02	.18	202	286	124	190	97	96	98	95	
1538	.06	.18	.04	.10	201	287	124	192	92	92	89	93	
1539	.21	.25	.07	.04	202	287	124	192	89	95	90	95	
1540	.33	.36	.08	.12	200	283	123	190	30	27	30	28	
1541	.49	-.02	-.01	-.01	202	287	124	192	2	2	1	1	
1542	.26	.36	-.05	.07	202	286	124	192	49	43	48	45	
1543	.28	.26	.19	.25	202	287	124	192	78	84	77	83	
1544	.27	.36	-.04	.05	202	288	124	190	43	54	42	56	
1545	.15	.26	.11	.11	202	289	124	191	12	16	16	14	
1546	-.02	.11	.12	-.03	202	289	124	192	2	5	5	3	
1547	.14	-.02	-.03	-.03	202	288	124	192	3	2	3	3	
1548	.18	.24	.05	.02	202	288	123	192	19	20	23	23	
1549	.12	.18	.22	-.04	202	288	124	192	6	5	6	4	
1550	.33	.20	.09	.13	202	288	124	192	51	57	52	62	
1551	-.05	.07	.22	-.06	201	288	124	192	4	6	6	6	
1552	.36	.27	.10	.17	201	287	124	192	30	30	30	22	
1553	.32	.33	.05	.10	200	287	124	192	21	25	20	26	
1554	.27	.21	.00	.20	200	287	124	192	21	22	18	26	
1555	.26	.22	.03	.14	201	288	124	192	40	34	47	42	
1556	-.00	.21	.15	.01	200	288	124	192	79	83	81	84	
1557	.29	.29	-.00	-.04	201	286	124	192	16	26	25	23	
1558	.34	.40	.24	.10	200	288	124	192	31	54	32	54	
1559	.28	.24	.27	.10	201	288	124	192	30	33	33	41	
1560	.20	.30	.25	.12	200	288	123	191	45	24	53	32	
1561	.19	.24	.16	.18	201	288	124	192	27	20	27	24	
1562	.19	.23	.17	.11	200	289	124	192	34	27	46	33	
1563	.21	.25	.08	.20	201	288	124	192	36	45	46	48	
1564	.18	.27	.02	.10	201	288	124	192	71	75	81	81	
1565	.47	.25	.02	.18	201	288	122	192	48	39	50	36	
1566	.39	.34	.08	.24	201	288	124	192	46	30	43	37	
1567	.27	.18	-.01	-.00	200	288	124	192	92	91	91	90	
1568	.33	.13	.35	.26	201	286	122	192	10	15	11	14	
1569	.25	.31	-.01	.03	201	287	124	192	13	24	13	28	
1570	.17	.26	.13	.13	200	285	124	191	47	49	50	46	
1571	.31	.41	.02	-.03	201	288	124	191	22	16	25	16	
1572	.29	.40	.34	.28	201	287	124	190	10	57	16	54	

TWIN DATA (CONT.)

VAR. NO.	INTRACLASS R				PAIRS				MEAN OR PERCENT				SD
	IM	IF	FM	FF	IM	IF	FM	FF	IM	IF	FM	FF	NG

CPI SCALES

1573	.57	.49	.13	.36	202	288	124	193	27.82	25.66	28.05	27.12	5.92
1574	.54	.59	.35	.54	202	288	124	193	18.27	18.57	18.37	18.69	3.97
1575	.52	.54	.24	.33	202	288	124	193	24.87	24.21	24.66	24.13	5.07
1576	.51	.55	.14	.31	202	288	124	193	34.81	32.89	34.50	33.00	5.51
1577	.42	.55	.14	.37	202	288	124	193	21.25	20.78	21.38	20.99	3.75
1578	.54	.45	.33	.27	202	288	124	193	36.28	35.83	35.84	35.29	4.55
1579	.57	.43	.29	.40	202	288	124	193	31.39	33.14	31.63	33.19	4.04
1580	.52	.55	.15	.48	202	288	124	193	39.50	41.29	38.91	40.98	4.92
1581	.56	.57	.27	.36	202	288	124	193	28.47	29.88	27.67	28.82	7.69
1582	.59	.47	.30	.39	202	288	124	193	22.24	22.65	22.36	22.74	4.80
1583	.49	.46	.32	.28	202	288	124	193	17.36	17.06	16.59	16.23	5.91
1584	.31	.42	.25	.12	202	288	124	193	25.97	25.47	26.02	26.48	1.81
1585	.48	.44	.06	.25	202	288	124	193	27.45	27.66	26.85	27.04	4.44
1586	.57	.52	.40	.42	202	288	124	193	19.38	19.76	19.38	19.65	4.21
1587	.57	.47	.29	.38	202	288	124	193	38.71	38.93	38.84	38.57	5.00
1588	.47	.37	.28	.19	202	288	124	193	11.26	10.65	10.90	10.55	2.65
1589	.43	.51	.25	.18	202	288	124	193	9.35	9.35	9.33	9.15	3.70
1590	.41	.30	.25	.14	202	288	124	193	16.87	24.08	16.50	23.88	3.43
1591	.56	.55	.29	.33	202	288	124	193	72.60	74.33	70.35	72.66	13.55
1592	.55	.59	.18	.39	202	288	124	193	30.95	29.77	30.93	29.82	7.85
1593	.45	.48	.13	.23	202	288	124	193	13.14	13.48	13.20	13.40	3.53
1594	.60	.56	.23	.42	202	288	124	193	144.19	140.85	144.07	141.26	17.97
1595	.47	.39	.11	.23	202	288	124	193	15.29	15.00	15.53	15.10	3.35
1596	.47	.50	.21	.39	202	288	124	193	19.62	19.55	19.18	18.98	4.31

VPI SCALES

1597	.38	.26	.25	.30	215	292	133	195	3.07	1.34	3.20	1.11	2.55
1598	.48	.42	.30	.32	215	292	133	195	5.49	4.30	5.15	3.98	4.34
1599	.37	.48	.14	.23	215	292	133	195	3.74	5.83	3.36	6.62	3.48
1600	.34	.32	.21	.10	215	292	133	195	2.46	2.06	2.43	2.03	2.51
1601	.41	.40	.19	.25	215	292	133	195	3.36	2.72	3.09	2.38	2.81
1602	.46	.46	.22	.34	215	292	133	195	3.20	5.15	3.02	4.95	3.98
1603	.32	.44	.25	.29	215	292	133	195	8.82	4.69	9.04	4.74	2.22
1604	.48	.42	.26	.22	215	292	133	195	8.36	9.07	8.09	9.02	2.27
1605	.41	.48	.12	.29	215	292	133	195	9.08	10.72	9.03	10.74	3.48
1606	.36	.43	.14	.31	215	292	133	195	4.74	4.45	4.80	4.27	3.73
1607	.40	.51	.05	.29	215	292	133	195	5.58	5.86	5.51	6.68	2.90
1608	.33	.40	.17	.35	215	292	133	195	44.18	43.40	42.90	41.46	24.11

TWIN DATA (CONT.)

VAR. NO.	INTRACLASS R IM	IF	FM	FF	PAIRS IM	IF	FM	FF	MEAN OR PERCENT IM	IF	FM	FF	SD WG

EYSENCK CPI SCALES

| 1609 | .58 | .48 | .26 | .23 | 197 | 284 | 122 | 190 | 19.47 | 22.45 | 20.42 | 23.83 | 9.11 |
| 1610 | .57 | .62 | .20 | .28 | 197 | 284 | 122 | 190 | 23.04 | 22.19 | 23.41 | 22.96 | 6.83 |

PARENT QUESTIONNAIRE DATA

NOTE--PERCENT DIFF IS PERCENT OF PAIRS FOR WHICH A DIFFERENCE IS REPORTED.
FOR BINARY VARIABLES, PERCENT AGREEING IS GIVEN INSTEAD OF MEAN.

| VAR. | PERCENT DIFF. | | | | PAIRS | | | | MEAN OR PERCENT | | | | SD |
NO.	IM	IF	FM	FF	IM	IF	FM	FF	IM	IF	FM	FF	WG

BACKGROUND INFORMATION

VAR	IM	IF	FM	FF	IM	IF	FM	FF	IM	IF	FM	FF	WG
4					214	293	134	195	1.12	1.08	1.07	1.20	.57
5					216	293	135	195	1.06	1.03	1.01	1.04	.18
6					205	277	129	184	1.14	1.12	1.10	1.13	.33
7					210	285	129	188	45.95	46.19	47.31	47.24	5.34
8					209	283	128	187	48.91	49.56	50.08	50.35	6.39
9					210	288	132	190	3.33	3.35	3.58	3.49	1.21
10					209	284	133	189	3.53	3.57	3.68	3.66	1.51
11					204	271	126	176	3.00	3.29	3.33	3.30	1.54

INFANCY

VAR	IM	IF	FM	FF	IM	IF	FM	FF	IM	IF	FM	FF	WG
12	3	2	12	16	209	288	133	192	23	18	16	18	
13	3	4	9	14	208	283	129	191	19	23	19	23	
14	0	1	5	1	187	262	121	175	10	12	7	6	
15	10	11	15	17	206	289	131	186	22	12	19	18	
16	2	1	7	6	210	287	134	191	52	52	57	55	
17	4	5	8	9	209	284	131	184	11	11	13	8	
18	2	4	14	6	211	291	134	191	9	7	9	8	
19	1	2	6	11	212	292	133	188	17	20	11	17	
20	0	0	2	3	212	288	132	189	55	50	55	54	
21	0	2	3	4	211	289	132	191	50	40	49	37	
22	0	0	0	0	213	292	134	188	6	7	2	6	
23	2	2	17	10	211	283	130	185	57	63	63	62	
24	5	6	23	23	211	288	133	192	77	81	78	79	
25	2	2	2	3	212	291	134	193	16	18	19	19	
26	6	4	10	15	209	292	133	192	19	15	13	14	
27	0	0	5	6	210	293	132	192	54	63	49	63	
28	0	0	0	1	214	292	134	192	87	88	89	86	
29	0	0	0	1	211	293	135	193	86	82	78	80	
30	1	0	3	5	214	293	135	193	82	84	81	90	
31	0	0	6	4	211	290	133	191	10	13	10	7	
32	0	0	4	2	212	293	135	191	92	95	91	93	
33	0	0	0	0	213	292	133	192	67	66	59	67	
34	0	1	0	2	211	293	134	193	3	5	7	3	
35	3	6	13	12	213	293	133	192	14	15	10	11	
36	0	0	1	2	213	291	134	189	51	47	46	41	

PARENT QUESTIONNAIRE DATA (CONT.)

VAR.	PERCENT DIFF.				PAIRS				MEAN OR PERCENT				SD
NO.	IM	IF	FM	FF	IM	IF	FM	FF	IM	IF	FM	FF	WG
37	0	1	2	2	206	285	126	186	48	40	39	34	
38	1	2	7	6	206	287	123	186	9	10	10	6	
39	0	0	2	0	201	274	122	181	32	25	23	23	

PRE-SCHOOL

VAR.	PERCENT DIFF.				PAIRS				MEAN OR PERCENT				SD
40	0	0	2	2	210	292	135	191	19	23	23	16	
41	0	0	0	0	212	290	132	188	66	58	64	64	
42	0	0	0	0	214	293	135	193	80	80	82	78	
43	0	1	2	1	214	292	134	192	59	68	69	74	
44	0	1	4	4	208	287	134	189	4	5	7	4	
45	0	0	0	0	213	293	135	193	84	84	86	85	
46	0	0	0	0	211	291	135	191	77	76	78	75	
47	0	0	0	2	213	291	135	193	65	67	72	70	
48	6	8	24	21	211	293	135	191	30	32	34	20	
49	8	7	12	14	212	291	133	192	17	27	15	21	
50	0	0	0	1	211	292	134	190	82	83	79	82	
51	13	18	35	25	212	290	133	191	42	41	38	38	
52	4	5	19	19	212	293	134	193	20	24	16	20	
53	0	0	0	0	213	292	135	193	7	13	8	8	
54	0	0	0	1	213	291	135	193	81	77	85	74	
55	5	5	8	10	212	293	134	190	6	8	5	7	
56	7	7	20	15	211	292	135	193	18	12	14	12	
57	0	0	0	4	211	287	131	192	62	52	57	48	
58	0	0	10	5	212	292	135	191	88	92	89	92	
59	0	0	0	0	210	289	132	192	10	15	16	11	
60	8	8	12	14	206	291	132	190	27	38	37	35	
61	0	1	9	9	205	280	131	184	20	27	19	19	
62	0	1	7	1	210	289	135	193	19	10	14	7	
63	6	7	24	9	211	291	135	192	77	77	66	78	
64	3	2	7	8	214	293	134	192	14	17	13	12	
65	3	3	8	9	213	292	135	193	17	16	13	14	
66	0	0	0	2	213	292	132	193	61	64	68	58	
67	4	6	18	20	212	292	135	192	42	50	41	42	
68	6	10	16	15	212	293	135	192	13	18	14	16	
69	3	2	16	9	214	289	134	193	24	17	28	18	
70	10	15	22	31	212	293	134	191	24	27	28	33	
71	1	1	4	4	209	291	135	192	9	10	9	13	
72	0	0	0	0	213	293	135	193	80	83	73	82	
73	0	0	0	0	213	293	135	193	4	8	0	5	
74	2	3	5	4	212	287	131	192	22	24	18	17	
75	1	0	2	2	213	291	133	191	4	1	3	3	
76	4	5	13	17	212	291	135	191	12	15	15	16	
77	3	3	16	11	209	287	129	190	42	59	40	57	
78	0	1	0	0	212	291	133	192	58	45	55	43	

PARENT QUESTIONNAIRE DATA (CONT.)

VAR.	PERCENT DIFF.				PAIRS				MEAN OR PERCENT				SD
NO.	IM	IF	FM	FF	IM	IF	FM	FF	IM	IF	FM	FF	WG
79	0	0	0	0	213	290	134	191	29	30	22	37	
80	0	0	0	0	213	292	133	190	83	79	86	85	

CHILDHOOD

81	0	0	0	0	216	293	135	192	92	93	94	93	
82	3	3	17	20	215	293	134	190	87	85	87	73	
83	0	0	0	0	214	293	135	190	89	86	91	88	
84	1	0	14	5	215	291	133	191	13	9	15	7	
85	0	0	1	2	214	291	135	189	14	25	24	22	
86	2	0	8	2	213	291	131	191	13	6	15	6	
87	5	5	6	6	214	293	135	192	12	6	6	4	
88	6	2	12	3	212	293	134	192	4	3	6	2	
89	4	4	18	14	215	292	133	191	17	19	19	16	
90	8	8	15	14	214	291	135	192	9	7	8	8	
91	0	0	1	0	215	292	135	192	2	1	2	0	
92	0	0	0	0	212	293	133	189	77	74	78	75	
93	0	0	0	0	213	288	135	191	31	39	33	36	
94	0	0	3	0	214	292	135	190	96	96	95	98	
95	2	1	1	2	215	293	135	193	5	3	4	2	
96	0	0	3	0	215	293	135	193	79	87	84	90	
97	5	4	22	21	211	290	132	192	41	46	31	44	
98	0	0	0	0	215	289	134	193	60	37	54	29	
99	0	0	2	1	215	292	135	191	70	68	71	66	
100	0	0	1	3	215	289	135	193	15	37	17	39	
101	24	19	42	36	213	291	135	191	30	24	27	28	
102	3	0	8	2	213	293	135	191	43	53	37	51	
103	0	0	0	0	215	291	134	192	79	82	79	83	
104	3	3	5	3	213	293	132	193	3	4	5	3	
105	16	19	40	38	213	291	135	192	26	36	30	33	
106	0	0	0	0	215	291	135	192	63	56	61	57	
107	8	9	20	18	214	292	135	192	27	33	27	27	
108	5	7	7	13	215	293	135	191	8	17	10	18	
109	0	0	0	0	214	293	135	193	71	69	71	66	
110	0	0	6	0	216	291	135	190	25	16	21	17	
111	0	0	6	4	213	284	126	185	8	4	8	6	
112	0	0	2	2	216	290	133	190	50	72	50	78	
113	6	3	13	5	213	291	134	191	11	5	14	6	
114	0	0	1	1	215	291	134	192	18	22	17	24	
115	5	6	6	6	215	291	135	192	7	7	8	7	
116	0	0	0	0	211	291	131	185	65	62	70	70	

PARENT QUESTIONNAIRE DATA (CONT.)

VAR. NO.	PERCENT DIFF.				PAIRS				MEAN OR PERCENT				SD WG
	IM	IF	FM	FF	IM	IF	FM	FF	IM	IF	FM	FF	

ADOLESCENCE

VAR. NO.	IM	IF	FM	FF	IM	IF	FM	FF	IM	IF	FM	FF	
117	7	9	35	22	213	289	133	191	45	57	41	52	
118	0	0	1	2	216	293	135	193	85	85	87	88	
119	0	1	0	2	213	291	134	193	44	57	43	63	
120	0	0	8	3	213	292	134	193	66	66	71	67	
121	4	5	18	10	211	292	134	192	49	46	40	48	
122	2	3	8	8	215	291	133	190	72	80	72	81	
123	0	2	1	4	214	293	134	192	0	2	1	5	
124	3	5	16	12	208	291	133	191	13	20	18	24	
125	16	19	34	34	212	290	134	193	22	27	25	28	
126	14	8	23	8	213	293	133	193	10	6	16	5	
127	0	0	1	0	214	293	134	193	38	32	35	22	
128	0	3	1	3	211	293	134	192	17	23	11	25	
129	3	3	14	13	213	293	135	192	19	22	15	24	
130	0	0	0	0	215	293	135	193	75	80	83	80	
131	7	4	8	10	215	292	135	193	5	4	7	8	
132	0	0	0	0	214	291	132	190	49	45	50	49	
133	1	1	5	2	215	292	135	192	50	46	43	49	
134	5	8	18	20	214	291	134	193	36	35	33	41	
135	0	0	0	0	213	290	132	193	44	45	39	46	
136	9	14	41	23	210	287	133	190	50	48	50	57	
137	8	8	36	28	216	292	135	193	48	56	44	54	
138	4	7	13	20	216	290	134	192	27	32	18	32	
139	18	19	35	44	213	291	135	193	38	54	34	53	
140	39	36	69	75	204	283	129	189	40	50	38	49	
141	42	40	68	70	200	274	129	188	43	34	38	40	
142	23	25	23	19	216	293	134	193	14	14	12	10	
143	22	23	37	33	215	292	134	192	28	23	23	22	
144	2	3	11	5	215	290	134	189	16	18	21	15	
145	5	3	10	7	215	292	135	192	18	12	21	16	
146	2	10	13	13	214	289	134	190	17	17	16	15	
147	10	3	17	9	212	286	133	187	10	13	12	14	
148	0	0	0	2	213	289	134	190	28	31	18	27	
149	2	4	7	5	215	288	133	190	62	56	68	55	
150	3	0	8	2	214	292	135	190	74	95	73	94	
151	0	0	0	1	215	291	134	192	84	88	85	90	
152	7	11	18	19	214	293	135	193	16	21	17	21	
153	0	0	0	0	214	292	135	192	53	42	53	38	
154	5	3	13	5	215	293	134	193	9	4	11	5	
155	0	0	2	0	213	289	131	189	52	58	53	59	
156	6	12	20	24	213	290	133	190	9	15	14	18	
157	0	0	0	0	212	286	131	190	42	47	38	45	
158	0	0	0	3	213	289	135	190	18	26	28	24	
159	0	0	2	1	215	292	134	190	16	15	16	15	
160	2	0	1	0	216	292	135	192	3	1	1	0	

PARENT QUESTIONNAIRE DATA (CONT.)

VAR. NO.	PERCENT DIFF.				PAIRS				MEAN OR PERCENT				SD WG
	IM	IF	FM	FF	IM	IF	FM	FF	IM	IF	FM	FF	

EARLY HOME ENVIRONMENT

VAR. NO.					IM	IF	FM	FF	IM	IF	FM	FF	
161					214	293	134	192	92	94	94	94	
162					212	292	135	192	60	57	65	54	
163					212	292	134	192	6	10	3	6	
164					213	292	133	193	79	84	85	84	
165					213	290	135	192	13	13	8	8	
166					212	292	135	193	91	92	93	93	
167					212	293	135	193	58	60	57	66	
168					212	293	135	192	26	29	21	20	
169					210	290	135	192	34	36	27	26	
170					214	292	134	193	55	60	65	61	
171					213	290	134	193	75	77	82	79	
172					212	290	133	193	15	16	13	11	
173					213	292	133	192	72	82	62	79	
174					209	289	134	189	13	8	11	6	
175					213	292	135	193	23	15	17	12	
176					213	293	135	193	66	67	64	66	

SEPARATIONS

VAR. NO.					IM	IF	FM	FF	IM	IF	FM	FF	
177					216	293	135	193	13	16	16	14	
178					215	293	134	193	2	3	2	2	
179					216	293	135	193	21	23	20	22	
180					216	293	135	192	58	48	63	45	
181					216	292	135	192	61	49	57	48	
182					216	293	135	193	48	50	50	44	
183					216	293	134	193	56	61	49	61	
184					216	293	135	193	8	10	14	9	
185					216	293	135	193	8	8	9	9	
186					216	293	135	193	60	58	56	67	
187					216	293	135	193	4	3	5	3	
188					216	293	135	193	4	4	4	3	
189					216	293	135	193	58	54	64	67	
190					216	293	135	193	58	54	61	64	
191					216	293	135	193	33	58	46	63	
192					216	293	135	193	33	58	41	62	
193					216	293	135	193	4	3	2	2	

PARENT QUESTIONNAIRE DATA (CONT.)

VAR.	PERCENT DIFF.				PAIRS				MEAN OR PERCENT				SD
NO.	IM	IF	FM	FF	IM	IF	FM	FF	IM	IF	FM	FF	WG

DISCIPLINE

VAR. NO.	IM	IF	FM	FF	IM	IF	FM	FF	SD WG
194	209	292	133	192	2.21	2.12	2.22	2.08	.45
195	207	288	131	190	1.80	1.60	1.76	1.76	.63
196	207	289	130	192	2.00	1.99	2.02	1.98	.62
197	204	287	130	184	1.31	1.31	1.37	1.22	.55
198	206	287	130	186	1.57	1.46	1.56	1.48	.64
199	208	289	132	191	2.12	2.15	2.27	2.17	.61
200	208	285	135	189	2.64	2.62	2.70	2.54	.55
201	208	285	131	188	1.08	1.08	1.05	1.05	.27
202	210	291	135	192	2.70	2.67	2.74	2.67	.50
203	207	289	130	190	1.36	1.40	1.40	1.38	.54
204	209	289	131	190	1.05	1.02	1.02	1.03	.20
205	206	284	132	190	1.52	1.47	1.55	1.53	.54
206	207	287	131	188	1.92	1.82	1.96	1.92	.63
207	203	285	132	185	1.64	1.61	1.62	1.65	.62
208	204	285	129	184	1.50	1.50	1.64	1.46	.66
209	207	282	129	184	1.49	1.38	1.40	1.38	.58
210	208	283	133	188	2.12	2.14	2.23	2.19	.62
211	207	282	133	188	2.65	2.62	2.71	2.69	.55
212	207	280	130	186	1.11	1.10	1.07	1.07	.33
213	207	285	133	188	2.66	2.60	2.73	2.58	.53
214	206	285	132	187	1.43	1.44	1.48	1.46	.57
215	208	286	131	189	1.07	1.06	1.02	1.02	.26
216	214	292	134	192	2.97	3.03	2.92	3.05	.76
217	213	290	134	193	1.94	1.94	1.93	1.97	.52
218	215	286	131	189	2.13	2.13	2.06	2.13	.68

CHILD REARING PATTERNS

VAR. NO.	IM	IF	FM	FF	IM	IF	FM	FF	SD WG
219	207	285	131	192	3.13	2.88	3.15	2.84	1.40
220	202	279	127	189	4.50	4.32	4.25	4.45	1.76
221	207	281	132	189	3.20	2.94	3.04	2.99	1.79
222	208	286	132	192	2.23	2.05	2.18	2.18	1.37
223	208	288	132	192	3.82	3.60	3.42	3.44	2.24
224	210	287	131	193	3.97	4.22	4.57	4.06	2.04
225	208	285	130	190	3.47	3.40	3.37	3.61	1.73
226	206	282	127	190	4.15	3.86	3.97	3.94	1.71
227	209	285	131	193	5.16	5.05	5.22	5.16	1.62
228	208	281	131	192	2.98	2.94	2.76	2.83	1.72
229	210	285	130	192	2.26	2.91	1.97	2.71	2.06
230	211	285	130	189	2.27	2.46	2.09	2.24	1.68
231	207	285	129	191	2.83	2.76	2.71	2.58	1.80
232	212	287	131	191	.28	.25	.30	.20	.73

PARENT QUESTIONNAIRE DATA (CONT.)

VAR.	PERCENT DIFF.				PAIRS				MEAN OR PERCENT				SD
NO.	IM	IF	FM	FF	IM	IF	FM	FF	IM	IF	FM	FF	WG
233			.		204	286	130	187	.65	.55	.75	.47	1.30

WHICH TWIN

234	99	100	100	100	215	292	135	192
235	94	96	96	96	214	289	135	192
236	45	56	67	80	212	290	135	192
237	23	22	41	39	213	289	134	191
238	7	13	18	20	213	293	134	193
239	5	11	11	19	209	293	134	193
240	31	24	54	52	213	290	131	193
241	35	34	61	63	213	287	132	191
242	22	23	55	54	210	290	133	193
243	19	19	31	31	210	289	133	192
244	13	18	21	29	208	286	131	192
245	30	28	42	43	211	293	133	192
246	2	4	15	8	210	291	131	192
247	9	7	15	11	210	292	131	192
248	63	58	70	81	212	285	132	188
249	43	45	45	66	212	286	132	193
250	35	32	63	41	210	284	131	191
251	38	13	66	29	210	283	133	192
252	45	45	66	54	212	282	132	191
253	29	19	49	35	210	284	132	193
254	27	27	43	39	210	283	134	192
255	40	34	67	56	208	286	131	192
256	39	44	67	65	209	283	129	191
257	27	25	45	39	211	283	130	191
258	60	57	82	74	210	289	134	190
259	48	46	83	73	212	291	133	192
260	25	31	59	53	210	288	135	192
261	45	51	67	72	208	290	135	192
262	61	47	71	72	210	290	133	191
263	53	49	65	62	211	287	134	191
264	11	11	32	30	210	291	135	193
265	9	11	21	26	210	289	135	193
266	14	17	34	39	209	289	134	193
267	26	36	54	52	208	289	134	192
268	34	38	53	58	205	289	134	188
269	31	48	48	50	210	287	129	191
270	0	85	50	94	2	290	6	191
271	39	0	67	67	204	7	132	9
272	37	44	56	51	207	283	134	192
273	41	42	63	56	208	286	131	193
274	42	42	71	65	209	288	133	193

PARENT QUESTIONNAIRE DATA (CONT.)

VAR.	PERCENT DIFF.				PAIRS				MEAN OR PERCENT				SD
NO.	IM	IF	FM	FF	IM	IF	FM	FF	IM	IF	FM	FF	WG
275	45	49	72	76	210	287	133	192					
276	46	47	66	70	209	287	131	191					
277	64	64	83	81	209	291	133	191					
278	64	65	81	80	212	291	134	192					
279	61	67	77	79	210	290	134	192					
280	69	70	84	82	212	289	135	192					
281	54	62	71	74	211	291	134	192					
282	52	64	69	76	211	291	134	190					

TWIN TREATMENT

VAR. NO.					IM	IF	FM	FF	IM	IF	FM	FF	SD WG
283					209	282	134	190	.66	.54	.99	.81	.62
284					216	293	135	193	.27	.33	.60	.55	.55
285					216	293	135	193	.81	.67	1.22	.96	.68
286					215	293	134	193	.70	.65	.80	.82	.74
287					216	292	135	192	.36	.45	.64	.44	.81
288					214	288	133	193	.94	.94	1.31	1.23	1.08
289					216	288	132	193	.94	.68	3.27	3.18	1.42

DERIVED SCORES

VAR. NO.					IM	IF	FM	FF	IM	IF	FM	FF	SD WG
290					212	292	133	191	.08	.08	.34	.31	.52
291					213	293	135	193	.17	.14	.67	.69	.83
292					213	293	134	193	.24	.32	.72	.68	.78
293					213	292	135	193	.05	.09	.19	.28	.36
294					213	293	135	193	.73	.92	2.47	2.07	1.66
295					215	293	135	192	.07	.07	.13	.09	.31
296					215	293	135	191	.86	.82	2.16	1.87	1.35
297					215	292	135	192	.27	.34	.76	.58	.69
298					214	293	135	193	1.83	2.01	4.07	4.01	1.92
299					212	290	133	190	.48	.57	1.43	1.27	1.07
300					212	293	135	191	3.59	3.88	9.36	8.63	4.25
301					211	290	134	192	5.76	6.17	7.95	7.89	3.15
302					211	284	131	193	3.21	2.82	5.15	4.24	2.19
303					212	292	135	193	2.95	2.81	4.27	4.07	1.64
304					214	293	134	193	.44	.57	1.13	1.14	1.21
305					209	292	134	191	4.08	5.11	5.75	6.43	2.03
306					207	283	130	192	11.86	11.83	17.45	16.20	5.65
307					209	289	131	190	19.71	19.34	20.07	19.28	2.43
308					206	285	131	189	19.00	18.63	19.34	18.81	2.60
309					211	286	131	193	23.90	23.98	25.76	24.06	6.47
310					199	278	127	189	62.65	61.85	65.27	62.19	8.82
311					216	293	135	193	2.17	2.29	2.24	2.26	1.36

PARENT QUESTIONNAIRE DATA (CONT.)

VAR. NO.	PERCENT DIFF.				PAIRS				MEAN OR PERCENT				SD WG
	IM	IF	FM	FF	IM	IF	FM	FF	IM	IF	FM	FF	
312					216	293	135	193	9.72	9.55	11.56	10.81	2.63
313					211	290	133	190	10.59	10.71	14.17	13.25	3.47

References

Allen, G. 1955. Comments on the analysis of twin samples. *Acta Geneticae Medicae et Gemellologiae* 4:143–160.

——. 1970. Within and between group variation expected in human behavioral characters. *Behavior Genetics* 1:175–194.

Anastasi, A. 1958. *Differential psychology*. New York: Macmillan.

Babson, S. G.; J. Kangas; N. Young; and J. L. Bramhall. 1964. Growth and development of twins of dissimilar size at birth. *Pediatrics* 33:327–333.

Barr, A., and A. C. Stevenson. 1961. Stillbirths and infant mortality in twins. *Annals of Human Genetics* 25:131–140.

Blewett, D. B. 1954. An experimental study of the inheritance of intelligence. *Journal of Mental Science* 100:922–933.

Bock, R. D., and S. G. Vandenberg. 1968. Components of heritable variation in mental test scores. In *Progress in human behavior genetics*, edited by S. G. Vandenberg, pp. 233–260. Baltimore: Johns Hopkins University Press.

Breland, N. S. 1972. *Hereditary and environmental sources of trait variation and covariation.* Ann Arbor, Mich.: University Microfilms, no. 72-27,239.

Burt, C. 1966. The genetic determination of differences in intelligence. *British Journal of Psychology* 57:137–153.

Byrns, R., and J. Healy. 1936. The intelligence of twins. *Journal of Genetic Psychology* 49:474–478.

Caldwell, B. M. 1964. The effects of infant care. In *Review of child development research*, edited by M. L. Hoffman and L. W. Hoffman, 1:9–87. New York: Russell Sage.

Carter, H. D. 1933. Twin-similarities in personality traits. *Journal of Genetic Psychology* 43:312–321.

Cattell, R. B.; D. B. Blewett; and J. R. Beloff. 1955. The inheritance of personality. *American Journal of Human Genetics* 7:122–146.

Cederlöf, R.; L. Friberg; E. Jonsson; and L. Kaij. 1961. Studies on similarity diagnosis in twins with the aid of mailed questionnaires. *Acta Genetica et Statistica Medica* 11:338–362.

Collins, R. L. 1970. The sound of one paw clapping: An inquiry into the origin of left-handedness. In *Contributions to behavior-genetic analysis: The mouse as a prototype*, edited by G. Lindzey and D. D. Thiessen, pp. 115–136. New York: Appleton-Century-Crofts.

Dahlberg, G. 1926. *Twin births and twins from a hereditary point of view.* Stockholm: Tidens.

Eaves, L. J. 1973a. Assortative mating and intelligence: An analysis of pedigree data. *Heredity* 30:199–210.

——. 1973b. The structure of genotypic and environmental covariation for personality measurements: An analysis of the PEN. *British Journal of Social and Clinical Psychology* 12:275–282.

Eaves, L. J., and J. S. Gale. 1974. A method for analyzing the genetic basis of covariation. *Behavior Genetics* 4:253–267.

Erlenmeyer-Kimling, L., and L. F. Jarvik. 1963. Genetics and intelligence: A review. *Science* 142:1477–1479.

Falconer, D. S. 1960. *Introduction to quantitative genetics*. New York: Ronald Press.

Fuller, J. L., and W. R. Thompson. 1960. *Behavior genetics*. New York: Wiley.

Galton, F. 1875. The history of twins, as a criterion of the relative powers of nature and nurture. *Fraser's Magazine* 92:566–576.

Goldberg, L. R., and L. G. Rorer. 1964. *Test-retest item statistics for the California Psychological Inventory*. Oregon Research Institute Research Monographs, vol. 4, no. 1. Eugene: Oregon Research Institute.

Gottesman, I. I. 1963. Heritability of personality: A demonstration. *Psychological Monographs* 77 (whole no. 572).

——. 1966. Genetic variance in adaptive personality traits. *Journal of Child Psychology and Psychiatry* 7:199-208.

Gough, H. B. 1957. *CPI manual*. Palo Alto: Consulting Psychologists Press. [Revised 1964.]

Hegmann, J. P., and J. C. DeFries. 1968. Open-field behavior in mice: Genetic analysis of repeated measures. *Psychonomic Science* 13:27-28.

——. 1970. Are genetic correlations and environmental correlations correlated? *Nature* 226:284-285.

Herrman, L., and L. Hogben. 1933. The intellectual resemblance of twins. *Proceedings of the Royal Society of Edinburgh* 53:105-129.

Holland, J. L. 1958. A personality inventory employing occupational titles. *Journal of Applied Psychology* 42:336-342.

Huntley, R. M. C. 1966. Heritability of intelligence. In *Genetic and environmental factors in human ability*, edited by J. E. Meade and A. S. Parkes, pp. 201-218. Edinburgh: Oliver and Boyd.

Husén, T. 1959. *Psychological twin research*. Stockholm: Almqvist & Wiksell.

——. 1960. Abilities of twins. *Scandinavian Journal of Psychology* 1:125-135.

——. 1963. Intra-pair similarities in the school achievements of twins. *Scandinavian Journal of Psychology* 4:108-114.

Jablon, S.; J. V. Neel; H. Gershowitz; and G. F. Atkinson. 1967. The NAS-NRC twin panel. *American Journal of Human Genetics* 19:133-161.

Jarvik, L. F., and L. Erlenmeyer-Kimling. 1967. Survey of familial correlations in measured intellectual functions. In *Psychopathology of mental development*, edited by J. Zubin and G. A. Jervis, pp. 447-459. New York: Grune & Stratton.

Jarvik, L. F.; F. J. Kallman; I. Lorge; and A. Falek. 1962. Longitudinal study of intellectual changes in senescent twins. In *Social and psychological aspects of aging*, edited by C. Tibbitts and W. Donohue, pp. 839-859. New York: Columbia University Press.

Jensen, A. R. 1967. Estimation of the limits of heritability of traits by comparison of monozygotic and dizygotic twins. *Proceedings of the National Academy of Sciences* 58:149-156.

——. 1970. IQ's of identical twins reared apart. *Behavior Genetics* 1:133-148.

Jinks, J. L., and D. W. Fulker. 1970. Comparison of the biometrical genetical, MAVA, and classical approaches to the analysis of human behavior. *Psychological Bulletin* 73:311-349.

Kaiser, H. F. 1960. The application of electronic computers to factor analysis. *Educational and Psychological Measurement* 20:141-151.

Kamitake, M. 1971. *Seishin kinō ni okeru iden to kankyō* [Genetic and environmental influences on mental functions]. Tokyo: Seibundo Shinkosha.

Kempthorne, O., and R. H. Osborne. 1961. The interpretation of twin data. *American Journal of Human Genetics* 13:320-339.

Koch, H. L. 1966. *Twins and twin relations*. Chicago: University of Chicago Press.

Lehtovaara, A. 1938. *Psychologische Zwillingsuntersuchungen*. Helsinki: Finnish Academy of Science.

Loehlin, J. C. 1965. A heredity-environment analysis of personality inventory data. In *Methods and goals in human behavior genetics*, edited by S. G. Vandenberg, pp. 163-170. New York: Academic Press.

Loehlin, J. C., and S. G. Vandenberg. 1968. Genetic and environmental components in the covariation of cognitive abilities: An additive model. In *Progress in human behavior genetics*, edited by S. G. Vandenberg, pp. 261-285. Baltimore: Johns Hopkins University Press.

Lykken, D. T.; A. Tellegen; and K. Thorkelson. 1974. Genetic determination of EEG frequency spectra. *Biological Psychiatry* 1:245-259.

Manosevitz, M.; G. Lindzey; and D. D. Thiessen. 1969. *Behavioral genetics: Method and research*. New York: Appleton-Century-Crofts.

Matheny, A. P., Jr., and A. M. Brown. 1971. The behavior of twins: Effects of birth weight and birth sequence. *Child Development* 42:251-257.

Mehrotra, S. N., and J. Maxwell. 1949. The intelligence of twins: A comparative study of eleven-year-old twins. *Population Studies* 3:295-302.

Meredith, W. 1968. Factor analysis and the use of inbred strains. In *Progress in human behavior genetics*, edited by S. G. Vandenberg, pp. 335-348. Baltimore: Johns Hopkins University Press.

Merrell, D. J. 1957. Dominance of eye and hand. *Human Biology* 29:314-328.

Mittler, P. 1969. Genetic aspects of psycholinguistic abilities. *Journal of Child Psychology and Psychiatry* 10:165-176.

Myrianthopoulos, N. C.; P. L. Nichols; S. H. Broman; and V. E. Anderson. 1972. Intellectual development of a prospectively studied population of twins and comparison with singletons. In *Human genetics: Proceedings of the Fourth International Congress of Human Genetics, Paris, September 1971*, edited by J. de Grouchy, F. J. G. Ebling, and I. W. Henderson, pp. 244-257. Amsterdam: Excerpta Medica.

Nagylaki, T., and J. Levy. 1973. "The sound of one paw clapping" isn't sound. *Behavior Genetics* 3:279-292.

Newman, H. H.; F. N. Freeman; and K. J. Holzinger. 1937. *Twins: A study of heredity and environment*. Chicago: University of Chicago Press.

Nichols, R. C. 1964. A statistical model for twin research. Mimeographed. Evanston, Ill.: National Merit Scholarship Corp.

———. 1965. The National Merit twin study. In *Methods and goals in human behavior genetics*, edited by S. G. Vandenberg, pp. 231-243. New York: Academic Press.

———. 1966. The resemblance of twins in personality and interests. *National Merit Scholarship Corporation Research Reports* 2, no. 8. [Reprinted in M. Manosevitz, G. Lindzey, and D. D. Thiessen, 1969, pp. 580-596.]

Nichols, R. C., and W. C. Bilbro, Jr. 1966. The diagnosis of twin zygosity. *Acta Genetica et Statistica Medica* 16:265-275.

Nichols, R. C., and R. R. Schnell. 1963. Factor scales for the California Psychological Inventory. *Journal of Consulting Psychology* 27:228-235.

Partanen, J.; K. Bruun; and T. Markkanen.1966. *Inheritance of drinking behavior*. Helsinki: Finnish Foundation for Alcohol Studies.

Petrinovich, L. F., and C. D. Hardyck. 1969. Error rates for multiple comparison methods. *Psychological Bulletin* 71:43-54.

Record, R. G.; T. McKeown; and J. H. Edwards. 1970. An investigation of the difference in measured intelligence between twins and single births. *Annals of Human Genetics* 34:11-20.

Robbins, L. C. 1963. The accuracy of parental recall of aspects of child development and of child rearing practices. *Journal of Abnormal and Social Psychology* 66:261-270.

Roberts, C. A., and C. B. Johansson. 1974. The inheritance of cognitive interest styles among twins. *Journal of Vocational Behavior* 4:237-243.

Roudabush, G. E. 1968. Analyzing dyadic relationships. In *Progress in human behavior genetics*, edited by S. G. Vandenberg, pp. 303-333. Baltimore: Johns Hopkins University Press.

Ryan, T. A. 1959. Multiple comparisons in psychological research. *Psychological Bulletin* 56:26-47.

——. 1962. The experiment as the unit for computing rates of error. *Psychological Bulletin* 59:301–305.

Sammalisto, L. 1961. The determination of zygosity in a study of Finnish twins. *Acta Genetica et Statistica Medica* 11:251–264.

Scarr, S. 1968. Environmental bias in twin studies. *Eugenics Quarterly* 15:34–40.

——. 1969a. Effects of birth weight on later intelligence. *Social Biology* 16:249–256.

——. 1969b. Social introversion-extraversion as a heritable response. *Child Development* 40:823–832.

Schoenfeldt, L. F. 1968. The hereditary components of the Project TALENT two-day test battery. *Measurement and Evaluation in Guidance* 1:130–140.

Scottish Council for Research in Education. 1953. *Social implications of the 1947 Scottish mental survey*. London: University of London Press.

Shields, J. 1962. *Monozygotic twins*. London: Oxford University Press.

Siegel, S. 1956. *Nonparametric statistics for the behavioral sciences*. New York: McGraw-Hill.

Smith, R. T. 1965. A comparison of socioenvironmental factors in monozygotic and dizygotic twins, testing an assumption. In *Methods and goals in human behavior genetics*, edited by S. G. Vandenberg, pp. 45–61. New York: Academic Press.

Stocks, P. 1933. A biometric investigation of twins and their brothers and sisters. *Annals of Eugenics* 5:1–55.

Tabah, L., and J. Sutter. 1954. Le niveau intellectuel des enfants d'une même famille. *Annals of Human Genetics* 19:120–150.

Thompson, W. R., and G. J. S. Wilde. 1973. Behavior genetics. In *Handbook of general psychology*, edited by B. B. Wolman, pp. 206–229. Englewood Cliffs, N.J.: Prentice-Hall.

Tienari, P. 1966. On intrapair differences in male twins with special reference to dominance-submissiveness. *Acta Psychiatrica Scandinavica* 42, suppl. 188.

Trankell, A. 1955. Aspects of genetics in psychology. *American Journal of Human Genetics* 7:264–276.

Turpin, R., and J. Lejeune. 1969. *Human afflictions and chromosomal aberrations*. Oxford: Pergamon Press.

U.S. Public Health Service. 1947. *Vital statistics of the United States, 1945*. Washington, D.C.: Government Printing Office.

Vandenberg, S. G. 1965. Innate abilities, one or many? *Acta Geneticae Medicae et Gemellologiae* 14:41–47.

——. 1967. Hereditary factors in normal personality traits (as measured by inventories). In *Recent advances in biological psychiatry*, edited by J. Wortis, 9:65–104. New York: Plenum Press.

——. 1968. The nature and nurture of intelligence. In *Genetics*, edited by D. C. Glass, pp. 3–58. New York: Rockefeller University Press.

——. 1969. A twin study of spatial ability. *Multivariate Behavioral Research* 4:273–294.

——. 1972. Assortative mating, or who marries whom? *Behavior Genetics* 2:127–157.

Vandenberg, S. G.; A. L. Comrey; and R. E. Stafford. 1967. Hereditary factors in personality and attitude scales: A twin study. *Research Report No. 16*, Louisville Twin Study. Louisville: Child Development Unit, University of Louisville School of Medicine.

Vandenberg, S. G.; R. E. Stafford; and A. M. Brown. 1968. The Louisville Twin Study. In *Progress in human behavior genetics*, edited by S. G. Vandenberg, pp. 153–204. Baltimore: Johns Hopkins University Press.

Wictorin, M. 1952. *Bidrag till räknefärdighetens psykologi: En twillingundersökning*. Göteborg: Elanders Boktryckeri Aktiebolag.

Wilde, G. J. S. 1964. Inheritance of personality traits. *Acta Psychologica* 22:37-51.

Willerman, L., and J. A. Churchill. 1967. Intelligence and birth weight in identical twins. *Child Development* 38:623-629.

Wilson, P. T. 1934. A study of twins with special reference to heredity as a factor determining differences in environment. *Human Biology* 6:324-354.

Wingfield, A. H., and P. Sandiford. 1928. Twins and orphans. *Journal of Educational Psychology* 19:410-423.

Yerushalmy, J., and S. E. Sheerar. 1940. Studies on twins: I. The relation of order of birth and age of parents to the frequency of like-sexed and unlike-sexed twin deliveries. *Human Biology* 12:95-113.

Zazzo, R. 1960. *Les jumeaux: Le couple et la personne*. Paris: Presses Universitaires de France.

Index